Acknowledgements

P9-CAT-073

It takes a village to write a grammar series. I am humbled by the expertise of all those who have contributed in so many ways.

I am grateful to Cheryl Pavlik for her intellectual curiosity, creativity, wit, and for her friendship. A special thanks goes to Stephanie Karras for putting all of the pieces together with such commitment and superb organizational and problem-solving skills, mixed with just the right amount of levity. I owe a special debt of gratitude to Janet Aitchison for her continued support and encouragement from the very beginning, and for her help with the big issues as well as the small details.

It has been a pleasure working closely with Andrew Gitzy, James Morgan, Nan Clarke, Randee Falk, and Marietta Urban. Their comments, questions, grammar insights, and creative solutions have been invaluable. Many thanks also go to the talented editorial, production, and design staff at Oxford University Press; to Susan Lanzano for her role in getting this project started; and to Susan Mraz for her help in the early stages.

Finally, I owe everything to my family, Bob, Jenny, and Scott, for always being there for me, as well as for their amusing views about everything, especially grammar.

This book is dedicated to my parents, Sam and Bess Kesner.

Susan Kesner Bland,
Series Director and Author of Student Book 3

The Series Director and Publisher would like to acknowledge the following individuals for their invaluable input during the development of this series:

Harriet Allison, Atlanta College of Art, GA; **Alex Baez,** Southwest Texas State University, TX; **Nathalie Bailey,** Lehman College, CUNY, NY; **Jamie Beaton,** Boston University, MA; **Michael Berman,** Montgomery College, MD; **Angela Blackwell,** San Francisco State University, CA; **Vera Bradford,** IBEU, Rio de Janerio, Brazil; **Glenda Bro,** Mount San Antonio Community College, CA; **Jennifer Burton,** University of California, San Francisco, CA; **Magali Duignan,** Augusta State University, GA; **Anne Ediger,** Hunter College, CUNY, NY; **Joyce Grabowski,** Flushing High School, NY; **Virginia Heringer,** Pasadena City College, CA; **Rocia Hernandez,** Mexico City, Mexico; **Nancy Herzfeld-Pipkin,** University of California, San Diego, CA; **Michelle Johnstone,** Mexico City, Mexico; **Kate de Jong,** University of California, San Diego, CA; **Pamela Kennedy,** Holyoke Community College, MA; **Jean McConochie,** Pace University, NY; **Karen McRobie,** Golden Gate University, CA; **Elizabeth Neblett,** Union County College, NJ; **Dian Perkins,** Wheeling High School, IL; **Fausto Rocha de Marcos Rebelo,** Recife, Brazil; **Mildred Rugger,** Southwest Texas State University, TX; **Dawn Schmidt,** California State University, San Marcos, CA; **Katharine Sherak,** San Francisco State University, CA; **Lois Spitzer,** University of Nebraska-Lincoln, NE; **Laura Stering,** University of California, San Francisco, CA; **Annie Stumpfhauser,** Morelios, Mexico; **Anthea Tillyer,** Hunter College, CUNY, NY; **Julie Un,** Massasoit Community College, MA; **Susan Walker,** SUNY New Paltz, NY; **Cheryl Wecksler,** California State University, San Marcos, CA; **Teresa Wise,** Georgia State University, GA.

Contents

PART 3: Modals

PART 4: The Passive, Gerunds, and Infinitives

PART 5: Modifying Nouns

Introduction

Grammar Sense: A Discourse-Based Approach

Grammar Sense is a comprehensive three-level grammar series based on the authentic use of English grammar in discourse. The grammar is systematically organized, explained, and practiced in a communicative, learner-centered environment, making it easily teachable and learnable.

Many people ask, why learn grammar? The answer is simple: meaningful communication depends on our ability to connect form and meaning appropriately. In order to do so, we must consider such factors as intention, attitude, and social relationships, in addition to the contexts of time and place. All of these factors make up a discourse setting. For example, we use the present continuous not only to describe an activity in progress (*He's working.*), but also to complain (*He's always working.*), to describe a planned event in the future (*He's working tomorrow.*), and to describe temporary or unusual behavior (*He's being lazy at work.*). It is only through examination of the discourse setting that the different meanings and uses of the present continuous can be distinguished from one another. A discourse-based approach provides students with the tools for making sense of the grammar of natural language by systematically explaining *who, what, where, when, why,* and *how* for each grammatical form.

Systematically Organized Syllabus

Learning grammar is a developmental process that occurs gradually. In *Grammar Sense* the careful sequencing, systematic repetition, recycling, review, and expansion promote grammatical awareness and fluency.

Level 1 (basic level) focuses on building an elementary understanding of form, meaning, and use as students develop basic oral language skills in short conversations and discussions. Level 1 also targets the grammar skills involved in writing short paragraphs, using basic cohesive devices such as conjunctions and pronouns.

At **Level 2 (intermediate level)** the focus turns to expanding the basic understanding of form, meaning, and use in longer and more varied discourse settings and with more complex grammatical structures and academic themes. Level 2 emphasizes grammar skills beyond the sentence level, as students begin to initiate and sustain conversations and discussions, and progress toward longer types of writing.

Finally, at **Level 3 (high intermediate to advanced level)** the focus moves to spoken and written grammar in academic discourse settings, often in contexts that are conceptually more challenging and abstract. Level 3 emphasizes consistent and appropriate language use, especially of those aspects of grammar needed in extended conversations and discussions, and in longer academic and personal writing.

Introduction of Form Before Meaning and Use

Form is introduced and practiced in a separate section before meaning and use. This ensures that students understand what the form looks like and sounds like at the sentence level, before engaging in more challenging and open-ended activities that concentrate on meaning and use.

Focus on Natural Language Use

Grammar Sense uses authentic reading texts and examples that are based on or quoted verbatim from actual English language sources to provide a true picture of natural language use. To avoid unnatural language, the themes of the introductory reading texts are only subtly touched upon throughout a chapter. The focus thus remains on typical examples of the most common meanings and uses.

Exposure to authentic language helps students bridge the gap between the classroom and the outside world by encouraging awareness of the "grammar" all around them in daily life: in magazines, newspapers, package instructions, television shows, signs, and so on. Becoming language-aware is an important step in the language learning process: Students generalize from the examples they find and apply their understanding to their independent language use in daily living, at work, or as they further their education.

Special Sections to Extend Grammatical Knowledge

Understanding grammar as a system entails understanding how different parts of the language support and interact with the target structure. *Grammar Sense* features special sections at strategic points throughout the text to highlight relevant lexical and discourse issues.

- **Beyond the Sentence** sections focus on the structure as it is used in extended discourse to help improve students' writing skills. These sections highlight such issues as how grammatical forms are used to avoid redundancy, and how to change or maintain focus.

- **Informally Speaking** sections highlight the differences between written and spoken language. This understanding is crucial for achieving second language fluency. Reduced forms, omissions, and pronunciation changes are explained in order to improve aural comprehension.

- **Vocabulary Notes** provide succinct presentations of words and phrases that are commonly used with the target structure, such as time expressions associated with the simple past, or the use of *say*, *tell*, and *ask* in reported speech.

Student-Centered Presentation and Practice

Student-centered presentation and practice allow learners at all levels to discover the grammar in pairs, groups, and individually, in both the Form and in the Meaning and Use sections of each chapter. Numerous inductive activities encourage students to use their problem-solving abilities to gain the skills, experience, and confidence to use English outside of class and to continue learning on their own.

Flexibility to Suit Any Classroom Situation

Grammar Sense offers teachers great flexibility with hundreds of intellectually engaging exercises to choose from. Teachers may choose to skip chapters or sections within chapters, or teach them in a different order, depending on student needs and time constraints. Each Student Book is self-contained so teachers may choose to use only one book, or the full series, if they wish.

Components at Each Level

- The **Student Book** is intended for classroom use and offers concise charts, level-appropriate explanations, and thorough four-skills practice exercises. Each Student Book is also a useful reference resource with extensive Appendices, a helpful Glossary of Grammar Terms, and a detailed Index.

- The **Audio Cassettes and CDs** feature listening exercises that provide practice discriminating form, understanding meaning and use, and interpreting non-standard forms.

- The **Workbook** has a wealth of additional exercises to supplement those in the Student Book. It is ideal for homework, independent practice, or review. The Answer Key, on easily removable perforated pages, is provided at the back of the book.

- The **Teacher's Book** has many practical ideas and techniques for presenting the Form and the Meaning and Use charts. It also includes troubleshooting advice, cultural notes, and suggestions for additional activities. The Answer Key for the Student Book and the complete Tapescript are also provided.

- **TOEFL®-Style Tests** and Answer Keys, along with advice on conducting the tests and interpreting the results, are available for teachers to download from the Internet. (See *Grammar Sense Teacher's Book 3* for the website address.)

Tour of a Chapter

Each chapter in *Grammar Sense* follows this format:

The **Grammar in Discourse** section introduces the target structure in its natural context via a high-interest authentic reading text.

- *Authentic reading texts show how language is really used.*

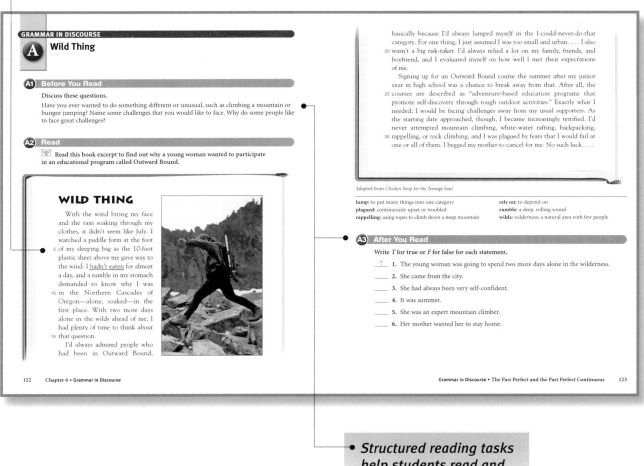

GRAMMAR IN DISCOURSE

A Wild Thing

A1 Before You Read

Discuss these questions.

Have you ever wanted to do something different or unusual, such as climbing a mountain or bungee jumping? Name some challenges that you would like to face. Why do some people like to face great challenges?

A2 Read

Read this book excerpt to find out why a young woman wanted to participate in an educational program called Outward Bound.

WILD THING

With the wind biting my face and the rain soaking through my clothes, it didn't seem like July. I watched a puddle form at the foot
5 of my sleeping bag as the 10-foot plastic sheet above me gave way to the wind. I hadn't eaten for almost a day, and a rumble in my stomach demanded to know why I was
10 in the Northern Cascades of Oregon—alone, soaked—in the first place. With two more days alone in the wilds ahead of me, I had plenty of time to think about
15 that question.

I'd always admired people who had been in Outward Bound,

basically because I'd always lumped myself in the I-could-never-do-that category. For one thing, I just assumed I was too small and urban. . . . I also
20 wasn't a big risk-taker. I'd always relied a lot on my family, friends, and boyfriend, and I evaluated myself on how well I met their expectations of me.

Signing up for an Outward Bound course the summer after my junior
25 year in high school was a chance to break away from that. After all, the courses are described as "adventure-based education programs that promote self-discovery through tough outdoor activities." Exactly what I needed; I would be facing challenges away from my usual supporters. As the starting date approached, though, I became increasingly terrified. I'd never attempted mountain climbing, white-water rafting, backpacking,
30 rappelling, or rock climbing, and I was plagued by fears that I would fail at one or all of them. I begged my mother to cancel for me. No such luck. . . .

Adapted from *Chicken Soup for the Teenage Soul*

lump: to put many things into one category
plagued: continuously upset or troubled
rappelling: using ropes to climb down a steep mountain

rely on: to depend on
rumble: a deep, rolling sound
wilds: wilderness; a natural area with few people

A3 After You Read

Write *T* for true or *F* for false for each statement.

_T_ 1. The young woman was going to spend two more days alone in the wilderness.

____ 2. She came from the city.

____ 3. She had always been very self-confident.

____ 4. It was summer.

____ 5. She was an expert mountain climber.

____ 6. Her mother wanted her to stay home.

- *Structured reading tasks help students read and understand the text.*

The **Form** section(s) provides clear presentation of the target structure, detailed notes, and thorough practice exercises.

• Inductive **Examining Form** exercises encourage students to think about how to form the target structure.

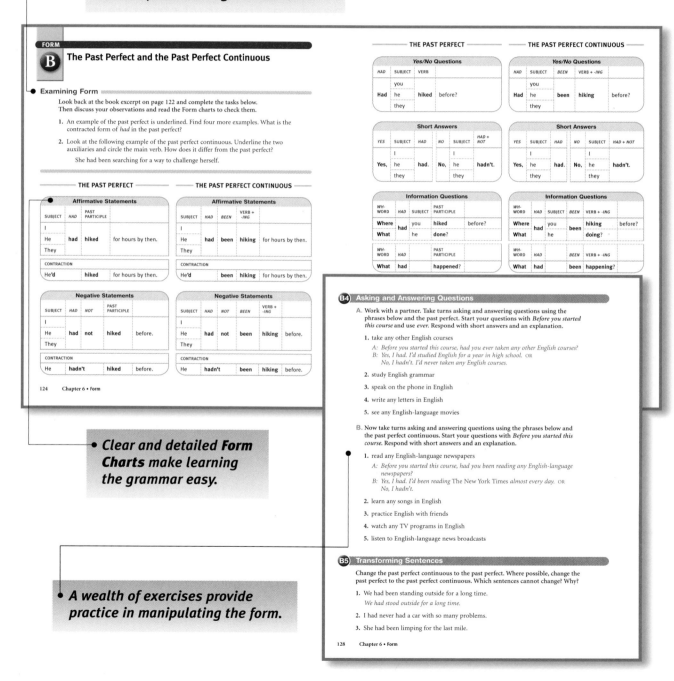

FORM

B The Past Perfect and the Past Perfect Continuous

Examining Form

Look back at the book excerpt on page 122 and complete the tasks below.
Then discuss your observations and read the Form charts to check them.

1. An example of the past perfect is underlined. Find four more examples. What is the contracted form of *had* in the past perfect?

2. Look at the following example of the past perfect continuous. Underline the two auxiliaries and circle the main verb. How does it differ from the past perfect?

   She had been searching for a way to challenge herself.

• Clear and detailed **Form Charts** make learning the grammar easy.

• A wealth of exercises provide practice in manipulating the form.

THE PAST PERFECT — THE PAST PERFECT CONTINUOUS

Affirmative Statements

SUBJECT	HAD	PAST PARTICIPLE	
I			
He	had	hiked	for hours by then.
They			

CONTRACTION		
He'd	hiked	for hours by then.

Affirmative Statements

SUBJECT	HAD	BEEN	VERB + -ING	
I				
He	had	been	hiking	for hours by then.
They				

CONTRACTION			
He'd		been	hiking	for hours by then.

Negative Statements

SUBJECT	HAD	NOT	PAST PARTICIPLE	
I				
He	had	not	hiked	before.
They				

CONTRACTION		
He	hadn't	hiked	before.

Negative Statements

SUBJECT	HAD	NOT	BEEN	VERB + -ING	
I					
He	had	not	been	hiking	before.
They					

CONTRACTION			
He	hadn't	been	hiking	before.

124   Chapter 6 • Form

— THE PAST PERFECT — — THE PAST PERFECT CONTINUOUS —

Yes/No Questions

HAD	SUBJECT	VERB	
	you		
Had	he	hiked	before?
	they		

Yes/No Questions

HAD	SUBJECT	BEEN	VERB + -ING	
	you			
Had	he	been	hiking	before?
	they			

Short Answers

YES	SUBJECT	HAD	NO	SUBJECT	HAD + NOT
	I			I	
Yes,	he	had.	No,	he	hadn't.
	they			they	

Short Answers

YES	SUBJECT	HAD	NO	SUBJECT	HAD + NOT
	I			I	
Yes,	he	had.	No,	he	hadn't.
	they			they	

Information Questions

WH-WORD	HAD	SUBJECT	PAST PARTICIPLE	
Where	had	you	hiked	before?
What		he	done?	

WH-WORD	HAD		PAST PARTICIPLE	
What	had		happened?	

Information Questions

WH-WORD	HAD	SUBJECT	BEEN	VERB + -ING	
Where	had	you	been	hiking	before?
What		he	been	doing?	

WH-WORD	HAD		BEEN	VERB + -ING	
What	had		been	happening?	

B4 Asking and Answering Questions

A. Work with a partner. Take turns asking and answering questions using the phrases below and the past perfect. Start your questions with *Before you started this course* and use *ever*. Respond with short answers and an explanation.

1. take any other English courses

   A: Before you started this course, had you ever taken any other English courses?
   B: Yes, I had. I'd studied English for a year in high school. OR
   No, I hadn't. I'd never taken any English courses.

2. study English grammar

3. speak on the phone in English

4. write any letters in English

5. see any English-language movies

B. Now take turns asking and answering questions using the phrases below and the past perfect continuous. Start your questions with *Before you started this course*. Respond with short answers and an explanation.

1. read any English-language newspapers

   A: Before you started this course, had you been reading any English-language newspapers?
   B: Yes, I had. I'd been reading The New York Times almost every day. OR
   No, I hadn't.

2. learn any songs in English

3. practice English with friends

4. watch any TV programs in English

5. listen to English-language news broadcasts

B5 Transforming Sentences

Change the past perfect continuous to the past perfect. Where possible, change the past perfect to the past perfect continuous. Which sentences cannot change? Why?

1. We had been standing outside for a long time.
   We had stood outside for a long time.

2. I had never had a car with so many problems.

3. She had been limping for the last mile.

128   Chapter 6 • Form

The **Meaning and Use** section(s) offers clear and comprehensive explanations of how the target structure is used, and exercises to practice using it appropriately.

• *Inductive **Examining Meaning and Use** exercises encourage students to analyze how we use the target structure.*

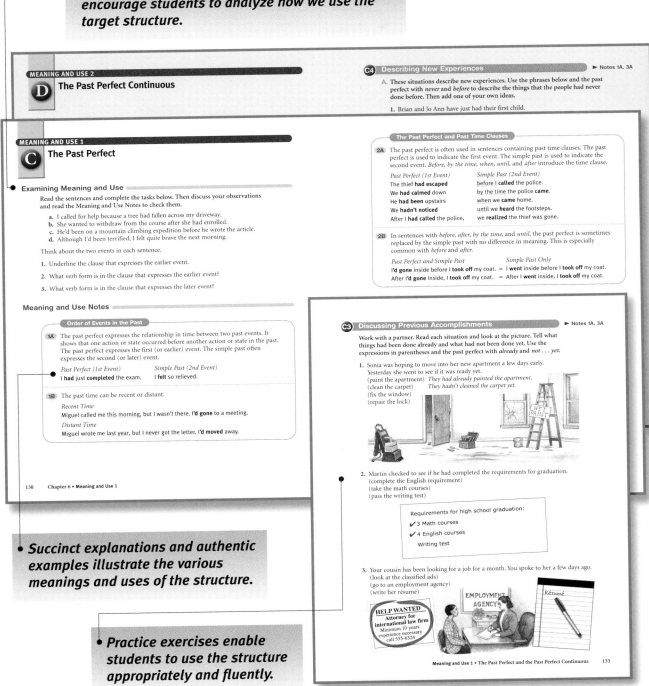

MEANING AND USE 2

D The Past Perfect Continuous

C4 Describing New Experiences ► Notes 1A, 3A

A. These situations describe new experiences. Use the phrases below and the past perfect with *never* and *before* to describe the things that the people had never done before. Then add one of your own ideas.

1. Brian and Jo Ann have just had their first child.

MEANING AND USE 1

C The Past Perfect

Examining Meaning and Use

Read the sentences and complete the tasks below. Then discuss your observations and read the Meaning and Use Notes to check them.

   a. I called for help because a tree had fallen across my driveway.
   b. She wanted to withdraw from the course after she had enrolled.
   c. He'd been on a mountain climbing expedition before he wrote the article.
   d. Although I'd been terrified, I felt quite brave the next morning.

Think about the two events in each sentence.

1. Underline the clause that expresses the earlier event.

2. What verb form is in the clause that expresses the earlier event?

3. What verb form is in the clause that expresses the later event?

Meaning and Use Notes

Order of Events in the Past

1A The past perfect expresses the relationship in time between two past events. It shows that one action or state occurred before another action or state in the past. The past perfect expresses the first (or earlier) event. The simple past often expresses the second (or later) event.

| *Past Perfect (1st Event)* | *Simple Past (2nd Event)* |
| I **had** just **completed** the exam. | I **felt** so relieved. |

1B The past time can be recent or distant.

Recent Time
Miguel called me this morning, but I wasn't there. I**'d gone** to a meeting.

Distant Time
Miguel wrote me last year, but I never got the letter. I**'d moved** away.

130   Chapter 6 • Meaning and Use 1

The Past Perfect and Past Time Clauses

2A The past perfect is often used in sentences containing past time clauses. The past perfect is used to indicate the first event. The simple past is used to indicate the second event. *Before, by the time, when, until,* and *after* introduce the time clause.

Past Perfect (1st Event)	*Simple Past (2nd Event)*
The thief **had escaped**	before I **called** the police.
We **had calmed** down	by the time the police **came**.
He **had been** upstairs	when we **came** home.
We **hadn't noticed**	until we **heard** the footsteps.
After I **had called** the police,	we **realized** the thief was gone.

2B In sentences with *before, after, by the time,* and *until,* the past perfect is sometimes replaced by the simple past with no difference in meaning. This is especially common with *before* and *after*.

Past Perfect and Simple Past	*Simple Past Only*
I**'d gone** inside before I **took off** my coat. =	I **went** inside before I **took off** my coat.
After I**'d gone** inside, I **took off** my coat. =	After I **went** inside, I **took off** my coat.

C3 Discussing Previous Accomplishments ► Notes 1A, 3A

Work with a partner. Read each situation and look at the picture. Tell what things had been done already and what had not been done yet. Use the expressions in parentheses and the past perfect with *already* and *not . . . yet*.

1. Sonia was hoping to move into her new apartment a few days early. Yesterday she went to see if it was ready yet.
(paint the apartment)   *They had already painted the apartment.*
(clean the carpet)   *They hadn't cleaned the carpet yet.*
(fix the window)
(repair the lock)

2. Martin checked to see if he had completed the requirements for graduation.
(complete the English requirement)
(take the math courses)
(pass the writing test)

Requirements for high school graduation:
✔ 3 Math courses
✔ 4 English courses
   Writing test

3. Your cousin has been looking for a job for a month. You spoke to her a few days ago.
(look at the classified ads)
(go to an employment agency)
(write her résumé)

HELP WANTED
**Attorney for
international law firm**
Minimum 10 years
experience necessary
call 555-6324

EMPLOYMENT AGENCY

Résumé

Meaning and Use 1 • The Past Perfect and the Past Perfect Continuous   133

• *Succinct explanations and authentic examples illustrate the various meanings and uses of the structure.*

• *Practice exercises enable students to use the structure appropriately and fluently.*

The **Review** section allows students to demonstrate their mastery of all aspects of the structure. It can be used for further practice or as a test.

• **Thinking About Meaning and Use** exercises consolidate students' understanding of all aspects of the structure.

• **Editing** exercises teach students to correct their own writing.

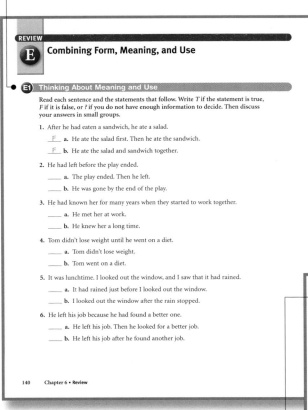

REVIEW

E Combining Form, Meaning, and Use

E1 Thinking About Meaning and Use

Read each sentence and the statements that follow. Write *T* if the statement is true, *F* if it is false, or *?* if you do not have enough information to decide. Then discuss your answers in small groups.

1. After he had eaten a sandwich, he ate a salad.
   _F_ **a.** He ate the salad first. Then he ate the sandwich.
   _F_ **b.** He ate the salad and sandwich together.

2. He had left before the play ended.
   ____ **a.** The play ended. Then he left.
   ____ **b.** He was gone by the end of the play.

3. He had known her for many years when they started to work together.
   ____ **a.** He met her at work.
   ____ **b.** He knew her a long time.

4. Tom didn't lose weight until he went on a diet.
   ____ **a.** Tom didn't lose weight.
   ____ **b.** Tom went on a diet.

5. It was lunchtime. I looked out the window, and I saw that it had rained.
   ____ **a.** It had rained just before I looked out the window.
   ____ **b.** I looked out the window after the rain stopped.

6. He left his job because he had found a better one.
   ____ **a.** He left his job. Then he looked for a better job.
   ____ **b.** He left his job after he found another job.

140   Chapter 6 • Review

7. The hospital didn't lose power, although there had been a power failure in the city.
   ____ **a.** The hospital had a power failure.
   ____ **b.** The city lost power.

8. The two men had been working on a project together when I met them.
   ____ **a.** They worked together before I met them.
   ____ **b.** They finished the project.

E2 Editing

Find the errors in these paragraphs and correct them, using either the simple past or the present perfect.

In 1953, Edmund Hillary and Tenzing Norkay ~~had been~~ *were* the first climbers to reach the top of Mount Everest. Since then, many people had climbed Mount Everest, especially in recent years. Before 1953, no human had ever stood on top of the world's highest peak, although some had tried. George Mallory and Sandy Irvine, for example, had died almost 30 years earlier on a perilous path along the North Ridge.

Since 1953, many more people had set world records. In 1975, Junko Tabei of Japan had become the first woman on a mountaineering team to reach the top. In 1980, Reinhold Messner of Italy had become the first person to make the climb to the top alone, without other people and without oxygen. In 1995, Alison Hargreaves of Scotland had duplicated Messner's triumph. She became the first woman to climb Mount Everest solo and without oxygen.

▶ **Beyond the Classroom**

Searching for Authentic Examples

Find examples of English grammar in everyday life. Choose one of the tasks below. Be prepared to discuss your findings.

A. Look in a newspaper, in a magazine, or on the Internet. Write down five examples of the past perfect and the past perfect continuous and bring them to class. Why do you think the past perfect or the past perfect continuous was used? Where in the article did you find the examples? Could you substitute the simple past instead?

B. Find examples of the past perfect and the past perfect continuous in a short story and bring them to class. Why do you think the past perfect and the past perfect continuous were used? Where in the story did you find the examples? Could you substitute the simple past instead?

Speaking

In small groups, follow these steps to prepare a description of a famous "mystery person."

1. Think of a famous person in history or sports who accomplished something that had never been done before. You are going to role-play that person by describing yourself and your accomplishment without revealing your identity to your group. You may wish to find out more about this person in the library or on the Internet.

2. Prepare a description of your mystery person using the first person. Give background information using the past perfect, the past perfect continuous, time clauses, and other tenses, where appropriate.

3. Present your description to your group and ask them to guess who you are. The group may wish to ask more questions.

142   Chapter 6 • Review

• **Beyond the Classroom** activities offer creative suggestions for further practice in new contexts.

Special Sections appear throughout the chapters, with clear explanations, authentic examples, and follow-up exercises.

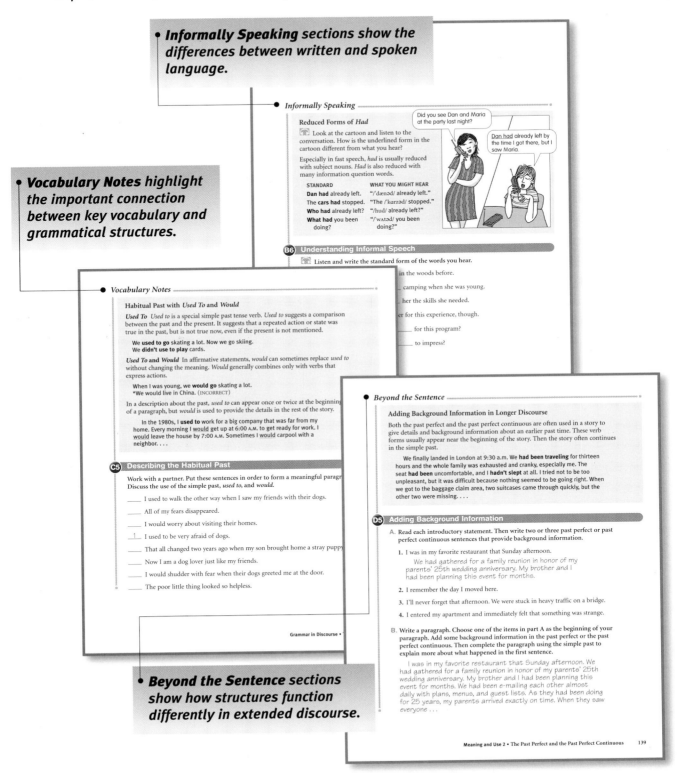

• **Informally Speaking** sections show the differences between written and spoken language.

• **Vocabulary Notes** highlight the important connection between key vocabulary and grammatical structures.

• **Beyond the Sentence** sections show how structures function differently in extended discourse.

● *Informally Speaking*

Reduced Forms of *Had*

🔊 Look at the cartoon and listen to the conversation. How is the underlined form in the cartoon different from what you hear?

Especially in fast speech, *had* is usually reduced with subject nouns. *Had* is also reduced with many information question words.

STANDARD	WHAT YOU MIGHT HEAR
Dan had already left.	"/'dɛnəd/ already left."
The **cars had** stopped.	"The /'kɑrzəd/ stopped."
Who had already left?	"/hud/ already left?"
What had you been doing?	"/'wʌtəd/ you been doing?"

Did you see Dan and Maria at the party last night?

Dan had already left by the time I got there, but I saw Maria.

B6 **Understanding Informal Speech**

🔊 Listen and write the standard form of the words you hear.

_____ in the woods before.
_____ camping when she was young.
_____ her the skills she needed.
_____ for this experience, though.
_____ for this program?
_____ to impress?

● *Vocabulary Notes*

Habitual Past with *Used To* and *Would*

Used To *Used to* is a special simple past tense verb. *Used to* suggests a comparison between the past and the present. It suggests that a repeated action or state was true in the past, but is not true now, even if the present is not mentioned.

> We **used to go** skating a lot. Now we go skiing.
> We **didn't use to play** cards.

Used To* and *Would In affirmative statements, *would* can sometimes replace *used to* without changing the meaning. *Would* generally combines only with verbs that express actions.

> When I was young, we **would go** skating a lot.
> *We would live in China. (INCORRECT)

In a description about the past, *used to* can appear once or twice at the beginning of a paragraph, but *would* is used to provide the details in the rest of the story.

> In the 1980s, I **used to** work for a big company that was far from my home. Every morning I would get up at 6:00 A.M. to get ready for work. I would leave the house by 7:00 A.M. Sometimes I would carpool with a neighbor. . . .

C5 **Describing the Habitual Past**

Work with a partner. Put these sentences in order to form a meaningful paragraph. Discuss the use of the simple past, *used to*, and *would*.

____ I used to walk the other way when I saw my friends with their dogs.
____ All of my fears disappeared.
____ I would worry about visiting their homes.
__1_ I used to be very afraid of dogs.
____ That all changed two years ago when my son brought home a stray puppy.
____ Now I am a dog lover just like my friends.
____ I would shudder with fear when their dogs greeted me at the door.
____ The poor little thing looked so helpless.

Grammar in Discourse •

● *Beyond the Sentence*

Adding Background Information in Longer Discourse

Both the past perfect and the past perfect continuous are often used in a story to give details and background information about an earlier past time. These verb forms usually appear near the beginning of the story. Then the story often continues in the simple past.

> We finally landed in London at 9:30 a.m. We **had been traveling** for thirteen hours and the whole family was exhausted and cranky, especially me. The seat **had been** uncomfortable, and I **hadn't slept** at all. I tried not to be too unpleasant, but it was difficult because nothing seemed to be going right. When we got to the baggage claim area, two suitcases came through quickly, but the other two were missing.

D5 **Adding Background Information**

A. Read each introductory statement. Then write two or three past perfect or past perfect continuous sentences that provide background information.

1. I was in my favorite restaurant that Sunday afternoon.

> We had gathered for a family reunion in honor of my parents' 25th wedding anniversary. My brother and I had been planning this event for months.

2. I remember the day I moved here.

3. I'll never forget that afternoon. We were stuck in heavy traffic on a bridge.

4. I entered my apartment and immediately felt that something was strange.

B. Write a paragraph. Choose one of the items in part A as the beginning of your paragraph. Add some background information in the past perfect or the past perfect continuous. Then complete the paragraph using the simple past to explain more about what happened in the first sentence.

> I was in my favorite restaurant that Sunday afternoon. We had gathered for a family reunion in honor of my parents' 25th wedding anniversary. My brother and I had been planning this event for months. We had been e-mailing each other almost daily with plans, menus, and guest lists. As they had been doing for 25 years, my parents arrived exactly on time. When they saw everyone . . .

The Present, Past, and Future

The Present

A You Snooze, You Win at Today's Workplace

A1 Before You Read

Discuss these questions.

How much sleep do you get each night? Do you usually get enough sleep?
Why or why not? Do you ever take naps?

A2 Read

Read this magazine article to find out how some businesses are helping their
tired employees.

You Snooze, You Win at Today's Workplace

It's early afternoon and lunch is over.
You're sitting at your desk and plowing
through paperwork. Suddenly you're
fighting to keep your eyes open. The
5 words on your computer are zooming
in and out of focus, and your head is
beginning to bob in all directions. A
nap sounds good right about now—so
does a La-Z-Boy leather recliner.

10   Well, a growing number of companies
are beginning to accept the idea of
sleeping on the job. No, it's not a
dream. Americans are increasingly
sleeping less and working longer hours
15 at the office. Some employers, therefore,
are warming up to the idea that a
midday nap helps increase productivity,
creativity, and safety.

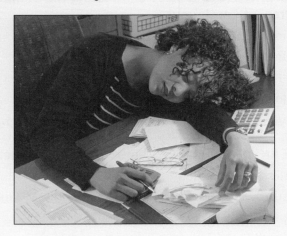

An architectural firm in Kansas City
20 now has three tents in a corner of its
office. Each one contains a sleeping
bag, a foam pad, a Walkman, eye
shades, and yes, an alarm clock. And
an engineering firm in California

publicizes its "quiet room," where employees often take a pillow and a blanket and stretch out on the couch.

Professor William Anthony, author of *The Art of Napping*, predicts that people will see the benefits of napping more and more, especially because the workplace is getting more competitive and the workforce is aging.

It's no secret that Americans are not getting enough sleep. The average American needs about 500 more hours of sleep per year, based on the assumption that eight hours of sleep per night is normal. Two out of three Americans get less than eight hours of sleep a night during the work week, according to a study by the National Sleep Foundation. Forty percent say they're so tired that it interferes with their daily activities.

Professor Anthony rarely misses a nap. He says that companies should permit napping during breaks. "Workers are sleepy, and when they're sleepy on the job, they're not productive."

Nevertheless, at most companies, napping on the job is not yet acceptable. In fact, it sometimes leads to dismissal. Still, that doesn't stop some nappers, according to Professor Anthony. He found that "they're napping in their cars, in the bathroom, or in vacant rooms. Others are trying to hide their naps in their cubicles. They're putting the phone to their ear, or pretending to write or read something."

Adapted from *The Christian Science Monitor*

bob: to move repeatedly up and down
cubicle: a small enclosed area
dismissal: telling an employee that he or she is fired
plow through: to force one's way through

productivity: the amount of work you can do in a certain time
snooze: to nap
warm up to: to begin to like

A3 **After You Read**

Write *T* for true or *F* for false for each statement.

__T__ 1. Tired workers produce fewer products.

_____ 2. Some employers provide special napping areas.

_____ 3. People need to sleep a total of five hundred hours a year.

_____ 4. One study shows that most adults get eight hours of sleep per night.

_____ 5. Most companies do not encourage napping.

_____ 6. Employees only nap at the office.

B The Simple Present and the Present Continuous

Examining Form

Look back at the article on page 4 and complete the tasks below. Then discuss your observations and read the Form charts to check them.

1. Look at the underlined verb forms. Draw one line under six more simple present verb forms. Draw two lines under six more present continuous verb forms.

2. Find a negative statement in the simple present and the present continuous. Describe the differences between them.

3. Change the following sentences to *Yes/No* questions. What changes do you have to make?

   a. The average American sleeps six hours a night.

   b. Americans are sleeping less.

THE SIMPLE PRESENT

Affirmative Statements

SUBJECT		VERB or VERB + -S/-ES	
I	usually	work	on weekends.
She		works	
They		work	

Negative Statements

SUBJECT	DO/DOES + NOT	VERB	
I	don't	sleep	enough.
She	doesn't		
They	don't		

THE PRESENT CONTINUOUS

Affirmative Statements

SUBJECT + BE	VERB + -ING	
I'm	working	right now.
She's		
They're		

Negative Statements

SUBJECT + BE + NOT	VERB + -ING	
I'm not	sleeping	well.
She's not / She isn't		
They're not / They aren't		

THE SIMPLE PRESENT

Yes/No Questions

DO/DOES	SUBJECT	VERB	
Do	you		
Does	she	**work**	on weekends?
Do	they		

Short Answers

	AFFIRMATIVE		NEGATIVE
	I **do.**		I **don't.**
Yes,	she **does.**	**No,**	she **doesn't.**
	they **do.**		they **don't.**

Information Questions

WH- WORD	DO/DOES	SUBJECT	VERB	
Why	**do**	you	**work**	late?
Where	**does**	she	**live?**	
What	**do**	they	**think?**	

WH- WORD			VERB + -S/-ES	
Who			**works**	late?
What			**happens**	now?

THE PRESENT CONTINUOUS

Yes/No Questions

BE	SUBJECT	VERB + -ING	
Are	you		
Is	she	**working**	now?
Are	they		

Short Answers

	AFFIRMATIVE		NEGATIVE
	I **am.**		I'm **not.**
Yes,	she **is.**	**No,**	she**'s not.** / she **isn't.**
	they **are.**		they**'re not.** / they **aren't.**

Information Questions

WH- WORD	BE	SUBJECT	VERB + -ING	
Why	**are**	you	**working**	late?
Where	**is**	she	**living?**	
What	**are**	they	**thinking?**	

WH- WORD	IS		VERB + -ING	
Who	**is**		**working**	late?
What			**happening?**	

The Simple Present

- Affirmative statements can use *do* or *does*, but only for emphasis.
  You're wrong. I **do** like her.
- See Appendices 1 and 2 for spelling and pronunciation rules for verbs ending in *-s* and *-es*.
- See Appendix 14 for contractions with *do.*

(Continued on page 8)

The Present Continuous

- To combine present continuous sentences with *and*, use the subject and *am/is/are* only once.

    You**'re sitting** at your desk and **going** through paperwork.

- *Is not / are not* can be used instead of the contracted form for emphasis in negative short answers.

    No, he **is not.**   No, they **are not.**

- Stative verbs (verbs that do not express actions) are not usually used with the present continuous. The simple present is used instead.

    I **own** a house.   * I'm **owning** a house. (INCORRECT)

- See Appendix 3 for spelling rules for verbs ending in *-ing*.

- See Appendix 14 for contractions with *be*.

B1 Listening for Form

Lee is a student who is living away from home. Listen to the questions that his family asks him over the phone. Choose the best response for each question.

1. **a.** Yes, I am.
   b. Yes, I do.
   c. Yes, it is.

2. **a.** Yes, I do.
   b. Yes, they are.
   c. Yes, I am.

3. **a.** Yes, I have.
   b. Yes, I do.
   c. Yes, I am.

4. **a.** Yes, she is.
   b. Yes, we are.
   c. Yes, they are.

5. **a.** Yes, I do.
   b. Yes, I am.
   c. Yes, I have.

6. **a.** No, it doesn't.
   b. No, I don't.
   c. No, they don't.

7. **a.** Yes, he does.
   b. No, he's not.
   c. Yes, he is.

8. **a.** No, it doesn't.
   b. Yes, it is.
   c. Yes, there are.

Working on Verb Forms

Complete the verb chart. Add *-s/-es* and *-ing* where necessary and make spelling changes.

	BASE FORM	SIMPLE PRESENT	PRESENT CONTINUOUS
1.	sleep	sleep/sleeps	sleeping
2.	open		
3.	fix		
4.	stop		
5.	wake		
6.	say		
7.	rest		
8.	dry		

B3 **Working on Present Continuous Statements and Questions**

Complete these conversations with the words in parentheses and the present continuous. Use contractions when possible.

Conversation 1: A child walks into the house on a rainy day.

Parent: Please take off your boots.

   Child: <u>I'm not wearing boots.</u> (I/not/wear/boots) _____
                   1   2

(I/wear/shoes) Do I need to take them off, too?

Conversation 2: Amy sees Sam at the vending machine.

Amy: _____ (you/buy/a soda?)
                       1

Sam: No, _____ (I/not/get/anything)
                       2

Amy: _____ (what/you/do?)
                       3

Sam: _____ (I/try/to get back/my money)
                       4

Conversation 3: Ann is taking everything out of the desk drawer.

Bill: _____ (what/you/do?)
                       1

Ann: _____ (I/look for/a pencil)
                       2

Bill: _____ (why/you/make/such a mess?)
                       3

There are pencils in the kitchen.

A. Work with a partner. The statements below are false. Make each one true by changing it to a negative statement. Then write a true statement using the word in parentheses instead of the underlined word.

1. Water freezes at 0° <u>Fahrenheit</u>. (centigrade)

   Water doesn't freeze at 0° Fahrenheit. It freezes at 0° centigrade.

2. The earth revolves around the <u>moon</u>. (sun)

   _____

3. Palm trees grow in <u>cold</u> climates. (warm)

   _____

4. Bees live in <u>ponds</u>. (hives)

   _____

5. The sun rises in the <u>north</u>. (east)

   _____

6. Penguins live in <u>the desert</u>. (the Antarctic)

   _____

7. Flowers bloom in the <u>winter</u>. (summer)

   _____

8. Spiders have <u>six</u> legs. (eight)

   _____

B. Make up a question related to each fact above. Then take turns asking and answering the questions with your partner.

A: *What temperature does water freeze at?*
B: *Water freezes at 0° centigrade.*
OR
A: *Does water freeze at 0° Fahrenheit?*
B: *No, it doesn't. It freezes at 0° centigrade.*

Informally Speaking

Omitting Auxiliaries and *You*

Are you feeling OK?

No. I have a headache. Do you have any aspirin?

🎧 Look at the cartoon and listen to the conversation. How is each underlined form in the cartoon different from what you hear?

Simple Present Questions In informal speech, *do* is often omitted from *Yes/No* questions with *you. You* is omitted only if the question is easy to understand without it.

STANDARD FORM	WHAT YOU MIGHT HEAR
Do you take the subway to work?	"You take the subway to work?"
Do you want some help?	"(You) want some help?"

Present Continuous Questions In informal speech, *are* is often omitted from *Yes/No* questions with *you. You* may also be omitted.

STANDARD FORM	WHAT YOU MIGHT HEAR
Are you having a good time?	"(You) having a good time?"
Are you feeling OK?	"(You) feeling OK?"

B5 Understanding Informal Speech

🎧 Listen to the advertisements and write the standard form of the words you hear.

1. <u>Are you feeling</u> tired in the morning?

2. _____ a vacation?

3. _____ car problems again?

4. _____ it yourself?

5. _____ any old clothes in your closets?

6. _____ to shop late?

7. _____ too hard?

8. _____ a house sitter?

Contrasting the Simple Present and the Present Continuous

Examining Meaning and Use

Look at the pictures and answer the questions below. Then discuss your observations and read the Meaning and Use Notes to check them.

1. In which picture is the conversation about something that is in progress at the moment (happening now)?

2. In which picture is the conversation about a repeated action or routine?

Meaning and Use Notes

Using the Simple Present

1A The simple present is used to talk about repeated activities, such as habits, routines, or scheduled events. Adverbs of frequency and time expressions (such as *usually* and *every hour*) often occur with the simple present.

Routines: I <u>usually</u> **drink** two cups of coffee in the morning.
Schedules: The bus **comes** <u>every hour</u>.

1B The simple present can also describe factual information, such as general truths or definitions.

General Truths: Some babies **don't sleep** at night.
Definitions: A recliner **is** a comfortable chair that **leans** back.

Using the Present Continuous

2A In contrast to the simple present, the present continuous is used for activities in progress at the exact moment of speaking. Adverbs and time expressions such as *now, right now,* and *at this moment* often occur with the present continuous.

Activities in Progress at This Exact Moment
I'm drinking a cup of coffee right now.
It's 3:00 A.M.! Why **isn't** the baby **sleeping**?

2B The present continuous can also express the extended present—an activity in progress over a period of time that includes the present, such as *this week* and *these days.* The activity may be ongoing or may stop and start repeatedly during the time. The extended present is often used to express changing situations.

Activities in Progress over a Period of Time (Extended Present)
I'm drinking a lot of coffee this week.
The baby **is sleeping** better these days.

Changing Situations
The bus **is coming** later and later this semester.

Permanent Situations vs. Temporary Situations

3 Sometimes the simple present and present continuous are close in meaning, but not exactly the same. If a situation is permanent or habitual, choose the simple present. If a situation is new or temporary, choose the present continuous.

Simple Present (Permanent or Habitual)	*Present Continuous (New or Temporary)*
We **live** on Eddy Street. We moved there ten years ago.	We**'re living** on Eddy Street. We just moved in.
I **stay** here every summer.	I**'m staying** here for the summer.

Expressing Complaints vs. Expressing Facts

4 Present continuous sentences with adverbs of frequency that mean "all of the time" (such as *always, constantly, continually,* and *forever*) often express complaints. Sentences in the simple present are more neutral or factual—they do not generally express complaints.

Simple Present (Neutral Attitude)	*Present Continuous (Expressing Complaints)*
They <u>always</u> **call** me early Sunday morning.	They **are** <u>always</u> **calling** me early Sunday morning. I hate when they wake me up.
My uncle <u>constantly</u> **smokes** cigars.	My uncle **is** <u>constantly</u> **smoking** cigars. I hate the smell.

C1 Listening for Meaning and Use

🎧 Listen and choose the best answer for each question.

1. **a.** I'm relaxing.
   b. I read books.
   c. Listen to music.

2. **a.** Two kids.
   b. Yes, I do.
   c. No, it's true.

3. **a.** I'm resting.
   b. Working at night.
   c. I'm a sales associate.

4. **a.** Yes, she does.
   b. I know.
   c. He leaves.

5. **a.** No, just in the morning.
   b. Because I like it.
   c. Yes, I am.

6. **a.** I mean it.
   b. A short period of sleep.
   c. Yes, he's mean.

7. **a.** Yes, he does.
   b. No, he isn't.
   c. To Jonah.

8. **a.** Yes, it's hard.
   b. Because of my work.
   c. Yes, I am.

C2 Contrasting Activities in Progress with Routine Activities

A. Work in small groups. Use the present continuous to discuss what is going on in the picture. What are the people doing? What is happening?

B. Work on your own. Use the present continuous to describe what you are doing right now. Then use the simple present to write sentences that describe your daily routines at work, school, and home.

ACTIVITIES IN PROGRESS AT THE MOMENT	DAILY ROUTINES
I'm sitting in class.	I take the bus every morning at 7:00.
I'm listening to the English teacher.	I go to English class on Mondays and Wednesdays.

C3 **Describing Activities in the Extended Present** ▶ Note 2B

Write five sentences describing activities that you are involved in. Use the present continuous and *this year, these days,* or *this semester.* Then discuss your answers in small groups. Were any of your answers the same?

I'm learning to ski this year. I'm also running a lot.

C4 **Contrasting Permanent and Temporary Situations** ▶ Note 3

Work in small groups. Match each sentence on the left with the sentence on the right that provides the best context. Discuss your choices.

<u> c </u> **1.** Tomek lives on Dryden Road.   **a.** He usually wears jeans and a T-shirt.

_____ **2.** Peter is living on Dryden Road.   **b.** He has worked there since 1990.

_____ **3.** Alex wears a tie to school.   **c.** He has lived there for a long time.

_____ **4.** Matt is wearing a tie to school.   **d.** He started the job a few days ago.

_____ **5.** Luis works at the bank.   **e.** He's a very formal dresser.

_____ **6.** Andrew is working at the bank.   **f.** He just moved there a few weeks ago.

C5 Expressing Complaints ► Note 4

Work in small groups. Complain about the behavior of people you know, politicians, or other famous people. Use *always, constantly, continually,* and *forever* with the present continuous.

My father is always smoking cigars.
My neighbor's stereo is constantly playing.
The governor is continually losing his temper in public.
She is forever talking on the phone.

Beyond the Sentence

Introducing a Topic with the Simple Present

The simple present is often used in the first sentence of a paragraph to express a general statement about a topic. The sentences that follow offer more specific details and may be in the simple present or other tenses. For example:

Many people **suffer** from a condition called insomnia. In fact, insomnia **is becoming** the most common sleep disorder in the United States. People with insomnia **are** unable to fall asleep easily, and they **wake up** many times during the night. As a result, they always **feel** tired during the day. Their constant fatigue **can affect** their work and all aspects of their lives.

C6 Introducing a Topic with the Simple Present

A. Write five or six general statements about people in the country or city you are living in. Write about children, adults, college students, teenagers, men, women, senior citizens, and so on.

College students don't get enough sleep.
In the United States, not many people retire before they're 60.

B. Choose one of your general statements as the topic sentence of a paragraph. Write a paragraph that explains the statement in more detail.

College students don't get enough sleep. They often stay up very late. Then they sleep for only four or five hours and drag themselves to morning classes.

Verbs with Stative Meanings vs. Verbs with Active Meanings

Examining Meaning and Use

Read the sentences and answer the questions below. Then discuss your observations and read the Meaning and Use Notes to check them.

    a. I have a new computer at work.
    b. I usually use it quite a bit.
    c. It's more powerful than my co-workers' computers.
    d. I do research on my computer.
    e. I feel good about my job.

1. Which sentences express actions?

2. Which sentences express states or conditions?

Meaning and Use Notes

States and Conditions

1 Stative verbs do not express actions. They express states and conditions. They commonly occur in the simple present.

My roommate's name **is** Peter. He**'s** tall and **has** brown hair. He **likes** sports cars and loud music.

Below are some common stative verbs.

Descriptions and Measurements
- be, appear, look, seem, look like, resemble
- sound, sound like
- cost, measure, weigh

Possession and Relationships
- have, possess, own
- belong, owe, depend on
- consist of, contain, include

Knowledge and Beliefs
- believe, guess, hope, feel (= think), know, think, doubt
- remember, forget, recognize, notice
- mean, understand, realize, suppose
- agree, disagree

Emotions and Attitudes
- dislike, fear, hate, like, love, despise
- care, mind
- need, prefer, want, desire, appreciate

Senses and Sensations
- hear, see, smell, taste
- ache, burn, feel, hurt, itch, sting

(Continued on page 18)

2A Some verbs with stative meanings also have active meanings and can express activities in the present continuous.

Simple Present (Stative)

I **think** this pie is delicious. (belief)

It **weighs** a lot. (measurement)

Present Continuous (Active)

We**'re thinking** about moving. (mental activity)

I**'m weighing** it on the scale. (physical activity)

2B When *have* means "possess" it expresses a state and can be used in the simple present, but not in the present continuous. When *have* means "experience," "eat," or "drink," it has an active meaning and can be used in the continuous.

Simple Present (Stative)

Peter **has** two cars.

We **have** a computer at home.

Present Continuous (Active)

Are you **having** any problems? (experience)

I**'m having** dinner with Sue. (eating)

2C Sense verbs with stative meanings express involuntary (uncontrolled) states in the simple present. In the present continuous, *smell* and *taste* have active meanings that express voluntary actions.

Simple Present (Stative)

This soup **tastes** great.

I **smell** something awful.

Present Continuous (Active)

I**'m tasting** the soup to see if it's too hot.

I**'m smelling** each flower to find my favorite.

3 Verbs that express physical sensations can occur in the simple present or the present continuous without changing the meaning.

Simple Present (Stative)

My stomach **hurts** and I **feel** sick.

Present Continuous (Active)

My stomach **is hurting** and I**'m feeling** sick.

4 Adjectives such as *good, bad, rude,* and *foolish* describe behavior. To express typical behavior, use these adjectives with the simple present of *be*. If the behavior is temporary or not typical, however, use them with the present continuous of *be*.

Simple Present (Typical Behavior)

My kids **are good.** They always behave well in restaurants.

Present Continuous (Not Typical Behavior)

My kids **are being good** today! They usually don't behave well in restaurants.

D1 Listening for Meaning and Use

Listen to each situation. Is the speaker talking about a state or condition or about an activity? Check (✓) the correct column.

	STATE OR CONDITION	ACTIVITY
1.	✓	
2.		
3.		
4.		
5.		
6.		

D2 Making Critical Remarks with Stative Verbs

Work with a partner. You are in a bad mood. Respond to your friend's comments and questions with a critical remark. Use the words in the box. Then switch roles.

VERBS		ADJECTIVES	
be	look	awful	loud
cost	seem	cheap	small
feel	smell	crowded	strong
like	sound	expensive	terrible

1. **Your Friend:** Let's go into this store. There's a big sale.

   You: *I don't want to. It looks crowded.*

2. I think I'll buy some of this cologne. I really like it.

3. I like this shirt. The fabric is nice.

4. I love these shoes. How do they look on me?

5. Listen to this song. Doesn't it sound great?

6. I need a new tennis racket. This one looks like a good buy.

Work with a partner. Complete these conversations with the words in parentheses and the simple present or the present continuous. Use contractions when possible. Then practice the conversations.

Conversation 1

A: What course ___are you taking___ (you/take) with Professor Hale?
                        1

B: Psychology 101.

A: _____ (it/be) a good course?
              2

B: Well, that _____ (depend on) my mood.
                       3

   I _____ (guess) it _____ (be) OK, but
          4   5

   I _____ (have) trouble with our latest assignment.
          6

Conversation 2

A: Excuse me. I _____ (hope) I _____
                          1   2

   (not/interrupt), but I _____ (need) some help with my car.
                                   3

B: What _____ (seem) to be the problem?
                  4

A: I _____ (smell) something bad. Maybe it's the engine.
             5

Conversation 3

A: How often _____ (you/dream)? I _____
                        1   2

   (not/dream) very often at all these days.

B: That's not true. Everyone _____ (have) dreams every night.
                                          3

   You probably _____ (not/remember) most of your dreams.
                        4

Conversation 4

A: What _____ (you/do)?
                  1

B: I _____ (smell) the milk. I _____ (think)
             2   3

   it's spoiled.

A: Well, how _____ (it/smell)?
                        4

B: It _____ (seem) fine.
              5

Work with a partner. Use the simple present or the present continuous with these verbs to describe your symptoms for each of the problems below.

feel   hurt   ache   tingle   itch   burn

1. You have a sore throat.

   A: *What's wrong?*
   B: *My throat feels sore.* OR *My throat is feeling sore.*

2. You have a headache.

3. You have something in your eye.

4. You have a sprained ankle.

5. You have a stomachache.

6. You have a rash on your arm.

D5 Describing Behavior ▶ Note 4

A. Work in small groups. Build as many meaningful sentences as possible. Use an item from each column. Punctuate your sentences correctly. Discuss why some combinations are not appropriate.

The dogs are quiet. The dogs are being quiet.

the dogs the flowers the children	are are being	quiet sick rude purple

B. Imagine you have heard these comments at work. Explain the use of *is* or *is being* by giving more details about each situation.

1. Walter is being so polite.

   He is usually very rude. OR
   He often insults people.

2. Marta is very helpful.

3. The company is being generous.

4. The employees are being so quiet.

5. Mr. Johnson is unfair.

6. My boss is being difficult.

7. My neighbor is being unfriendly.

Expressing Emotions in the Continuous

Look at the cartoon and listen to the conversation. How is each underlined form in the cartoon different from what you hear?

In informal speech, some verbs may be used in the continuous form but keep their stative meaning. This is especially common with verbs of emotion such as *love, hate,* and *like.* Using the continuous shows a more intense or emotional situation. Adverbs such as *just* or *really* and special emphatic intonation are often used as well.

STANDARD FORM	WHAT YOU MIGHT HEAR
I **love** this novel.	"I'm just loving this novel!"
I **hate** this movie.	"I'm really hating this movie!"
I **like** it here.	"I'm really liking it here!"

D6 **Understanding Informal Speech**

Listen and write the standard form of the words you hear.

1. <u>I like</u> my apartment more and more each day!

2. _____ this new television show!

3. _____ the beautiful weather!

4. _____ this trip!

5. _____ this movie!

6. _____ my new job.

Follow these steps to write a summary about a favorite character in a book, movie, or TV show.

1. In small groups, brainstorm a list of three or four of your favorite books, movies, or TV shows. Discuss your favorite character in each and explain why you like him or her.

2. Choose one character that you have discussed. Write a description in the simple present about this person. Tell what happens to him or her, how the person looks, feels, and so on, using verbs with stative meaning where appropriate.

> The "Wizard of Oz" tells the story of Dorothy. She is a young girl and she lives on a farm in Kansas. Dorothy has a dog named Toto. After a big storm, she and Toto land in Oz. Dorothy feels frightened at first, but soon after, she meets three interesting characters: a lion, a tin man, and a scarecrow. Together they travel . . .

The Wizard of Oz

E Combining Form, Meaning, and Use

E1 Thinking About Meaning and Use

Read each sentence and answer the questions that follow with one of these choices:
Yes, No, Probably, Probably not, or *It's not clear.* Then discuss your answers in small
groups.

1. I'm writing a book.

   a. Is the speaker finished with the book yet? _No._____

   b. Did the speaker start writing the book a few days ago? _____

   c. Is the speaker writing at the moment of speaking? _____

2. The bus is stopping.

   a. Is the bus speeding up? _____

   b. Is the driver's foot on the brake? _____

   c. Are the passengers getting off the bus? _____

3. My sister works at the Computing Center.

   a. Is she working right now? _____

   b. Did she get the job yesterday? _____

   c. Does she work on Saturdays? _____

4. I'm sleeping much better this week.

   a. Is the speaker sleeping right now? _____

   b. Did the speaker sleep well last week? _____

   c. Will the speaker sleep well next week? _____

5. I'm taking a French course right now.

   a. Is the speaker in the French class right now? _____

   b. Has the course begun? _____

   c. Is the course over? _____

6. I watch the news during breakfast.

    a. Is the speaker watching the news? _____

    b. Is the speaker eating breakfast? _____

    c. Will the speaker watch the news during breakfast tomorrow? _____

E2   Editing

Find the errors in these paragraphs and correct them.

It's mid-afternoon at a busy law firm in Washington, D.C. The telephones ~~is~~ *are* ringing, voice mail piles up, and faxes are arriving. But what many of the lawyers are doing? They take naps at their desks! As more and more busy professionals works from morning until night, many are sleep in their offices for just 15 or 20

"You're late, Myers!"

minutes during the afternoon. And they are not embarrassed about it at all. It becomes a new trend, according to a recent survey on napping.

Some people sleeps in their chairs, while some are preferring the floor or couches. Everyone agrees that a little nap help them get through their very long workday. Meanwhile, many experts are asking "What means this new trend?" It's simple, according to the most experienced nappers. They are do what people in other cultures and climates do every day. And they are pleased that napping finally gets more common in the workplace.

Beyond the Classroom

Searching for Authentic Examples

Find examples of English grammar in everyday life. Choose one of the tasks below. Be prepared to discuss your findings.

A. Look in a newspaper or on the Internet for five simple present headlines and bring them to class. Do not choose simple present headlines that express past or future meanings. How do you know that the headlines express simple present meaning?

B. Listen to a news broadcast on the radio or watch the evening news. Write down five examples of the present continuous and bring them to class. Why did the speaker use the present continuous in each example?

Speaking

In small groups, follow these steps to conduct a survey.

1. In the book *Power Sleep* (1998), Dr. James Maas lists a number of suggestions for getting enough rest. These include suggestions about a healthy diet, regular exercise, relaxation, and the four "golden rules of sleep":

   1. Get an adequate amount of sleep every night.
   2. Establish a regular sleep schedule.
   3. Get continuous sleep.
   4. Make up for lost sleep.

   Use these ideas and some of your own to write a six-question survey about sleep habits. Use the simple present and the present continuous. For example:

   Are you getting enough sleep every night?
   Do you go to sleep at the same time every night?

2. Interview two people outside of your classroom and record their answers.

3. Compare your survey findings with the findings of the other people in your group. Are they similar or different? Prepare a group summary of six or seven sentences in the simple present about your group's findings. Be ready to report this summary to the class.

The Past

A A Night to Remember

Discuss these questions.

What are some important news events from your lifetime? Do you remember where you were when they occurred? What were you doing at that particular time?

Read this book excerpt to find out what was happening when the *Titanic* hit an iceberg.

A NIGHT TO REMEMBER

It <u>was</u> April 14, 1912, the fifth night of the *Titanic*'s first trip. At almost 11:40 P.M., Frederick Fleet and Reginald Lee, two of the ship's "lookouts," were on duty. They were watching for icebergs when Fleet suddenly saw something directly ahead. At first it was
5 small, but every second it grew larger and closer. Quickly, Fleet <u>banged</u> the bell three times to warn of danger ahead. He also lifted the phone and rang the bridge.

"What did you see?" asked a calm voice at the other end.

"Iceberg right ahead," replied Fleet.
10 "Thank you," said the voice calmly.

At this moment George Thomas Rowe, one of the ship's officers, was standing watch. Suddenly, he felt a curious motion break the steady rhythm of the engines. He glanced forward—and stared again. He thought he saw a ship before he
15 realized it was an iceberg. The next instant it was gone.

Meanwhile, down below in the first class dining room, four other members of the *Titanic*'s crew were sitting around one of the tables. They were doing what off-duty stewards often did—they were gossiping about the passengers. Then, while they
20 were talking, a grinding vibration seemed to come from deep inside the ship. It was not much, but it was enough to break their conversation and rattle the silver that was on the breakfast tables for the next morning.

In the kitchen, Chief Night Baker Walter Belford was making rolls for the following day. When the jolt came, it impressed Belford strongly. Perhaps this was because a pan of fresh rolls clattered off the top of 25 the oven and scattered about the floor.

Most of the *Titanic*'s passengers were in bed when the strange vibration occurred. But a few were still up. As usual, they were in the first class smoking room. Around one table, some men were enjoying a final cigar. At another table, the ship's younger passengers were enjoying a lively game of bridge. While they were playing and laughing, they suddenly felt that grinding vibration. Some 30 people ran out onto the deck. When they got there, they saw the iceberg. It was scraping the side of the ship. In another moment it faded into the darkness. The excitement, too, soon disappeared. The group went back inside, and the bridge game continued.

Down in Boiler Room No. 6, Fireman Fred Barrett was talking to an assistant engineer when the warning bell rang. A quick shout of warning—an ear-splitting crash—and the whole side of the 35 ship seemed to collapse. The sea rushed in and swirled around the pipes and valves. Before the watertight door slammed down, the two men leaped through the doorway into Boiler Room No. 5. Unfortunately, they found things almost as bad there. . . .

Adapted from *A Night to Remember*

clatter: to make a series of knocking noises
grinding: rubbing together harshly
jolt: a sudden forceful shake

stand watch: to be on duty on a ship
steward: a man who helps passengers and serves meals
vibration: a shaking movement

A3 After You Read

Choose the answer that best completes each sentence.

1. Crew members were watching for _____.
   a. seagulls
   b. rain
   c. icebergs

2. The dining room stewards were _____.
   a. cleaning up
   b. sleeping
   c. talking

3. The baker was making _____.
   a. pies
   b. rolls
   c. cakes

4. _____ of the passengers were in bed.
   a. All
   b. Most
   c. None

5. Some of the passengers _____.
   a. saw the iceberg
   b. warned the captain
   c. were worried

6. Water poured into _____ first.
   a. the kitchen
   b. the boiler rooms
   c. the captain's quarters

B The Simple Past, the Past Continuous, and Time Clauses

Examining Form

Look back at the book excerpt on page 28 and complete the tasks below. Then discuss your observations and read the Form charts to check them.

1. Two examples of the simple past are underlined. Find three regular and three irregular simple past verb forms.

2. An example of the past continuous is circled. Find six more examples. Sort your examples into singular and plural.

3. Find examples of clauses beginning with *when, while,* and *before*. Do these clauses come before or after the main clause they are connected to?

THE SIMPLE PAST

Affirmative Statements

SUBJECT	VERB + -D/-ED or IRREGULAR FORM	
I	**worked**	that night.
He	**felt**	scared.
They	**traveled**	by ship.

Negative Statements

SUBJECT	DID + NOT	VERB	
I		**work**	that night.
He	**didn't**	**feel**	scared.
They		**travel**	by ship.

THE PAST CONTINUOUS

Affirmative Statements

SUBJECT	WAS/WERE	VERB + -ING	
I	**was**	**working**	that night.
He	**was**	**feeling**	scared.
They	**were**	**traveling**	by ship.

Negative Statements

SUBJECT	WAS/WERE + NOT	VERB + -ING	
I	**wasn't**	**working**	that night.
He	**wasn't**	**feeling**	scared.
They	**weren't**	**traveling**	by ship.

THE SIMPLE PAST

Yes/No Questions

DID	SUBJECT	VERB	
	you	**work**	that night?
Did	he	**feel**	scared?
	they	**travel**	by ship?

Short Answers

AFFIRMATIVE			NEGATIVE		
	I			I	
Yes,	he	**did.**	**No,**	he	**didn't.**
	they			they	

Information Questions

WH- WORD	DID	SUBJECT	VERB	
When		you	**work**	there?
Why	**did**	he	**feel**	scared?
Where		they	**travel**	to?

WH- WORD		VERB + -D/-ED or IRREGULAR FORM	
Who		**worked**	late?
What		**happened**?	

THE PAST CONTINUOUS

Yes/No Questions

WAS/WERE	SUBJECT	VERB + -ING	
Were	you	**working**	that night?
Was	he	**feeling**	scared?
Were	they	**traveling**	by ship?

Short Answers

AFFIRMATIVE			NEGATIVE		
	I	**was.**		I	**wasn't.**
Yes,	he	**was.**	**No,**	he	**wasn't.**
	they	**were.**		they	**weren't.**

Information Questions

WH- WORD	WAS/WERE	SUBJECT	VERB + -ING	
When	**were**	you	**working**	there?
Why	**was**	he	**feeling**	scared?
Where	**were**	they	**traveling**	to?

WH- WORD	WAS		VERB + -ING	
Who			**working**	late?
What	**was**		**happening**?	

The Simple Past
- See Appendices 4 and 5 for spelling and pronunciation rules for verbs ending in *-ed*.
- See Appendix 6 for irregular verbs and their simple past forms and Appendix 14 for contractions with *did*.

The Past Continuous
- Stative verbs are not usually used in the past continuous. Use the simple past instead.
  I owned a house.   * I was owning a house. (INCORRECT)
- See Appendix 3 for spelling rules for verbs ending in *-ing* and Appendix 14 for contractions with *was/were*.

(Continued on page 32)

THE SIMPLE PAST AND THE PAST CONTINUOUS IN TIME CLAUSES

TIME CLAUSE	MAIN CLAUSE
While the crew **was working,**	the passengers **were sleeping.**
Before the noise **interrupted** them,	they **were playing** cards.

MAIN CLAUSE	TIME CLAUSE
The passengers **were sleeping**	while the crew **was working.**
Water **flooded** the ship	after it **struck** the iceberg.

- Time clauses begin with time words such as *while, when, before,* or *after.* They are dependent clauses and cannot stand alone as complete sentences. They must be attached to independent main clauses to complete their meaning.
- A time clause can come before or after the main clause. The meaning is the same. If the time clause comes first, it is followed by a comma.

B1 Listening for Form

Listen to this news report and write the verb forms you hear.

Where ___were___ you when the lights _____ out this morning? That's
        1   2
the question everyone is asking today. Early this morning, a construction crew

_____ on 33rd Street while people across the city _____ to work. At
      3   4
8:29 A.M., a simple mistake by the construction crew _____ a blackout that
                                                              5
_____ power to almost a million people.
      6

The blackout _____ airports to send incoming flights elsewhere. But
                     7
according to one report, an Alaskan jet liner _____ just when the power in
                                                      8
the control tower _____. After the jet _____ contact with the tower,
                          9   10
the pilot _____ the plane himself with no problems.
                 11

The mayor _____ a state of emergency. Fortunately, no major accidents
                 12
or injuries _____, and the power _____ after six hours and twenty
                  13   14
minutes, at 2:49 this afternoon.

Building Simple Past and Past Continuous Sentences

Build as many meaningful sentences as possible. Use an item from each column, or from the second and third columns only. Punctuate your sentences correctly.

When did you buy a computer?

when did	who	paid cash
what did	what	studying this morning
what were	you	buy a computer
did		happened last night
		do when the bell rang
		go online yesterday

B3 **Identifying Dependent and Independent Clauses**

Check (✓) the examples that can stand alone as full sentences. Correct the punctuation of those sentences.

✓ 1. ~~he~~ He was standing on the deck of the *Titanic.*

_____ 2. while the stewards were talking

_____ 3. something vibrated inside the ship

_____ 4. before midnight

_____ 5. the iceberg hit the ship

_____ 6. some passengers were getting ready for bed

_____ 7. after the incident

_____ 8. a group was still playing bridge

_____ 9. while others were wandering about

_____ 10. after the men escaped

B4) Combining Sentences with Time Clauses

Work with a partner. Combine the sentences with the time word in parentheses to form as many sentences with time clauses as possible.

1. I went home. I finished my work. (when)

   When I went home, I finished my work. OR *I finished my work when I went home.*
   When I finished my work, I went home. OR *I went home when I finished my work.*

2. He was reading. He was listening to music. (while)

3. He went to law school. He studied hard. (after)

4. She fell asleep. The doorbell rang. (before)

5. The fire started. We were sleeping. (when)

6. The TV show started. They went to bed. (before)

7. The phone was ringing. They were cooking dinner. (while)

8. The package arrived. She called the post office. (before)

B5) Asking and Answering Questions with Time Clauses

Work with a partner. Take turns asking and answering the questions.

1. What were you doing . . .
   before this class started?
   when the teacher walked in?
   when the class ended yesterday?
   while you were eating breakfast?

   A: What were you doing before this class started?
   B: I was talking to my friends.

2. Where were you living . . .
   when you were a child?
   while you were in high school?
   before you came to this town/city?

3. What were you thinking about . . .
   when you went to sleep last night?
   when you woke up this morning?
   while you were coming to class?
   before you walked in the door?

Contrasting the Simple Past and the Past Continuous

Examining Meaning and Use

Read the sentences and answer the questions below. Then discuss your observations and read the Meaning and Use Notes to check them.

1a. The warning bell rang.
1b. The warning bell was ringing.

2a. The bakers cleaned up.
2b. The bakers were cleaning up.

Which sentences describe a completed event? an unfinished event?

Meaning and Use Notes

The Simple Past for Completed Past Situations

1 The simple past describes an action or state that started and finished at a definite time in the past. The action or state can last for a short or long period of time, occur in the recent or distant past, and happen once or repeatedly.

Short Period of Time
The rain **lasted** for 30 seconds.

Long Period of Time
The rain **lasted** for many days.

Recent Past
She **was** very sick last week.

Distant Past
She **was** very sick last year.

Happened Once
She **arrived** late last week.

Happened Repeatedly
She always **arrived** late.

The Past Continuous for In-Progress Past Situations

2A The past continuous expresses an activity in progress at an exact moment in the past. The activity began before the specific point in time and might also have continued after that time.

Activities in Progress at an Exact Moment
He **was getting ready** for bed at 11:40 P.M. He still wasn't ready ten minutes later.

2B The past continuous may also express an activity in progress over an extended period of time in the past. The activity may have been ongoing or may have stopped and started repeatedly.

Activities in Progress over an Extended Period of Time
They **were working** on the project for two years.

(Continued on page 36)

Completed vs. In-Progress Past Situations

3A The past continuous and the simple past can be similar in meaning, but not exactly the same. To describe a situation as completed, choose the simple past. To describe the same situation in progress, choose the past continuous.

Simple Past (Completed)	*Past Continuous (In Progress)*
I **lived** on Eddy Street in 1986.	I **was living** on Eddy Street while I was in school.

3B The simple past implies the completion of an event. The past continuous often emphasizes the activity or process. The past continuous activity may or may not have been completed.

Simple Past	*Past Continuous*
He **wrote** a letter in the library and **mailed** it on his way home. (He finished the letter.)	He **was writing** a letter in the library when the lights went out. (We don't know if he finished the letter.)

The Past Continuous for Background Information

4 The past continuous often appears at the beginning of a narrative to describe background activities. It can express several background activities happening at the same time as the main event. The main event is in the simple past.

It **was raining** hard outside. I **was sleeping** and my roommate **was taking** a shower. At exactly 7:00 A.M., there <u>was</u> a huge clap of thunder. I <u>jumped up</u> as the house <u>shook</u> violently. . . .

C1 Listening for Meaning and Use ▶ Notes 3A, 3B

Listen to descriptions of these activities. Check (✓) whether the activity is completed at the end of the description or may continue after the end of the description.

	ACTIVITY	COMPLETED	MAY CONTINUE
1.	writing a book		✓
2.	eating dinner		
3.	taking a bath		
4.	painting his kitchen		
5.	baking a cake		
6.	writing a letter		

Look at the picture and describe the different activities that were happening yesterday afternoon at the public library. Use the past continuous.

Many people were waiting in line at the reference desk.
One man was chasing his child around the book carts.

C3 **Contrasting In-Progress and Completed Past Situations** ▶ Notes 3A, 3B

Read this interview by a dorm advisor who is investigating a theft in a college dorm. Choose the simple past or past continuous forms that best complete the conversation.

Advisor: What ((did you notice)/ were you noticing) last night?
                                1

Student: It was after dinner and I was in the student lounge. Four male students

(played / were playing) cards at a table. Three others (studied / were studying)
      2   3

together on the couches. A female student (read / was reading) a newspaper in
                                                          4

the corner. I (did / was doing) a crossword puzzle. At eight o'clock,
                  5

(I heard / was hearing) two of my friends in the hall. They (told / were telling)
          6   7

jokes, so I (went / was going) into the hall to talk to them. On the way back to
                  8

my seat, I (stopped / was stopping) to talk to the card players. The female
                      9

student suddenly (jumped / was jumping) up, (dropped / was dropping) her
                        10   11

newspaper, and (ran / was runnning) out of the lounge. I (sat / was sitting)
                      12   13

down and (saw / was seeing) that my backpack was missing.
              14

C4 **Describing Background Activities** ▶ Note 4

A. Write two past continuous sentences that describe activities that were happening at the same time as each of the simple past events.

1. My phone rang at 7:00 A.M.

   I was sleeping. My roommate was taking a shower.

2. We watched the evening news at 6:30.

3. Lightning struck a huge tree in our yard this afternoon.

4. I stopped at the supermarket on my way home from work.

5. My computer crashed last night.

6. The fire alarm rang during class.

B. Write a paragraph about an item in part A. Begin with background information in the past continuous. Then use the simple past to describe the main event.

   At 7:00 a.m., I was sleeping and my roommate was taking a shower. The dog was waiting to go out. The phone rang. I jumped out of bed, picked up the phone, and heard the news. . . .

Vocabulary Notes

Habitual Past with *Used To* and *Would*

Used To *Used to* is a special simple past tense verb. *Used to* suggests a comparison between the past and the present. It suggests that a repeated action or state was true in the past, but is not true now, even if the present is not mentioned.

> We **used to go** skating a lot. Now we go skiing.
> We **didn't use to play** cards.

Used To and *Would* In affirmative statements, *would* can sometimes replace *used to* without changing the meaning. *Would* generally combines only with verbs that express actions.

> When I was young, we **would go** skating a lot.
> *We would live in China. (INCORRECT)

In a description about the past, *used to* can appear once or twice at the beginning of a paragraph, but *would* is used to provide the details in the rest of the story.

> In the 1980s, I **used to** work for a big company that was far from my home. Every morning I <u>would</u> get up at 6:00 A.M. to get ready for work. I <u>would</u> leave the house by 7:00 A.M. Sometimes I <u>would</u> carpool with a neighbor. . . .

C5 Describing the Habitual Past

Work with a partner. Put these sentences in order to form a meaningful paragraph. Discuss the use of the simple past, *used to*, and *would*.

_____ I used to walk the other way when I saw my friends with their dogs.

_____ All of my fears disappeared.

_____ I would worry about visiting their homes.

_1_ I used to be very afraid of dogs.

_____ That all changed two years ago when my son brought home a stray puppy.

_____ Now I am a dog lover just like my friends.

_____ I would shudder with fear when their dogs greeted me at the door.

_____ The poor little thing looked so helpless.

Beyond the Sentence

Using the Simple Past in Discourse

Simple Present Introductions to Descriptions of the Past General statements in the simple present can often introduce simple past descriptions. The simple past gives specific details about the simple present statement.

> Voice mail systems **are** often frustrating. Last week, I <u>tried</u> to call an airline company. First, I <u>listened</u> to a menu with six different choices. Then I . . .

Time Expressions with the Simple Past In a simple past description, a time expression such as *last weekend* often appears in the description, but not in every sentence. Each sentence relates to this time until a new expression appears. Often a change of time expression (for example, *now*) signals a change in tense.

> I **called** Jill <u>last weekend</u>, and she **was** sick with the flu. She **sounded** terrible so we **didn't talk** very long. I **spoke** to her again <u>this morning</u>, and she **was** much better. She**'s** back at work <u>now</u>, and everything **seems** fine.

C6 Using the Simple Past in Discourse

A. Read each simple present introductory statement. Then write a sentence in the simple past that adds a detail. Tell when the particular experience happened.

1. You can't depend on the weather. <u>Last year, we ran into terrible fog</u>
   <u>during our trip through Austria.</u>

2. I still remember my childhood. _____

   _____

3. I don't like long lines. _____

   _____

B. Write a short paragraph. Choose one of the items in part A. Pay attention to your use of time expressions for keeping or changing sentences.

> You can't depend on the weather. Last year, we ran into terrible fog during our trip through Austria. It was our first time in the Austrian countryside, and we barely saw anything as we rode from town to town. The whole countryside was under a dense fog. We were very disappointed so we . . .

D The Simple Past and the Past Continuous in Time Clauses

Examining Meaning and Use

Read the sentences and answer the questions below. Then discuss your observations and read the Meaning and Use Notes to check them.

   a. They were talking about the passengers when they suddenly felt the vibration.
   b. Some people were sleeping while others were playing cards.
   c. When the bell rang, he yelled to his assistant.

1. Which sentence shows that one completed event happened after another completed event?

2. Which sentence shows that one event interrupted another event?

3. Which sentence shows that two events were happening at the same time?

Meaning and Use Notes

Sequential Events

1A Past time clauses describe the time relationship of two past events and show the order of those events. Sentences with two simple past clauses can show that one completed event happened after the other. *Before, after,* or *when* introduces the time clause.

Simple Past (1st Event)	*Simple Past (2nd Event)*
I wrote the letter	**before I heard the news.**
After I heard the news,	I wrote the letter.
When I heard the news,	I wrote the letter.

1B Sometimes a sentence with a *when* or *after* time clause expresses a cause-and-effect relationship. The first event causes the second event.

Cause (1st Event)	*Effect (2nd Event)*
When the power went out,	the room got completely dark.
After the power went out,	the room got completely dark.

(Continued on page 42)

2A Sentences with one simple past and one past continuous clause typically show that a simple past event interrupted a past continuous event.

He **was studying** for exams when the lights **went out**.

OR

Before the lights **went out**, he **was studying** for exams.

2B Both *while* and *when* introduce a past continuous clause that means "during the time."

Past Continuous (1st Event)	*Simple Past (2nd Event)*
While I was dancing,	I lost my necklace.
When I was dancing,	I lost my necklace.

2C *When* can also introduce a simple past clause that means "at the time," but *while* cannot.

Past Continuous (1st Event)	*Simple Past (2nd Event)*
I was dancing	**when I lost my necklace.**
* I was dancing	while I lost my necklace. (INCORRECT)

3 Sentences with two past continuous clauses typically show that two activities were happening at the same time. Both *while* and *when* can introduce the time clause.

Past Continuous	*Past Continuous*
They were laughing	**while they were playing cards.**
They were laughing	**when they were playing cards.**

🎧 Listen to the two events in each statement and choose the event that happened or started first.

1. **(a.)** I went home.
   b. I opened the mail.

2. **a.** I played tennis.
   b. I took a shower.

3. **a.** The phone rang.
   b. I was fixing the bathroom sink.

4. **a.** She came home.
   b. It started to rain.

5. **a.** I was waiting for John.
   b. I saw Erica.

6. **a.** The water ran out.
   b. I opened the drain.

7. **a.** I called the operator.
   b. She connected me with Bogotá.

8. **a.** I shouted.
   b. She turned around.

D2 **Using Past Time Clauses**   ▶ Notes 1A, 1B,
                                               2A–2C, 3

Work in groups. Read this account of the Johnstown Flood of 1889. Make notes about what happened. Then make up as many sentences as you can with *while*, *when*, *before*, and *after* time clauses. Include sequential, interrupted, and simultaneous events in your sentences.

Before the water crashed into Johnstown, the train engineer tried to warn people.

It was May 31, 1889. It was raining, and the waters of a nearby lake were rising. The South Fork Dam was sagging. A few minutes after 3:00 P.M. that day, the dam collapsed and a 40-foot wall of water headed toward Johnstown, 14 miles away. A train engineer outside of the town tried to warn people that the flood was coming. He sped down the track and blew his train whistle loudly. This time, he didn't toot the whistle three times in his usual friendly way. Instead, he made the whistle wail in a way that survivors remembered years later.

The water crashed into Johnstown at a very high speed. Some people called it a tidal wave. The flood destroyed everything in its path. It wiped out villages, bridges, and freight trains. Many people had no time to leave their homes. They ran to the upper floors of their houses and they climbed onto their roofs. The force of the water lifted some houses and knocked them into each other. Other people were luckier. They were able to escape to the hills right above Johnstown.

After the tragedy, people from around the world donated 4 million dollars to help Johnstown, and more than 200 photographers came to record the story. It was the first big international news event. Johnstown survived two more major floods in 1936 and 1977.

A. Describe the changes in each pair of pictures. Use *before* and *after*.

Situation 1: Her grades came in the mail.

Before her grades came in the mail, she was worried. After her grades came in the mail . . .

Situation 2: He tripped and fell.

Situation 3: Their parents came home.

B. Write a short story about one of the pairs of pictures. Use time clauses in your story to describe what happened before and after.

Elena was standing at the window, waiting for the mail. Her exam grades were late. . . .

Work with a partner. Read each pair of sentences and label the cause and the effect. Then combine the sentences, using *when* or *after* to express the cause. Discuss why more than one answer is possible in some sentences.

1. a. The roads became icy. _effect_

 b. The temperature dropped below freezing. _cause_

 When the temperature dropped below freezing, the roads became icy.

2. a. They had to call for help. _____

 b. They ran out of gas. _____

 _____

3. a. The lightning struck. _____

 b. The lights went out. _____

 _____

4. a. They painted their house bright pink. _____

 b. The neighbors refused to talk to them. _____

 _____

5. a. He went on a strict diet. _____

 b. His best suit didn't fit anymore. _____

 _____

6. a. Her arm started to itch. _____

 b. A mosquito bit her. _____

 _____

7. a. The doorbell rang. _____

 b. He answered the door. _____

 _____

8. a. She found the lost jewelry. _____

 b. She got a reward. _____

 _____

A. Complete this e-mail message by writing sentences with *when* and *while* time clauses about the events in parentheses. Use the simple past or the past continuous.

Hi Jeanne,

You wouldn't believe what a terrible day I had! <u>While I was trying to sleep,</u>
<u>the cat jumped on my chest</u> (I try to sleep / the cat jumps on my chest).
So I got up to let him go out, but _____ (I go down the
stairs / I trip on a shoe). By this time, I was fully awake even though it was just 5:15 in the
morning. So I decided to make breakfast. Would you believe that _____
_____ (I make coffee / I spill the whole can of coffee
on the floor)? I tried to calm down, eat my breakfast, and get ready for school. But
_____ (I take a shower / the phone rings). So I got out
of the shower to answer it, but _____ (I step out of the
shower / I slip on the wet floor). I finally answered the phone, and it was an old friend who
drives me crazy! He asked to come and visit me. I told him he couldn't come.
_____ (I try to explain / he gets mad and hangs up).

Well, I got to school all right. The most important thing that I had to do today was to type a
paper for my economics class. Well, guess what? _____
(I type the paper / the computer system goes down). I had to go to class without my paper.
Then _____ (I ride the elevator to class / it gets stuck).
I was 45 minutes late, so I missed most of my class. Fortunately, my professor has a
sense of humor.

Thanks for reading all of this nonsense! How was your day?

B. Work with a partner. Can you remember a day when something unexpected happened? Take turns telling each other what happened. Use time clauses and the simple past or the past continuous.

Combining Form, Meaning, and Use

E1 Thinking About Meaning and Use

Read each sentence and the statement that follows. Write *T* if the statement is true, *F* if it is false, or *?* if you do not have enough information to decide. Then discuss your answers in small groups.

1. Before the storm arrived, the weather stations were warning us about it.

   __F__ The storm began before the weather stations warned us.

2. The children were building a snowman while it was snowing.

   _____ They finished the snowman.

3. He wrote a book about the *Titanic*.

   _____ He completed the book.

4. We lost our power when a tree came down.

   _____ A tree came down after we lost our power.

5. He was listening to the news while she was sleeping.

   _____ She fell asleep before the news started.

6. At 4:00 Tim was driving to work.

   _____ Tim arrived at work.

E2 Editing

Some of these sentences have errors. Find the errors and correct them.

1. While he was taking a shower, ~~when~~ someone called.

2. After he fell asleep, he was reading a book.

3. Were you having your own car in college?

4. He didn't go to class yesterday.

5. Oh, no! I was dropping my earring. I can't find it.

6. I dialed again, after I heard the dial tone.

Follow these steps below to write about your childhood. Describe what it was like when you were ten. Talk about your school, your family, and your hobbies.

1. Brainstorm a list of items to write about. Use *used to, would,* and the simple past where appropriate. Try to use time clauses and the past continuous, too. Write your description.

2. Exchange papers with a partner. Check your partner's description for the appropriate use of the simple past, past continuous, *used to, would,* and time clauses. Underline any problems you find. Discuss them with your partner.

3. Rewrite your description, making any necessary corrections.

▶ Beyond the Classroom

Searching for Authentic Examples

Find examples of English grammar in everyday life. Choose one of the tasks below. Be prepared to discuss your findings.

A. Look in a newspaper, in a magazine, or on the Internet for five examples of the simple past in descriptions of past events. Bring your examples to class. What is the definite time that each of your simple past sentences refers to? Are there other tenses used in the same paragraphs? Why?

B. Look for the past continuous in a story about the past. Find an example of the introductory use of the past continuous and bring it to class. What other tenses are used in the same paragraph?

Gerald Celente

• Soon most of us <u>will be doing</u> all our shopping in electronic "virtual reality" stores.

35 • To make sure our foods are safe, we'll all own one of the "newly reliable portable food testers."

According to Gerald Celente:

40 • Health, fitness, and nutrition are going to be key. People are going to do more to take care of themselves.

• Napping will come 45 into vogue.

• People will spend more on chemical-free food as their fear of contaminated meat, vegetables, and fish increases.

50 • As consumers shop by computer, malls will die out.

• Videophones will become the hottest digital invention.

• Technology will make it 55 possible for people to test load a virtual washing machine or refrigerator in a virtual appliance department.

60 • More people will be working from their homes. Rural communities will be growing substantially.

---

come into vogue: to become popular
contaminated: unclean; unfit for use
key: very important
reliable: dependable

trend: a current style or fashion; what people generally seem to be doing
virtual reality: an imaginary world created by computer technology

---

A3 After You Read

Choose the products and trends that will become more popular according to the trend forecasters.

1. chemical-free foods

2. electric cars

3. robot housekeepers

4. virtual reality stores

5. videophones

6. personal helicopters

7. napping

8. safe cities

9. healthier cigarettes

10. larger and larger malls

11. do-it-yourself surgery

12. genetically engineered pets

B The Future Continuous and Review of Future Forms

Examining Form

Look back at the article on page 50 and complete the tasks below. Then discuss your observations and read the Form charts to check them.

1. Examples of three different future forms are underlined. Find all the other examples of these future forms and sort them into categories:

   am/is/are + *going to* + verb
   will + verb
   will be + verb + *-ing*

2. There is one example of the present continuous used as future. Can you find it?

3. Do you know any other tenses that can be used to express the future?

THE FUTURE CONTINUOUS

Affirmative Statements				
SUBJECT	WILL	BE	VERB + *-ING*	
I				
She	will	be	coming	later.
They				

Negative Statements					
SUBJECT	WILL	NOT	BE	VERB + *-ING*	
I					
She	will	not	be	coming	later.
They					

Yes/No Questions				
WILL	SUBJECT	BE	VERB + *-ING*	
	you			
Will	she	be	coming	later?
	they			

Short Answers							
YES	SUBJECT	WILL		NO	SUBJECT	WON'T
	I				I	
Yes,	she	will.	No,	she	won't.
	they				they	

Information Questions

WH- WORD	WILL	SUBJECT	BE	VERB + -ING	
When	**will**	you	**be**	**coming**?	
Where		they		**working**	tomorrow?

WH- WORD	WILL		BE	VERB + -ING	
Who	**will**		**be**	**coming**	later?
What				**happening**	next year?

- The future continuous has the same form with every subject.
- The future continuous has two auxiliary verbs: *will* and *be*. Only *will* forms contractions.
- Verbs with stative meanings are not usually used with the future continuous.
  - *I'll be knowing the answer later. (INCORRECT)
- See Appendix 3 for spelling rules for verbs ending in *-ing*.
- See Appendix 14 for contractions with *will*.

REVIEW OF FUTURE FORMS

The Future with *Be Going To*

AM/IS/ARE + *GOING TO* + VERB

It**'s going to rain** tonight.

It**'s not going to rain** tonight.

Is it **going to rain** tonight?
  Yes, it **is**. / **No**, it **isn't**.

When is it **going to rain**?

The Future with *Will*

WILL + VERB

I**'ll finish** this soon.

I **won't finish** this soon.

Will you **finish** this soon?
  Yes, I **will**. / **No**, I **won't**.

When will you **finish**?

The Present Continuous as Future

AM/IS/ARE + VERB + -ING

She**'s leaving** in a few minutes.

She**'s not leaving** in a few minutes.

Is she **leaving** in a few minutes?
  Yes, she **is**. / **No**, she **isn't**.

When are you **leaving**?

The Simple Present as Future

SIMPLE PRESENT VERB FORM

The store **opens** at ten tomorrow.

The store **doesn't open** until ten tomorrow.

Does the store **open** at ten tomorrow?
  Yes, it **does**. / **No**, it **doesn't**.

What time **does** the store **open** tomorrow?

(Continued on page 54)

> - All future forms can occur in the main clause of sentences with future time clauses.
> - Future time clauses begin with a time word such as *when, before,* or *after.*
> - In most sentences expressing future time, the time clause uses the simple present. Only the main clause uses a future form.
>
>   <u>After</u> you **get** home, I**'m leaving** for work.
>
>   I**'ll** probably **leave** for work <u>when</u> you **get** home.

B1 Listening for Form

Listen to each situation. Choose the future form that you hear.

1. **a.** I call
   b. I'll call
   c. I'll be calling
   d. I'm calling

2. **a.** It won't be raining
   b. It won't rain
   c. It's not going to rain
   d. It's not raining

3. **a.** The movie starts
   b. The movie will start
   c. The movie will be starting
   d. The movie is starting

4. **a.** We'll cruise
   b. We're cruising
   c. We'll be cruising
   d. We're going to cruise

5. **a.** We'll be leaving
   b. We're going to leave
   c. We're leaving
   d. We'll leave

6. **a.** They're sending
   b. They'll send
   c. They'll be sending
   d. They're going to send

7. **a.** John will arrive
   b. John will be arriving
   c. John is going to arrive
   d. John is arriving

8. **a.** Do you go skiing
   b. Are you going to go skiing
   c. Will you be going skiing
   d. Are you going skiing

Write five sentences that tell why Abdul can't go out with his friends this week.
Use Abdul's calendar to explain what he will be doing.

Abdul will be studying for a history exam. He'll also be . . .

Monday	Friday clean apartment for Mom's visit
Tuesday history exam English paper due	Saturday
Wednesday dinner with Kelly	Sunday
Thursday prepare speech for debate class	Notes

B3 Building Sentences Using Future Forms

Build as many meaningful sentences as possible. Use an item from each column, or
from the first and third columns only. Use contractions when possible and punctuate
your sentences correctly.

I'll (I will) leave tomorrow.

I who her family	is going to will will be am	leaving soon leave tomorrow

B4 Asking *When* Questions About the Future

Work with a partner. Take turns asking and answering questions with *when*. Use the phrases below and *be going to*, the present continuous as future, or the future continuous. Use future time words in your answers.

1. take a vacation

   A: *When are you going to take / are you taking / will you be taking a vacation?*
   B: *This summer.*

2. get a medical checkup

3. take the day off

4. clean your apartment

5. finish your work

6. go out to dinner

7. do your laundry

8. shop for groceries

B5 Working on the Simple Present as Future

A. Read this fall semester schedule from an American university. Use the simple present as future and the verbs *begin, start, last,* and *end* to make as many sentences as possible about the schedule.

Classes start on September 1.

University Fall Semester Schedule

September 1	First day of classes
October 12–15	Fall vacation
November 22–25	Thanksgiving break
December 6	Last day of classes
December 13–20	Final exams

B. Work with a partner. Write a current school schedule like the one in part A. Take turns saying simple present sentences to talk about the future events on your schedule.

Work with a partner. Combine the sentences with the time word in parentheses to form as many sentences with future time clauses as possible. Use the simple present in the time clause and *will* or *be going to* in the main clause. Are any combinations illogical?

1. He takes a shower.

   He gets out of bed. (after)

   After he gets out of bed, he'll take a shower.
   After he gets out of bed, he's going to take a shower.
   He'll take a shower after he gets out of bed.
   He's going to take a shower after he gets out of bed.
   ILLOGICAL:
   After he takes a shower, he'll get out of bed.
   After he takes a shower, he's going to get out of bed.

2. I go shopping.

   I call you. (before)

3. The mail arrives.

   I eat breakfast. (after)

4. He falls asleep.

   He reads the newspaper. (when)

5. He sets the table.

   He cooks dinner. (before)

6. I go home.

   I clean my house. (when)

Contrasting *Will* and the Future Continuous

Examining Meaning and Use

Read the sentences and answer the questions below. Then discuss your observations and read the Meaning and Use Notes to check them.

1a. Don't worry. I'll pick up the kids after work.
1b. I'll be picking up the kids after work. Then I'll be going straight home.

2a. Don't call Bob at six. He'll probably be eating dinner then.
2b. Don't call Bob at six. He'll probably eat dinner then.

1. Compare 1a and 1b. Which one describes a plan? Which one expresses a promise?

2. Compare 2a and 2b. Which one refers to an activity in progress? Which one refers to the beginning of an activity?

Meaning and Use Notes

> **Future Activities in Progress**
>
> **1** The future continuous expresses an activity in progress at a specific time in the future. Like all other continuous forms, the future continuous makes you think of a situation as ongoing.
>
> At this time tomorrow, **I'll be leaving** for Hawaii.
> **I'll be staying** in Hawaii for three weeks.

> **Promises and Requests vs. Plans and Expectations**
>
> **2A** Especially in the first person, *will* and the future continuous express different meanings. A sentence with *will* can be used to make a promise. However, the same sentence in the future continuous typically expresses a plan or expectation.
>
> *Future with* Will *(a Promise)*   *Future Continuous (a Plan or Expectation)*
> **I'll finish** this tomorrow.   **I'll be finishing** this tomorrow.

2B A question with *will* can be used to make a request. However, the same question in the future continuous asks about a plan or expectation. This question may lead to a request in a more indirect and polite way.

Future with Will *(a Request)*

A: **Will** you **stop** at the post office tomorrow to send this package?

B: Sure.

Future Continuous (a Question About a Plan)

A: **Will** you **be stopping** at the post office tomorrow?

B: Yes, I will.

A: Could you send this package?

C1 Listening for Meaning and Use

► Notes 1, 2A, 2B

Listen to each situation. Choose the sentence that most appropriately follows what you hear.

1. **a.** So hurry up. She'll be coming at 8:00.
   b. So hurry up. She'll come at 8:00.

2. **a.** Will you open it for me?
   b. Will you be opening it for me?

3. **a.** I won't be baking a cake today.
   b. I won't bake a cake.

4. **a.** I'll e-mail it to you by 9:00 A.M. tomorrow.
   b. I'll be e-mailing it to you by 9:00 A.M. tomorrow.

5. **a.** We'll be getting back to you as soon as possible.
   b. We'll get back to you as soon as possible.

6. **a.** Will you be getting some more from the supply room?
   b. Will you get some more from the supply room, please?

7. **a.** Will you go past the bus stop?
   b. Will you be going past the bus stop?

8. **a.** . . . she'll be getting married.
   b. . . . she'll get married.

C2 Expressing Promises, Plans, and Expectations

► Notes 1, 2A, 2B

Work with a partner. For each situation, finish writing the conversation using the future with *will* or the future continuous. Then act out your conversations.

1. **Student A:** You are the parent. You are going away for the weekend. You are nervous about leaving your teenage son or daughter alone. Discuss your concerns with him or her.

   Student B: You are the teenager. Reassure your parent.

   Parent: I hope you'll be home by 11:00.

   Teenager: I promise I won't break any rules. Anyway, I won't be going out much. I'll be studying for my exams tonight.

   Parent: When will you be . . . ?

2. **Student A:** You are the employee. You need to leave early because of a family problem. Make promises about your work.

   Student B: You are the boss. Your employee has a family problem and needs to leave work early. You are concerned about your employee's problem, but the project needs to get done.

   Employee: Could I leave early today? I need to help my mother.

   Boss: Will you be able to finish your work?

   Employee: I promise I'll . . .

C3 Using Direct and Indirect Requests

► Note 2B

A. Work with a partner. Write a conversation for each situation. Use *will* to make a direct request.

1. You want to borrow your friend's math notes.

   A: Will you please lend me your math notes?
   B: Sure. No problem.

2. You want your friend to drive you to school.

3. You would like to use your brother's car.

4. Your friend is going to buy concert tickets and you would like one, too.

B. Work with the same partner. Write another conversation for each situation in part A. Use the future continuous to make an indirect request that asks about a plan. Then respond to the indirect request.

   A: Will you be using your math notes this afternoon?
   B: No. Do you want to borrow them?
   A: Yes, I do. Thanks.

Contrasting *Be Going To,* the Present Continuous as Future, and the Simple Present as Future

Examining Meaning and Use

Read the sentences and answer the questions below. Then discuss your observations and read the Meaning and Use Notes to check them.

    a. <u>I'm going to exercise during my lunch hour everyday.</u>
    b. <u>Classes start on September 1</u>.
    c. I'm tired. <u>I'm not working tonight.</u>

Think about the meanings of the underlined sentences in each context.

1. Which two sentences describe a plan that may or may not actually happen?

2. Which sentence describes a scheduled event that is unlikely to change?

Meaning and Use Notes

> **Expressing Plans or Intentions**
>
> **1A** Both *be going to* and the present continuous as future are used to talk about a planned event or future intention. A future time expression is stated or implied with the present continuous.
>
> *Future with* Be Going To
> He**'s not going to take** any classes this summer. He**'s going to work** full-time.
>
> *Present Continuous as Future*
> He**'s not taking** any classes this summer. He**'s working** full-time.
>
> ---
>
> **1B** The meanings of *be going to* and the present continuous as future are sometimes similar, but not exactly the same. With *be going to,* the speaker may not have an exact plan. With the present continuous as future, the plan is often more definite.
>
> *Future with* Be Going To
> I**'m going to leave** my job (someday). I'm just so unhappy.
>
> *Present Continuous as Future*
> I**'m leaving** my job (next week). I've been unhappy for too long.

(Continued on page 62)

2A The simple present as future is used for scheduled events that usually cannot be changed. It is common in more formal contexts.

Simple Present as Future

Printed Program: The conference **starts** on Tuesday evening and **ends** on Saturday afternoon.

Trip Itinerary: The flight **leaves** Chicago at 10:02 and **arrives** in Palm Beach at 12:36.

Announcement: Our new branch office **opens** this Monday at the Cedar Mall.

2B When talking about scheduled events, the simple present, the present continuous, or *be going to* can express the same meaning. However, the simple present as future is more likely to imply that the schedule is beyond the control of the speaker.

Present Continuous as Future and Future with Be Going To

Student: **I'm leaving** at midnight. That's my plan.
I'm going to leave at midnight. That's my plan.

Simple Present as Future

Soldier: I **leave** at midnight. Those are my orders.

Making Predictions

3 Use *be going to* to make predictions. Do not use the present continuous or the simple present as future to make predictions.

Future with Be Going To

They**'re going to win** tonight.

Everyone thinks so.

*They're winning tonight. (INCORRECT)

*They win tonight. (INCORRECT)

It**'s going to rain** later.

*It rains later. (INCORRECT)

*It is raining later. (INCORRECT)

Listen to each pair of sentences. Do they have approximately the same meaning or different meanings? Check (✓) the correct column.

	SAME	DIFFERENT
1.		✓
2.		
3.		
4.		
5.		
6.		

D2 **Expressing Plans, Scheduled Events, and Predictions** ► Notes 1A, 2A, 2B, 3

A. Build as many logical sentences as possible. Use an item from each column. Punctuate your sentences correctly. Which sentences are plans or scheduled events? Which sentences can only be predictions?

We're having a party tomorrow.

we're having we're going to have we have	a party a storm an exam an election a sale	tomorrow

B. Choose the nouns below that can appropriately begin the sentence. Which nouns would make the sentence illogical? Discuss each of your choices.

_____ begins tomorrow.

An explosion	My new job
It	School
A snowstorm	Winter vacation

A. Work with a partner. Look at the European trip itinerary below and follow the instructions. When you are finished, switch roles for the U.S. trip itinerary.

Student A: You are the travel agent. Call your client and read the trip itinerary. Use the simple present as future to describe the itinerary.

Student B: You are the client. Take notes and ask questions.

Travel Agent: *You leave New York at 7:00 P.M. on July 5.*
Client: *What airline do I take?*
Travel Agent: *French Airways.*

United States Trip Itinerary

August 19	Leave New York, La Guardia Airport (Skyway Airlines, Flight 299 at 8:00 A.M.)
	Arrive Washington, D.C., Dulles Airport 9:30 A.M.
August 19–22	Washington, D.C.
August 22	Leave Washington, D.C., Dulles Airport (Northeast Airlines, Flight 137 at 2:00 P.M.)
	Arrive Atlanta, William B. Hartsfield Airport 4:00 P.M.
August 22–26	Atlanta
August 26	Leave Atlanta, William B. Hartsfield Airport (Northeast Airlines, Flight 201 at 9:00 A.M.)
	Arrive Orlando International Airport 10:30 A.M.
August 26–31	Orlando
September 1	Drive to Miami Beach
September 1–7	Miami Beach
September 7	Leave Miami International Airport (Skyway Airlines, Flight 122 at 1:00 P.M.)
	Arrive New York, La Guardia Airport 4:00 P.M.

European Trip Itinerary

July 5	Leave New York, Kennedy Airport (French Airways, Flight 139 at 7:00 P.M.)
July 6	Arrive Paris, Charles de Gaulle Airport 8:00 A.M. (Flight time: 7 hours)
July 6–11	Paris
July 11	Leave Paris, Charles de Gaulle Airport (Air Britain, Flight 267 at 11:00 A.M.)
	Arrive London Heathrow Airport 11:15 A.M. (Flight time: 1 hour, 15 minutes)
July 11–14	London
July 15–22	Car trip through Scotland
July 23	Return to London
July 24	Leave London Heathrow Airport (French Airways, Flight 298 at 12:00 PM.)
July 25	Arrive New York, Kennedy Airport 3:00 P.M. (Flight time: 8 hours)

B. Send an e-mail message to a friend who lives in one of the places you will be visiting in part A. Describe your itinerary and find out if your friend can meet you.

Dear Chris,

I'm hoping that we can meet for dinner during my trip to Florida next month. I leave New York on August 19, and then I stop in Washington D.C. and Atlanta for a few days. I arrive in Orlando on August 26 for three days. Are you going to be in town during that time?

Min-hee

Contrasting *Will*, the Future Continuous, and *Be Going To*

Examining Meaning and Use

Read the sentences and complete the tasks below. Then discuss your observations and read the Meaning and Use Notes to check them.

1a. Don't be disappointed about the canceled ski trip. It'll snow soon.
1b. Wear your hat. It's probably going to snow.

2a. **Hanna:** Can someone open that window for me?
     Shelley: I'll do it.
2b. **Kevin:** What's your decision about the job?
     Laura: I'm going to do it.

1. Underline the future verb forms in the sentences.

2. Which pair contrasts a quick decision with a plan thought about in advance?

3. Which pair expresses predictions that may or may not happen?

Meaning and Use Notes

> **Predictions and Expectations with Similar Meanings**
>
> **1A** *Will, be going to,* and the future continuous can be used to make predictions or state expectations with similar meaning. With predictions the speaker is less certain that an event will occur. With expectations, the speaker is more certain.
>
> | *Predictions* | *Expectations* |
> |---|---|
> | It **will warm up** tomorrow. | The bank **will close** early tomorrow. |
> | It **will be warming up** tomorrow. | The bank **will be closing** early tomorrow. |
> | It **is going to warm up** tomorrow. | The bank **is going to close** early tomorrow. |

(Continued on page 66)

1B *Will* and the future continuous are frequently used in more formal contexts than *be going to*. Information in a more formal context is usually restated with *be going to* in conversation.

Future with Will *and Future Continuous (More Formal)*
    Sign: The bank **will close** at 1:00 P.M. today.
Weather Report: It **will be warming up** tomorrow.

Future with Be Going To *(Less Formal)*
Speaker: The bank **is going to close** at 1:00 P.M. today.
Speaker: It**'s going to warm up** tomorrow.

More Certain and Less Certain Predictions

2 With predictions, the meanings of *will* and *be going to* are sometimes similar, but not exactly the same. Use *be going to* when an event is fairly certain to happen very soon because there is evidence for it. Do not use *will* in this situation.

Future with Be Going to *(More Certain Events)*
They**'re going to win** tonight. They're the best team.
Look at the clouds. It**'s going to rain.**

Future with Will *(Less Certain Events)*
They**'ll win** tonight if they can keep the ball.
*Look at the clouds. It will rain. (INCORRECT)

Quick Decisions vs. Advance Plans

3 Especially in first person, *will* and *be going to* express different meanings. A sentence with *will* can express a quick decision or offer. However, the same sentence with *be going to* expresses a plan thought about in advance.

Future with Will *(a Quick Decision)*
A: Does anyone want to help me?
B: I**'ll help.** What can I do first?

Future with Be Going To *(an Advance Plan)*
A: What are your plans for the weekend?
B: I**'m going to help** my sister move tomorrow.

4 Future time clauses show the order of two future events. The specific order of events usually depends on the choice of the time word, not on the choice of future form. *Before, after, until, as soon as* (= right after), *by the time* (= before), and *when* introduce the time clause.

First Event	*Second Event*
I'm going to buy the novel	**before I get on the plane.**
After I buy the novel,	I'll get on the plane.
I'll be reading the novel	**until the plane lands.**
As soon as I get off the plane,	I'll get my bags.
I'll be in the baggage area	**by the time you get to the airport.**

⚠ In sentences with *when*, the choice between using *will* or the future continuous can affect the order of events because the future continuous activity is in progress and the *will* activity is not.

First Event	*Second Event*	
I'll be making dinner	**when** you get home.	(I'll start dinner, and then you'll get home.)
When you get home,	**I'll make** dinner.	(You'll get home, and then I'll start dinner.)

E1 **Listening for Meaning and Use** ► Notes 1A, 1B, 2, 3

 Listen to each situation. Choose the sentence that most appropriately follows what you hear.

1. **a.** That glass is going to fall.
   b. That glass will fall.

2. **a.** An agent is going to be with you shortly.
   b. An agent will be with you shortly.

3. **a.** I'm going to get it.
   b. I'll get it.

4. **a.** I'm going to read.
   b. I'll read.

5. **a.** I'll do it.
   b. I'm going to do it.

6. **a.** It will rain.
   b. It's going to rain.

7. **a.** Sure. I'll get it for you.
   b. Sure. I'll be getting it for you.

8. **a.** I'll work in an art museum.
   b. I'm going to work in an art museum.

E2 Restating Formal Announcements

► Notes 1A, 1B

Work with a partner. Decide in what context you might hear or see each sentence. Then use *be going to* to state each one in a less formal way.

1. The weather will be cool tomorrow with a chance of rain.

   Context: radio weather forecast
   Restatement: It's going to be cool tomorrow with a chance of rain.

2. Flight 276 will be arriving at Gate 12.

3. On April 1, the fare will increase to $1.75.

4. Classes will resume on January 22.

5. Tonight we will begin with a short poem.

E3 Restating Predictions

► Note 2

Work with a partner. Restate these predictions with *will*, if possible. Discuss why *will* would be inappropriate in some contexts.

1. I think that genetic engineering is going to become more widespread.

   I think that genetic engineering will become more widespread.

2. That car is speeding and the road is icy. The driver is going to lose control.

3. Computers are probably going to cost much less in a few years.

4. There are two seconds left in the hockey game. The buzzer is going to sound.

5. In a few years, "smart refrigerators" are going to tell owners when they need milk.

6. The patient's heart is failing. I'm sorry. He's going to die.

E4 Making Quick Decisions and Stating Plans

► Note 3

A. Work in small groups. Brainstorm a list of what needs to be done for each situation. Then go around the group and have members volunteer for specific tasks using *will*.

1. Your kitchen is a mess. Your group has 15 minutes to clean it up before some important guests arrive.

   Benito: I'll clean the sink.
   Danilo: I'll sweep the floor.
   Mei: I'll . . .

2. Your group is going to have a potluck dinner tomorrow night.

3. Your group is going to have a garage sale to raise money for charity.

4. Your group will be going camping next weekend.

B. Use your list for a chain summary of each situation in part A. First, restate your quick decision using *going to.* Then, restate the other volunteers' jobs with *be going to.*

> Benito: *I'm going to clean the sink.*
> Danilo: *Benito is going to clean the sink, and I'm going to sweep the floor.*
> Mei: *Benito is going to clean the sink, Danilo is going to sweep the floor,*
>   *and I'm going to . . .*

E5 Understanding the Order of Future Events ► Note 4

A. Read these predictions. For each one, choose the situation that will happen or start first.

1. People will have more time after they open their home offices.
- **a.** People will have more time.
- **(b.)** They'll open their home offices.

2. We'll be doing all the housework until we get a robot.
- **a.** We'll be doing all the housework.
- **b.** We'll get a robot.

3. Many malls will close when on-line shopping becomes more reliable.
- **a.** Many malls will close.
- **b.** On-line shopping will become more reliable.

4. We'll all own portable food testers as soon as they become easier to use.
- **a.** We'll all own portable food testers.
- **b.** They'll become easier to use.

5. We won't use electric cars until gas gets too expensive.
- **a.** We'll use electric cars.
- **b.** Gas will get too expensive.

6. We'll all buy videophones as soon as the prices go down.
- **a.** We'll all buy videophones.
- **b.** The prices will go down.

B. Which predictions in part A do you think are likely to happen? Which ones are unlikely? Why? Discuss your opinions with your classmates.

Work in small groups. Read each example and the sentences that follow. Choose the sentence that is closest in meaning to the example. Discuss your answers.

1. Yes, Jeanne, I'll pick up the children later. Don't worry.
    a. I'm about to pick up the children.
    (b.) I'm willing to pick up the children.

2. Watch out! That ladder is going to fall.
    a. The ladder will fall.
    b. The ladder is about to fall.

3. I'm going to visit my aunt this week. Would you like to come?
    a. I intend to visit my aunt this week.
    b. I promise to visit my aunt this week.

4. I'm meeting Susan at six.
    a. I'm willing to meet Susan at six.
    b. I plan to meet Susan at six.

5. I'll do it when I get home. You have my word.
    a. I promise to do it when I get home.
    b. I expect to do it when I get home.

6. A: No one volunteered to help me.
    B: I'll help.
    a. I'm willing to help.
    b. I'm about to help.

7. I won't clean up tonight. It's your turn.
    a. I don't expect to clean up tonight.
    b. I refuse to clean up tonight.

8. She's going to get the job. The boss was very impressed.
    a. I expect her to get the job.
    b. She intends to get the job.

9. He's starting graduate school in the fall.

   a. He plans to start graduate school.

   b. He's willing to start graduate school.

10. I'm going to China when I have enough money.

   a. I intend to go to China.

   b. I'm willing to go to China.

Beyond the Sentence

Repeating Future Forms in Discourse

In a paragraph or conversation, *be going to* or the future continuous often introduces the topic. The sentences that follow usually use the shorter forms *will* or the present continuous as future to supply more details.

> **I'm going to visit** my aunt this afternoon. First, **I'll stop** at the bakery for her favorite cookies. Then **I'll pick up** my sister, and **we'll get** on the interstate. . . .

> **We're going to cook** a really nice dinner tonight. **I'm making** soup and a new pasta recipe. Kedra **is making** a salad, and Andy **is baking** a cake.

Notice how several future forms can be used, but *will* is the most simple and the most common one to repeat as the paragraph progresses.

> On Sunday, we**'re going to celebrate** my aunt's 40th birthday. We**'ll be taking** her out to her favorite restaurant where two of her friends **are joining** us. We**'ll order** her favorite meal and then, for dessert, we**'ll have** a cake with 40 candles. It**'ll be** fun to spend the afternoon with her.

E7 **Repeating Future Forms in Discourse**

Write a paragraph about something you are going to do in the next month, for example, take a trip or visit a friend. Be specific and explain exactly what you are going to do. Begin your paragraph with *be going to* or the future continuous, but use shorter future forms or other verbs to supply the details.

> I'm going to visit my sister and her family in two weeks. I'll stop there on my way to a conference in San Francisco. We'll probably go out to dinner. We also intend to . . .

F Combining Form, Meaning, and Use

F1 Thinking About Meaning and Use

Choose the best response to complete each conversation. Then discuss your answers in small groups.

1. **A:** The milk spilled.
   B: I'll be getting a sponge. / I'll get a sponge.

2. **A:** Why can't you come to our party this weekend?
   B: I'll work. / I'll be working.

3. **A:** Why did you leave the door open?
   B: I'm going to carry in the packages. / I'll carry in the packages.

4. **A:** The doorbell is ringing.
   B: I'll answer it. / I'll be answering it.

5. **A:** I'm ready to take your order.
   B: I'll have a bowl of soup. / I have a bowl of soup.

6. **A:** Why did you turn on the oven?
   B: I'm making a cake later. / I'll make a cake later.

7. **A:** What are your plans for dinner?
   B: I'm going to cook pasta. / I'll cook pasta.

8. **A:** What does your work schedule say about next week?
   B: I'll work Monday and Friday. / I work Monday and Friday.

9. **A:** You'll have some free time in an hour.
   B: Maybe I'll do my homework. / Maybe I'll be doing my homework.

10. **A:** Who volunteered before to pick up the pizza for tonight's party?
    B: I did. I'll get it. / I did. I'm going to get it.

Find the errors in these paragraphs and correct them. There may be more than one way to correct an error.

One of the most exciting advances in medicine in the next few years is ~~gonna~~ *going to be* ~~be~~ the widespread use of robots in the

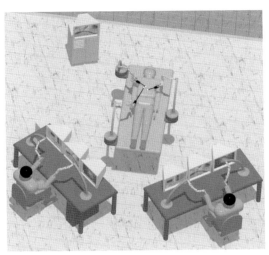

operating room. Experts predict that "robot assistants" are never replacing surgeons. Nevertheless, there is no doubt that robots going to revolutionize surgery.

In just a few years, robots become the standard in certain types of heart surgery, eye surgery, hip surgery, and brain surgery. Why this is going to happen? The answer is simple. No surgeon will ever be able to keep his or her hand as steady as the hand of a robot. No surgeon is ever being able to greatly magnify a microscopic blood vessel with his or her own eyes. These are simple and routine tasks for medical robots.

Some patients are still worried, however. In the words of one patient before hip surgery, "How do I know the robot doesn't go crazy? Maybe it drills a hole in my head instead of my hip!"

Surgeons are quick to reassure their patients. "That's impossible," says one optimistic surgeon. "I promise that isn't happening. Robots are medical assistants. They'll work when I am going to give them a command, and they'll stop when I will say so. I be right there the whole time."

Follow these steps to write a page in a personal journal.

1. It is the beginning of a new year, and you are thinking about your future. Try to picture your life in ten or twenty years from now. How is your life going to change? What improvements will there be? What problems will there be? What will your friends or relatives be doing? Make some brief notes to answer these questions.

2. Use your notes to write a first draft consisting of a few paragraphs about your future. Remember to use appropriate future forms to express your ideas. Pay attention to the forms you use in the introductions to paragraphs, and the ones that are repeated many times.

3. Read over your work carefully and circle grammar, spelling, and punctuation errors. Work with a partner to decide how to fix the errors. Then rewrite your draft with the changes that you and your partner discussed.

▶ Beyond the Classroom

Searching for Authentic Examples

Find examples of English grammar in everyday life. Choose one of the tasks below. Be prepared to discuss your findings.

A. Listen to a weather report on the radio or TV. Write down five examples of future forms and bring them to class. Why do you think these future forms were used?

B. Listen to recorded announcements, telephone answering machines, or news broadcasts. Write down five examples of future forms and bring them to class. Which forms did you hear? Why do you think the particular forms were used? Are there other forms that could replace them?

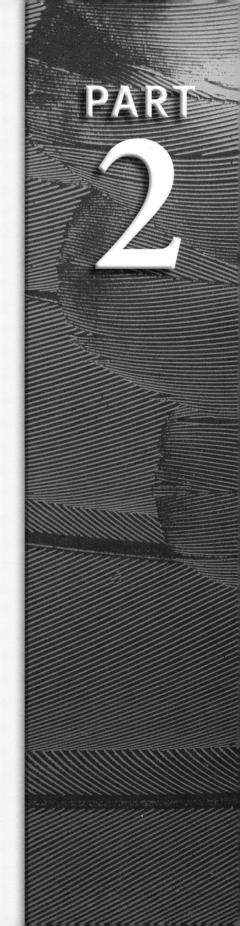

Connecting the Present, Past, and Distant Past

The Present Perfect

A The Questions That Stump the Scientists

A1 Before You Read

Discuss these questions.

Can you name some important scientific discoveries that happened recently? Why are they important? Do you think there are some questions that scientists will never be able to answer? What are they?

A2 Read

 Read this magazine article to find out what problems scientists still hope to solve.

The Questions That Stump the Scientists

We've come to "the end of science," writer John Horgan declared recently, saying that scientists have already made all the really important discoveries. With
5 future jobs on their minds, worried young scientists quickly responded with lists of what they don't know. After all, somewhere between the big unanswerable problems, like the meaning of life and the
10 very specialized subjects of most doctoral theses, there must be some questions that are both important and answerable. An informal survey of a variety of young scientists produced some topics that
15 might be worthwhile to look at:

Memory: How does the human brain store knowledge? The brain is a physical organ, so does this mean that memory has a physical part too? We haven't
20 discovered it yet, but if we do, the results will be earthshaking. Consider some possibilities: Will we be able to find certain memories in the brain, change

them, or move them from person to
25 person? And now ask yourself this
question: How many new technologies and
terrifying possibilities from science fiction
can you imagine?

Missing Matter: Very simply, we can't find
30 most of the universe. Physicists have
estimated the total quantity of material in
the universe, but they've observed only
about 10 percent of it. Are the equations
wrong, or haven't they found everything
35 yet? Are there entire new classes of matter
that are part of the universe?

Are We Alone? It's a simple yes or no
question. According to statistics, it's very
likely that life has evolved elsewhere in
40 the universe. However, we're still waiting
for the first bit of convincing evidence of
life somewhere else.

Have we reached the end of scientific
discovery? "No way," says one young
45 scientist from the University of British
Columbia. Like most scientists, he
cheerfully concludes that we've only just
begun to make important discoveries.
What do you think?

Adapted from *Newsweek*

---

doctoral theses: book-length papers written by university
  students to get advanced university degrees
matter: material that makes up the universe

physical: related to the body, not spiritual or mental
store: to collect and keep for later use
stump: to make someone unable to answer

After You Read

Write *T* for true or *F* for false. Change the false statements to true ones.

_F_ **1.** John Horgan thinks we are just beginning to make important discoveries.
  John Horgan thinks that we've come to the end of science.

_____ **2.** Young scientists think there are still many questions to study.

_____ **3.** Scientists know everything about the human brain.

_____ **4.** Scientists can move memories from one person to another person.

_____ **5.** Physicists are able to observe the whole universe.

_____ **6.** Scientists think there is probably life elsewhere in the universe.

B The Present Perfect

Examining Form

Look back at the article on page 78 and complete the tasks below. Then discuss your observations and read the Form charts to check them.

1. Two examples of the present perfect are underlined. Find seven more examples.

2. What are the two different forms of *have* in these examples? When is each one used?

3. Sort your examples into regular and irregular verbs. How do you know the difference?

Affirmative Statements

SUBJECT + *HAVE*	PAST PARTICIPLE	
You've	studied	physics.
He's	done	research.
They've	found	the answers.

Negative Statements

SUBJECT	*HAVE* + *NOT*	PAST PARTICIPLE	
You	haven't	studied	physics.
He	hasn't	done	research.
They	haven't	found	the answers.

Yes/No Questions

HAVE	SUBJECT	PAST PARTICIPLE	
Have	you	studied	physics?
Has	he	done	research?
Have	they	found	the answers?

Short Answers

AFFIRMATIVE			NEGATIVE		
	I	have.		I	haven't.
Yes,	he	has.	No,	he	hasn't.
	they	have.		they	haven't.

Information Questions

WH- WORD	HAVE	SUBJECT	PAST PARTICIPLE	
Where	**has**	he	**studied?**	
How long	**have**	they	**done**	research?

WH- WORD + HAVE			PAST PARTICIPLE	
Who's			**studied**	the problem?
What's			**happened**	lately?

- The past participle of regular verbs is the same as the simple past form (verb + -*ed*). See Appendices 4 and 5 for spelling and pronunciation rules for verbs ending in -*ed*.
- Irregular verbs have special past participle forms. See Appendix 6 for irregular verbs and their past participles.
- See Appendix 14 for contractions with *have*.

⚠ Do not confuse the contraction of *is* with the contraction of *has* in the present perfect.

He's **doing** research. = He **is doing** research. (He's currently doing research.)

He's **done** research. = He **has done** research. (He did research at some time in the past.)

⚠ Do not repeat *have/has* when present perfect verb phrases are connected by *and* or *or*.

He **has washed** his face and **brushed** his teeth.

B1 ▶ **Listening for Form**

🎧 **Listen to the sentences and choose the one that you hear.**

1. He's one of the racers. / (He's won the race.)

2. They called their senator in Washington. / They've called their senator in Washington.

3. Who's reading the book over there? / Who's read the book over there?

4. Where's the team playing this week? / Where's the team played this week?

5. She's worrying about her father. / She's worried about her father.

6. Who's going fishing? / Who's gone fishing?

7. You bought all of the equipment already. / You've bought all of the equipment already.

8. We looked up his telephone number. / We've looked up his telephone number.

Choose the ten verb forms below each sentence that can correctly complete it.

1. I haven't _____ it.

   (caught)   cooked   eaten   found   had   saw   took
   chose   did   forgotten   gotten   heard   sung   written

2. It hasn't _____.

   appeared   broken   exploded   froze   happened   rained   sunk
   began   came   fallen   gone   left   started   tore

3. Why haven't you _____ it?

   allowed   cut   drank   driven   rang   spent   thrown
   bought   destroyed   drawn   kept   sang   taken   wore

Build as many meaningful sentences as possible. Use an item from each column. Punctuate your sentences correctly.

I have arrived early.

I she it have	have hasn't you	arrived early snowed a lot melted quickly been sick forgotten your umbrella bought herself anything

Complete these conversations with the words in parentheses and the present perfect. Use contractions when possible. Then practice the conversations with a partner.

Conversation 1

A: <u>Have you eaten</u> (you/eat) in the new cafeteria yet?
1

B: No, but I _____ (hear) that it's very good and very fast. It
2
seems that the dean finally _____ (begin) to understand that
3
most students don't have time for long lunch breaks.

Conversation 2

A: How long _____ (Tom/be) married?
1

B: He _____ (be) married for only a year, but he and his wife
2
_____ (know) each other since they were ten.
3

Conversation 3

A: I _____ (not/send) my parents any e-mail for a week. They
1
probably think that something terrible _____ (happen) to me.
2

B: I'm surprised that they _____ (not/call) or
3
_____ (write) you.
4

Conversation 4

A: We had a long list of things to do. What _____ (we/do) so far?
1

B: Well, we _____ (make) a lot of progress. So far, I
2
_____ (do) the laundry, you _____ (sweep)
3   4
the kitchen, and Eric _____ (buy) the groceries. But we still
5
_____ (not/take) the clothes to the cleaners.
6

Informally Speaking

Omitting *Have* and *You*

 Look at the cartoon and listen to the conversation. How is the underlined form in the cartoon different from what you hear?

Have you seen any good movies lately?

Yes, as a matter of fact. Last night I saw that new Japanese movie.

In very informal speech, *have* and *has* are often omitted from questions. The subject *you* may also be omitted if it is clear from the context.

STANDARD FORM	WHAT YOU MIGHT HEAR
Has she **been** here already?	"She been here already?"
Have you **talked** to your brother lately?	"(You) talked to your brother lately?"

B5 Understanding Informal Speech

Listen and write the standard form of the words you hear.

1. <u>Have you heard</u> any good jokes lately?

2. _____ your vacation yet?

3. _____ to the beach yet this summer?

4. _____ at that new restaurant yet?

5. _____ yet?

6. _____ my keys?

7. _____ any programming?

8. _____ you lately?

C Indefinite Past Time

Examining Meaning and Use

Read the sentences and answer the questions below. Then discuss your observations and read the Meaning and Use Notes to check them.

a. I've traveled to Spain and Italy.
b. I traveled to Spain and Italy in July.

1. Which sentence talks about a definite period of time in the past?

2. In which sentence does the time seem less definite or less important?

Meaning and Use Notes

Indefinite Past Time

1A The present perfect often expresses an action or state that happened at an indefinite time in the past. It does not express a definite time in the past; the action happened at any time up to the present.

I've read that book. It's fascinating.

*I've read that book a week ago. (INCORRECT)

What have we learned about life?

*What have we learned about life last year? (INCORRECT)

1B The action or state may occur only once or may be repeated several times.

Ed has been to the exhibit once, but Al has been there many times.

Adverbs Used with Indefinite Past Time

2A Adverbs such as *already, yet, still, so far, ever,* and *never* are frequently used with the present perfect to express the connection between the past and the present.

We've already eaten.
They haven't found the answers yet.

They still haven't finished.
So far, I've visited 16 countries.

2B Use *ever* to ask if an event took place at any time in the past. Only use negative forms of *ever (not ever, never)* in statements (not in questions).

A: Have you ever taken a psychology course?
B: I've read a few popular psychology books, but I've never actually taken a course.

🎧 Listen and choose the best answer for each question.

1. **a.** Yes, I have.
    b. Twice.
    c. No, it hasn't.

2. **a.** Yes, several times.
    b. Here's one.
    c. No, she hasn't.

3. **a.** No, I haven't.
    b. She's coming soon.
    c. Yes, it has.

4. **a.** Not now.
    b. Yes, it has.
    c. Not yet.

5. **a.** No, never.
    b. No, she hasn't.
    c. No, I haven't.

6. **a.** No, not yet.
    b. Everything, except the laundry.
    c. I've already done it.

C2 **Talking About Life Experiences with *Ever*** ▶ Note 2B

A. Work with a partner. Take turns asking and answering questions about your life experiences. Make questions with the expressions below and the present perfect with *ever*. Respond with a present perfect short answer and *Have you?*

1. have a flat tire

    A: Have you ever had a flat tire?
    B: Yes, I have. Have you? OR *No, I haven't. Have you?*

2. bounce a check

3. lose your wallet

4. run out of gas

5. tell a lie

6. meet a famous person

7. see a comet

8. ride a motorcycle

B. Follow these steps to ask your classmates about their life experiences.

1. Make up five questions with *Have you ever* to ask your classmates.

2. Move around the classroom and ask different classmates the questions. Return to your seat and tell the class what you have learned.

    I'm going to tell you about Paula. She has flown an airplane and . . .

C3 **Making Up Reminders with Indefinite Past Time**   ▶ Notes 1A, 2A

A. List three or four things you need to do to prepare for each of these situations.

   1. You are going to mail your telephone bill.

      write a check to the telephone company, address the envelope, . . .

   2. You have your first job interview tomorrow.

   3. You have just picked out a used car to buy.

   4. You are going to the beach.

B. Work with a partner. Exchange lists and take turns. Use your partner's lists to make up reminders. Ask about what has been done for each situation. Use the present perfect and adverbs where appropriate.

   Have you written the check yet?
   Have you packed the sunscreen already?

C. Take turns asking and answering the questions on your lists. Reply using short answers.

   A: Have you written the check yet?
   B: Yes, I have. OR *No, I haven't. I'll do it tomorrow.*

C4 **Writing About Accomplishments and Progress**   ▶ Notes 1A, 1B, 2A

A. Choose an activity that you have already started planning (for example, a party). Write sentences about your progress using the suggested adverbs and the present perfect. Then tell a partner about your progress.

   1. Name three things that you've accomplished. Use *so far* or *already* in each sentence.

      So far, I've made a list of the guests. OR
      I've already made a list of the guests.

   2. Name three things you still need to do. Use *still* or *yet*.

      I still haven't invited the guests. OR
      I haven't invited the guests yet.

B. Write a paragraph using your ideas from part A.

   I am planning a small surprise dinner for my mother. So far, I have made a list of the guests, but I haven't invited them yet. I still haven't bought the invitations. . . .

D Recent Past Time and Continuing Time up to Now

Examining Meaning and Use

Read the sentences and answer the questions below. Then discuss your observations and read the Meaning and Use Notes to check them.

- **a.** I've worked for a publishing company.
- **b.** I've recently worked for a publishing company.
- **c.** I've worked for a publishing company for two years.

1. Which sentence suggests that the speaker is still working for the publishing company?

2. Which sentences suggest that the speaker doesn't work for the company anymore?

3. Which sentence refers to the recent past?

Meaning and Use Notes

> **Recent Past Time**
>
> **1** The present perfect often describes recent past actions and experiences, especially when their results are important in the present. Adverbs like *lately, recently,* and *just* emphasize this meaning of recent past time. (See the Vocabulary Notes on page 91 for more information about these adverbs.)
>
> *Conversations*
> A: Where**'s** your sister **been** <u>lately</u>? I **haven't seen** her.
> B: She **hasn't been** home very much <u>recently</u>. She's busy looking for a job.
>
> *Announcements*
> Flight 602 from Miami **has landed** at Gate 4.
>
> *News Broadcasts*
> We**'ve** <u>just</u> **learned** that the mayor **has resigned.**
>
> *Telephone Recordings*
> The number you **have dialed** is busy.
>
> *Conclusions*
> (The doorbell is ringing.) I think the guests **have** (<u>just</u>) **arrived.**

2A The present perfect expresses actions and states that began in the past and continue at the present time. These sentences often have expressions with *for, since,* or *all* to indicate how long the situation has lasted.

> A: **How long have** you **lived** here?
> B: **I've lived** here <u>for twenty years</u>. (I still live here.)
> **I've lived** here <u>since 1983</u>. (I still live here.)
> **I've lived** here <u>all my life</u>. (I still live here.)

2B Stative verbs like *be, have,* and *know,* and other verbs that can express duration, such as *keep* or *last,* are commonly used to express continuing time up to now.

> We**'ve known** about it for a long time.
> I**'ve kept** this secret for three months.

⚠️ Verbs that express an instant event such as *arrive, start, stop, hit,* or *realize* are not used to express continuing time up to now. However, they can be used with indefinite past time or recent past time.

Continuing Time up to Now   *Recent Past Time*
*We have arrived for an hour. (INCORRECT)   We **have** <u>just</u> **arrived**.

D1 **Listening for Meaning and Use**   ▶ Notes 1, 2A

A. Listen to each sentence. Does the sentence express recent past time or continuing time up to now? Check (✓) the correct column.

	RECENT PAST TIME	CONTINUING TIME UP TO NOW
1.	✓	
2.		
3.		
4.		
5.		
6.		

(Continued on page 90)

B. 🔊 Listen to each situation and the question that follows it. Choose the correct answer to the question.

1. **a.** 10:00 A.M.
   b. 1:00 P.M.
   c. 11:00 A.M.
   d. 4:00 P.M.

2. **a.** All day.
   b. Since 5:00 P.M.
   c. This morning.
   d. For four hours.

3. **a.** 1:00 P.M.
   b. 3:30 P.M.
   c. 3:00 P.M.
   d. 2:00 P.M.

4. **a.** Since midnight.
   b. For three hours.
   c. For nine hours.
   d. For fifteen hours.

D2 **Talking About Continuing Time up to Now**   ▶ Notes 2A, 2B

Work in groups of three. Switch roles for each phrase. When you are finished, think of two more phrases to ask about.

> **Student A:** Ask a question using *how long* and a phrase below.
> **Students B and C:** Answer using *for*, *all*, or *since*.

1. be in this room

   A: How long have you been in this room?
   B: I've been in this room for ten minutes.
   C: I've been in this room all morning.

2. know how to speak English

3. have your driver's license

4. own this book

5. be a student

6. live in your apartment / house / dorm

7. know the students in this class

8. own your car / bicycle

9. know how to use a computer

10. be in this city

Vocabulary Notes

Adverbs That Express Recent Past Time

Just means "right before now." It comes before the past participle.

The mayor has **just** resigned.

Recently means "not long ago." It comes before the past participle, or at the beginning or end of the sentence.

She's **recently** been away.   She's been away **recently**.

Recently, she's been away.

Lately also means "not long ago." It comes at the beginning or end of the sentence.

Lately, the weather has been awful.   The weather has been awful **lately**.

D3 Reaching Conclusions About Recent Past Time

Work in small groups and look at the pictures. Make up sentences using *just, lately,* and *recently* to describe what you think has just happened.

1.

3.

5.

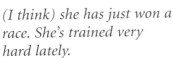

(I think) she has just won a race. She's trained very hard lately.

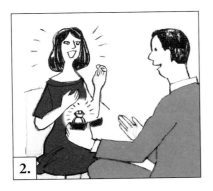

2.

4.

6.

A. These newspaper headlines tell about recent events. Use the information in the headline and the present perfect to complete the first line of each news article.

Mayor Powell Signs Antipollution Legislation

Research Center Receives Grant

Governor Miller Raises Gasoline Taxes

Geologist Makes Rare Discovery

Grocer Wins $2 Million in Lottery

1. For the second time in less than a year, Governor Miller <u>has raised</u> <u>gasoline taxes</u> by 5 percent.

2. Mayor Powell _____ that promises to reduce the amount of carbon monoxide in the air.

3. Douglas Lake, owner of Lake's Groceries, _____.

4. A geologist _____ in the William Robb State Forest, 20 miles west of the city.

5. The Human Behavior Research Center _____ to study the sleep patterns of children.

B. These sentences begin news articles. Write a related short headline with a simple present verb for each one.

1. Severe weather has caused serious delays at all major airports in the region.
   Severe Weather Causes Airport Delays

2. Technology stocks have risen sharply this week.

3. MCJ Industries has moved all of its offices to Texas.

4. State universities have lost millions of dollars in research grants this year.

5. President Perez has left for a 12-day trip to China and Japan.

Contrasting the Present Perfect and the Simple Past

Examining Meaning and Use

Read the sentences and answer the questions below. Then discuss your observations and read the Meaning and Use Notes to check them.

1a. I've worked in Los Angeles for three years. I love my job.
1b. I worked in Los Angeles for three years. I loved my job.

2a. When did you see the movie *Titanic*?
2b. Have you seen the movie *Titanic*?

1. Compare 1a and 1b. In which sentence does the speaker still work in Los Angeles? How do you know?

2. Compare 2a and 2b. Which sentence asks about the time of a past event? Which sentence does not ask about the time of a past event?

Meaning and Use Notes

Continuing Time up to Now vs. Completed Actions

1 The present perfect can express situations that continue at the present time, but the simple past can only express situations that are completed. The simple past can be used to talk about historical events, whereas the present perfect cannot.

Present Perfect	*Simple Past*
She**'s been** lucky all her life. (She is still alive and still lucky.)	She **was** lucky all her life. (She is no longer alive.)
I**'ve worked** there for ten years. (I still work there.)	I **worked** there for ten years. (I don't work there anymore.)
*Alexander Graham Bell has invented the telephone. (INCORRECT)	Alexander Graham Bell **invented** the telephone over 100 years ago.

Indefinite Past Time vs. Definite Past Time

2 Because present perfect sentences do not indicate a definite time, use the present perfect only to talk about an indefinite time. Use the simple past to talk about a definite time.

Present Perfect (Indefinite Past Time)	*Simple Past (Definite Past Time)*
Have you **visited** Maria lately?	**When did** you **visit** Maria?

(Continued on page 94)

3 It is common to use *just, already,* and *yet* with the simple past. The following sentences have the same meaning.

Present Perfect	*Simple Past*
A: You should call Jada.	A: You should call Jada.
B: I**'ve just called** her.	B: I **just called** her.
A: Don't forget to buy some milk.	A: Don't forget to buy some milk.
B: I**'ve already bought** some.	B: I **already bought** some.
A: **Have** you **eaten yet**?	A: **Did** you **eat yet**?
B: No, not yet.	B: No, not yet.

E1) Listening for Meaning and Use ▶ Note 1

Listen to each situation and choose the sentence you hear. Pay attention to the second sentence in each situation to help you understand the context.

1. **a.** I've lived there for a year.
   b. I lived there for a year.

2. **a.** We've worked with him for six months.
   b. We worked with him for six months.

3. **a.** He's kept the secret all week.
   b. He kept the secret all week.

4. **a.** She's studied physics for two years.
   b. She studied physics for two years.

5. **a.** I've had a dog for a long time.
   b. I had a dog for a long time.

6. **a.** I've owned a car for years.
   b. I owned a car for years.

7. **a.** They've worked there for three years.
   b. They worked there for three years.

8. **a.** I've played the piano for years.
   b. I played the piano for years.

Choose the simple past or present perfect forms that best complete the conversation.

Jeff: How long ((have you had) / did you have) this computer?
                                    1

Kim: Let's see. (I've bought / I bought) it when (I've moved / I moved) here,
                          2   3

so (I've owned / I owned) it for a long time.
       4

Jeff: Well, (I've had / I had) mine for two years, and it already seems to be outdated.
                     5

(It's been / It was) very slow lately. Do you think it needs more memory?
     6

Kim: I don't know. (Have you called / Did you call) Janet lately? She knows
                                7

everything about this stuff. (She's worked / She worked) for Computing World
                                        8

since (she's graduated / she graduated).
            9

Jeff: Well, actually, I have tried to reach her. (I've phoned / I phoned) her last night,
                                                         10

but (she was / she's been) out for the evening.
        11

Kim: What about your roommate? (Hasn't he taken / Didn't he take) all kinds of
                                              12

engineering and computing courses last year?

Jeff: Yeah, but he doesn't know much about personal computing. Anyway,

(he's left / he left) town yesterday because his uncle (has died / died) suddenly
     13   14

on Monday. (He lived / He's lived) with his uncle for two years. They were
                 15

very close.

Kim: Oh, I'm sorry to hear that. Why don't you call the Computer Center on

campus? (They were / They have been) very helpful last week when I
                 16

called them.

Jeff: That's a good idea.

Work with a partner. Take turns as Student A and Student B. Imagine today is the town festival.

Student A: Ask about the festival events using the words in parentheses.
Student B: Answer the questions using the schedule.

GALESBURG TOWN FESTIVAL SCHEDULE

12:00 – 12:30	Welcome Speech by Mayor Ferrara
12:30 – 1:00	Jerry's Juggling Show
1:00 – 1:30	The Melodians Barbershop Quartet
1:30 – 2:00	Storytellers
2:00 – 2:30	Three-legged Race
2:30 – 3:00	Pie-eating Contest
3:00 – 3:30	Line Dancers from Green Apple Ranch
3:30 – 4:00	Folk-Dancing Club: Dances from Around the World
4:00 – 4:30	Jazz from the *Blues Men*
4:30 – 7:30	Picnic Dinner
7:30 – 8:00	Request-a-Song Sing-Along
8:00 – 8:45	Fireworks

1. It's 2:00 P.M. (the juggler/perform)

   A: *Has the juggler already performed?*   OR   A: *Did the juggler perform already?*
   B: *Yes, he has. He finished an hour ago.*   B: *Yes, he did. He finished an hour ago.*

2. It's 3:00 P.M. (the jazz band/play)

   A: *Has the jazz band played yet?*   OR   A: *Did the jazz band play yet?*
   B: *No, they haven't. They play at four.*   B: *No, they didn't. They play at four.*

3. It's 11:00 A.M. (the mayor/speak)

4. It's 5:00 P.M. (the picnic/start)

5. It's 7:00 P.M. (the fireworks/begin)

6. It's 3:00 P.M. (the three-legged race/happen)

7. It's 3:45 P.M. (the pie-eating contest/end)

8. It's 2:00 P.M. (The Melodians/sing)

9. It's 6:00 P.M. (the sing-along/take place)

10. It's 4:10 P.M. (the line dancers/perform)

Beyond the Sentence

Introducing Topics with the Present Perfect

The present perfect has a special introductory use in larger contexts. It is often used at the beginning of a written text (or conversation) to introduce a general idea with indefinite past time. The text often continues with the simple past to give more specific details about the general idea.

> *A Newspaper Article*
>
> For the second time in two weeks, an inmate **has escaped** from the local prison. Last night at 2:00 A.M., several guards **heard** strange noises coming from an underground tunnel. An investigation **revealed** . . .

E4 Introducing Topics with the Present Perfect

A. **Read each present perfect introductory sentence. Then write a sentence in the simple past that adds a detail. Tell when the particular experience happened.**

1. Computers have helped me a lot with my schoolwork. For example,

   I did all my assignments on a computer last semester.

2. There have been several disasters in recent years. For example,

   _____

3. I've made many mistakes in my life. For example,

   _____

4. There have been many changes in my country / town / family lately. For example,

   _____

5. I've learned a lot of important things in recent years. For example,

   _____

6. I've taken long trips by bus / train / car. For example,

   _____

B. **Write a paragraph. Choose one of the six items in part A as the beginning of your paragraph. Use the simple past to develop specific examples and details.**

> Computers have helped me a lot with my schoolwork. For example, I did all my assignments on a computer last semester. I was able to type and edit my work quickly. Most importantly, I found a lot of useful information on the Internet without leaving home.

F Combining Form, Meaning, and Use

F1 Thinking About Meaning and Use

Read each sentence and the statements that follow. Write *T* if the statement is true, *F* if it is false, or *?* if you do not have enough information to decide. Then discuss your answers in small groups.

1. I've studied Russian.

   _F_ a. I'm still studying Russian.

   _T_ b. I studied Russian at some time in the past.

2. I haven't eaten breakfast this morning.

   _____ a. It's still morning.

   _____ b. I'm going to eat breakfast.

3. I've worked there for many years.

   _____ a. I don't work there anymore.

   _____ b. I'm changing jobs next week.

4. I still haven't visited the exhibit.

   _____ a. I didn't visit the exhibit.

   _____ b. I expect to visit the exhibit.

5. I've owned a house.

   _____ a. I still own a house.

   _____ b. I bought a house some time in the past.

6. I've had this cold for two weeks already.

   _____ a. I don't have this cold anymore.

   _____ b. I caught this cold two weeks ago.

7. I lived there for two years.

_____ **a.** I still live there.

_____ **b.** I moved two years ago.

8. I've already finished my work.

_____ **a.** I finished sooner than expected.

_____ **b.** I finished it a few minutes ago.

F2 Editing

Find the errors in this paragraph and correct them.

Since 1993, the Hubble space telescope has ~~provide~~ _provided_ us with extraordinary pictures of the universe. It has shown us new comets and black holes. It is found exploding stars. Astronomers have been amazed that the Hubble space telescope have sent back so many spectacular images. But it hasn't always been this way. The Hubble space telescope was actually been in space since 1990. However, for the first three years, there was a problem with the main mirror. The pictures that it sent back to earth were not at all clear. In 1993, two astronauts have fixed the problem. They took a space walk and dropped a special lens over the mirror. Since then, there was no problem with the space telescope.

Beyond the Classroom

Searching for Authentic Examples

Find examples of English grammar in everyday life. Choose one of the tasks below. Be prepared to discuss your findings.

A. Look in newspapers, in magazines, or on the Internet. Write down five examples of the introductory use of the present perfect and bring them to class. What tense or tenses are used in the sentences that immediately follow your examples?

B. Look in a newspaper for sentences in the present perfect. Write down two examples each of indefinite past time, recent past time, and continuing time up to now, and bring them to class. Which is the easiest to find?

C. Listen to conversations, movies, TV shows, or radio or TV news broadcasts. Write down five examples of the simple past with *just, already,* and *yet,* and bring them to class. Rewrite each sentence in the present perfect. Do the simple past and the present perfect sentences have the same meanings?

Speaking

In small groups, follow these steps to prepare a role-play of a reporter conducting an interview.

1. Find a short article in a newspaper or magazine about a recent discovery in science or a recent news event. Bring it to class to share with your group. Explain the contents of the article to your group using the present perfect and past forms where appropriate.

2. Choose one of the articles to work with. Pretend that one student is a reporter and the others are participants in the discovery or other event described in the article.

3. The reporter should interview the participants, and they should provide details about the incident or discovery in their own words. Use the present perfect and the simple past where appropriate.

The Present Perfect Continuous

A Aging—New Answers to Old Questions

A1 Before You Read

Discuss these questions.

Do you look forward to old age? Why or why not? Why do people want to stay young? What are some things that people do in order to stay young?

A2 Read

Read this magazine article to find out what researchers are learning about the process of growing old.

Aging—New Answers to Old Questions

SISTER ESTHER SCOOTS DOWN A corridor toward the ceramics studio in the convent where she lives. She <u>has been enjoying</u> pottery since she retired
5 from her career as a schoolteacher. "That was six years ago," she says, doing the math quickly in her head. Back when she was 96. "I thought it was time to slow down a little," she continues, as she moves
10 actively about the studio.

Then there is Sister Matthia, 103 years old. For the past several years, her active fingers have been knitting a pair of mittens every day for charity. That day she
15 was knitting her 1,378th pair.

These women, along with about 550 others from around the United States, have been participating in a long-term study of aging. The "Nun Study" has been
20 trying to find out how and why we change

as we age, and whether there is anything we can do about it. Researchers have chosen the convent as a perfect place to study aging because all the nuns have such
25 similar backgrounds. They have all eaten similar foods, gotten similar educations, and had similar careers. They have all avoided cigarettes, alcohol, marriage, and

childbearing. Their similarities make
30 it easier to figure out which biological
factors make the difference between those
who age quickly and those who don't.

Current research on aging has already
discovered a great deal about Alzheimer's
35 disease, special genes for aging, cells, and
hormones. But researchers still disagree
on the exact cause of aging. Is it related to
our genes, or is it mostly gradual damage
that occurs as time passes?
40 Meanwhile, researchers at Tufts
University have shown that exercise,
including weight training, has a dramatic
effect on 72- to 98-year-olds. They report
great improvement in muscle strength,
45 walking speed, and the ability to climb

stairs. It seems that exercise naturally
influences many of the same factors in
the aging process that scientists have been
studying. And it's not only the body that
50 needs exercise. The same is true for the
mind. When elderly adults have been
reading, learning, and interacting with
others, they are much less likely to lose
their memories or become senile.
55 Scientists still haven't found the
"fountain of youth," but they have been
getting closer to understanding aging. In
fact, many have already begun to worry
about an entirely new set of questions: Are
60 longer lives necessarily better lives? For how
long should we extend life? How will society
care for more and more elderly people? ■

Adapted from *National Geographic*

aging: growing old
charity: an organization that helps people in need
convent: a building where nuns live
elderly: old
factor: condition

genes: basic parts of a cell that determine characteristics in living things
nun: a woman who has devoted herself to religious life
scoot: to move quickly
senile: weak of mind because of old age

A3 After You Read

Complete these sentences with appropriate words.

1. In the article, Sister Esther is ___102 years old___ .

2. Sister Matthia _____ every day.

3. The Nun Study is research on _____ .

4. Scientists have chosen to study nuns because their lives are very _____ .

5. Scientists wonder whether aging is related to _____ or if it is caused by gradual damage.

6. Research shows that _____ is good for the mind as well as the body.

B The Present Perfect Continuous

Examining Form

Look back at the article on page 102 and complete the tasks below. Then discuss your observations and read the Form charts to check them.

1. An example of the present perfect continuous is underlined. Find five more examples.

2. How many auxiliaries are there in each example? What ending is added to the main verb?

3. What are the two forms of *have* in your examples? When is each one used?

Affirmative Statements				
SUBJECT	*HAVE*	*BEEN*	VERB + *-ING*	
I	**have**			
She	**has**	**been**	**getting**	better.
They	**have**			

Negative Statements					
SUBJECT	*HAVE*	*NOT*	*BEEN*	VERB + *-ING*	
I	**have**				
She	**has**	**not**	**been**	**getting**	better.
They	**have**				

Yes/No Questions				
HAVE	SUBJECT	*BEEN*	VERB + *-ING*	
Have	you			
Has	she	**been**	**getting**	better?
Have	they			

Short Answers					
YES	SUBJECT	*HAVE*	NO	SUBJECT	*HAVE + NOT*
	I	**have.**		I	**haven't.**
Yes,	she	**has.**	**No,**	she	**hasn't.**
	they	**have.**		they	**haven't.**

Information Questions

WH- WORD	HAVE	SUBJECT	BEEN	VERB + -ING	
Who	have	you	been	talking	to?
How	has	she		doing?	

WH- WORD	HAVE		BEEN	VERB + -ING	
What	has		been	happening?	
Who				calling	you?

- The present perfect continuous has two auxiliary verbs: *have* and *been*. Only *have* and *has* form contractions.
- Verbs with stative meanings are not usually used with the present perfect continuous.
    *I have been knowing her. (INCORRECT)
- See Appendix 3 for spelling rules for verbs ending in *-ing*.
- See Appendix 14 for contractions with *have*.

B1 Listening for Form

Listen to the sentences and choose the one you hear.

1. **a.** What's been happening this week?
   (b.) What's happening this week?

2. **a.** Jack has been visiting his grandparents.
   b. Jack has visited his grandparents.

3. **a.** It's rained all day.
   b. It's been raining all day.

4. **a.** They've been living in Florida.
   b. They're living in Florida.

5. **a.** He's been sleeping on the sofa.
   b. He's sleeping on the sofa.

6. **a.** She's been exercising at the gym.
   b. She's exercising at the gym.

Work with a partner. Complete these conversations with the words in parentheses and the present perfect continuous. Use contractions when possible. Then practice the conversations.

Conversation 1

A: What's wrong?

B: I 've been trying _____ (try) to call the doctor for an hour, but the line is
      ___1___
      still busy.

A: It's not an emergency, is it?

B: No, but I _____ (not/feel) well, and I'm starting to worry.
      _____2_____

A: You do look tired. _____ (you/get) enough sleep?
      _____3_____

B: Well, no, I really _____ (not/sleep) very well.
      _____4_____

Conversation 2

A: I _____ (not/go) to the movies at all this summer.
      ___1___

B: Why not?

A: I _____ (help) my parents almost every weekend.
      ___2___
      We _____ (pack up) their house because they're
      ___3___
      going to retire to Arizona next month. The house is very large, so it

      _____ (take) a lot of my time.
      ___4___

Conversation 3

A: We normally don't get any homework in this course, but lately the

      instructor _____ (give) us an hour or two each night.
      ___1___

B: Maybe you _____ (not/make) enough progress, or
      ___2___

      maybe the material _____ (get) more difficult.
      ___3___

Conversation 4

A: You look wonderful. What _____ (you/do)?
      ___1___

B: I _____ (exercise) a lot at the gym, and I
      ___2___

      _____ (not/eat) junk food.
      ___3___

A. Work with a partner. Reorder the words to form a question in the present perfect continuous. Make sure you use every word and correct punctuation.

1. you/how/been/have/lately/feeling

   How have you been feeling lately?

2. who/you/writing to/have/lately/been

3. recently/sleeping/you/well/have/been

4. been/you/working/semester/hard/this/have

5. enough/lately/you/exercising/been/have

6. time/what/recently/getting up/have/you/been

7. doing/you/what/in/the/been/have/evening

8. been/have/where/semester/you/eating/this/lunch

B. Now take turns asking and answering the questions. Respond to each question and then ask *What about you?*

   A: *How have you been feeling lately?*
   B: *I've been feeling fine. What about you?*
   A: *I've been feeling great.*

Use these verbs or your own to write two responses for each sentence below.

daydream	read	stand	talk	work
listen	sit	study	think	write

1. Describe something you have been doing since you came to class.

   I've been sitting in the back of the room. I've been . . .

2. Describe something you haven't been doing since you came to class.

3. Describe two people in your class have been doing since they came to class.

4. Make questions about what your classmates have been doing since they came to class.

Informally Speaking

Omitting *Have*

🎧 Look at the cartoon and listen to the conversation. How is each underlined form in the cartoon different from what you hear?

> Have you been going to the study sessions?

> No. I've been writing my English paper all week. It's due tomorrow.

In informal speech, some speakers may omit *have*. Other speakers may say *have* very quickly so that it is difficult to hear. This happens most often in statements with *I* and in questions with *you*. Notice that the subject *you* may also be omitted if it is clear from the context.

STANDARD FORM	WHAT YOU MIGHT HEAR
I **have been** studying so hard.	"I been studying so hard."
Have you **been doing** the homework lately?	"(You) been doing the homework lately?"

B5 Understanding Informal Speech

🎧 Listen and write the standard form of the words you hear.

1. **A:** _What have you been doing_____ all day?

2. **B:** _____ my friend.

3. **A:** _____ OK?

4. **B:** No, _____ some problems with my back.

5. **A:** _____ at all?

6. **B:** _____ a lot.

Focus on Continuing or Recent Past Activities

Examining Meaning and Use

Read the sentences and answer the questions below. Then discuss your observations and read the Meaning and Use Notes to check them.

a. Look at this library book. Someone has been writing all over it.
b. She's been trying to find information on the Internet, and she's still searching for it.
c. Look. It's finally done! I've been knitting this sweater for months.

1. Which sentence focuses on an activity that began in the past and is continuing into the present?

2. Which sentence is used to reach a conclusion about a current situation?

3. Which expresses an activity that was in progress but just ended?

Meaning and Use Notes

Focus on Continuing Activities up to Now

1 The present perfect continuous most often describes activities that began in the past and are continuing at the present time. The present perfect continuous emphasizes that the activity is ongoing. This meaning can be understood in context, but time expressions with *for* and *since* often help to show continuing time up to now.

I've been reading that novel, too. It's so good. (I'm still reading it.)
I've been writing this letter <u>since four o'clock</u>. (I'm still writing it.)
<u>For the past several years</u>, she**'s been knitting** a pair of mittens every day.
    (She's still knitting a pair every day.)

Focus on Recent Past Activities

2 The present perfect continuous also describes recent situations or activities that were in progress, but have just ended. To emphasize the recent past, adverbs like *recently, just,* and *lately* may be used with the present perfect continuous.

I've been thinking about you <u>recently</u>.
I've <u>just</u> **been reading** the most wonderful book.
What **have** you **been doing** <u>lately</u>?

(Continued on page 110)

> **Common Uses of the Present Perfect Continuous**

3 The present perfect continuous is frequently used to make an excuse along with an apology. It is also often used to reach a conclusion about a current situation.

An Excuse: I'm sorry I haven't called you. I **haven't been feeling** well lately.

A Conclusion: Half of my cake is gone. Someone **has been eating** it!

C1 **Listening for Meaning and Use** ▶ Notes 1–3

🎧 Listen to the conversations between Max and Helen. Check (✓) the correct column to answer each question.

		MAX	HELEN
1.	Who is reading a John Grisham novel?	✓	
2.	Who is no longer sick?		
3.	Who still volunteers at a hospital?		
4.	Who has been to Chicago more than once this year?		
5.	Who has tried to call Eddie more recently?		
6.	Who is playing chess these days?		

C2 **Making Apologies and Excuses** ▶ Note 3

Work with a partner. Use the present perfect continuous to make excuses for your behavior. Begin with an apology. Then practice the conversations.

1. **A:** What's the matter? You're not listening to me.

   B: *I'm sorry. I've been thinking about something else.*

2. **A:** You're really late. What took you so long?

   B: _____

3. **A:** I thought we were going to the movies sometime this week.

   B: _____

4. **A:** You never come home right after school anymore. What's going on?

   B: _____

5. A: Is something wrong? You keep looking out the window.

B: _____

6. A: It was your turn to go grocery shopping, wasn't it? We're out of milk.

B: _____

C3 **Reaching Conclusions**   ► Note 3

Work in small groups. Look at the picture. What can you conclude about what has just been happening? Write as many sentences as possible.

The TV is on. Someone has been watching TV.

A. Work with a partner. The advertisements below are missing introductory sentences that will attract attention. Write one or two present perfect continuous questions to begin each advertisement.

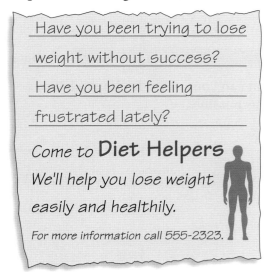

Have you been trying to lose weight without success?

Have you been feeling frustrated lately?

Come to **Diet Helpers**
We'll help you lose weight easily and healthily.

For more information call 555-2323.

1.

_____

_____

_____

Call Apartment Finders Rental Agency at 555-4949.

We'll help you find the kind of apartment you need today.

3.

_____

_____

You need
MORE EXERCISE!
Join the
Aurora Health & Fitness Club
Reasonable rates, friendly staff
Stop by for more information about
a free trial membership.
298 Ridgewood Road
555-0908

2.

_____

_____

You need to get away!

We offer discounted plane and bus fares for students.
Let us help you plan your trip.
Mills Travel Agency
209 West Main St.

4.

B. Create a newspaper, radio, or TV advertisement for one of the businesses below. Begin your advertisement with one or more attention-getting questions in the present perfect continuous. Be prepared to share your ad with the class.

a clothing store   an ice-cream shop   a photocopy center

a dating service   an Internet provider   a take-out restaurant

D Contrasting the Present Perfect Continuous and the Present Perfect

Examining Meaning and Use

Read the sentences and answer the questions below. Then discuss your observations and read the Meaning and Use Notes to check them.

1a. Kathy has been reading the book.
1b. Vera has read the book.

2a. I've been working here for ten years.
2b. I've worked here for ten years.

1. Which pair of sentences express the same meaning?

2. Which pair express different meanings?

3. In sentences 1a and 1b, who has probably finished the book? In which sentence is the activity continuing up to the present?

Meaning and Use Notes

> ### Similar Meanings with Continuing Time up to Now
>
> **1A** Certain common verbs can be used in the present perfect or the present perfect continuous with *for* or *since* with no difference in meaning. These verbs include *live, teach, wear, work, study, stay,* and *feel.*
>
> | *Present Perfect* | *Present Perfect Continuous* |
> |---|---|
> | Mr. Ortiz **has lived** here since 1960. | Mr. Ortiz **has been living** here since 1960. |
> | He**'s taught** English for a long time. | He**'s been teaching** English for a long time. |
> | He**'s worn** the same jacket for years. | He**'s been wearing** the same jacket for years. |
>
> **1B** The meanings of the present perfect and the present perfect continuous are not always the same. Sometimes the focus on the ongoing activity is stronger in the continuous, so you can choose the continuous to emphasize the length of time a situation lasted. Remember, using the continuous can show a more intense or emotional situation.
>
> | *Present Perfect* | *Present Perfect Continuous* |
> |---|---|
> | I**'ve waited** for an hour. | I**'ve been waiting** for an hour. I'm very annoyed. |
> | I**'ve thought** about this for days. | I**'ve been thinking** about this for days. I can't stop. |

(Continued on page 114)

Completed vs. Continuing or Recent Past Activities

2 The present perfect can express a completed activity that may or may not have been recent. In contrast, the present perfect continuous suggests that an activity is continuing up to the present time or was very recently completed.

Present Perfect	*Present Perfect Continuous*
I've read a book about astronomy. (I finished it at some indefinite time in the past.)	**I've been reading** a book about astronomy. (I'm not finished. OR I've just finished.)

⚠️ A sentence with the present perfect continuous usually does not tell how many times an activity is repeated.

Present Perfect	*Present Perfect Continuous*
I've read the report three times.	*I've been reading the report three times. (INCORRECT)

D1 **Listening for Meaning and Use** ► Notes 1A, 1B, 2

🎧 Listen to each situation. Decide whether the situation is completed or continues. Check (✓) the correct column.

	COMPLETED	CONTINUES
1.		✓
2.		
3.		
4.		
5.		
6.		
7.		
8.		

A. Complete this letter with the words in parentheses and the present perfect or the present perfect continuous. In some sentences, either one is acceptable.

Dear Ellen,

How are you and how's your family? <u>Has your father been feeling</u>
₁
(your father / feel) better? I hope so. I _____ (think) about
₂
you a lot and _____ (wonder) if everything is OK.
₃

I _____ (read) the novel that you sent me for my
₄
birthday. So far, I _____ (read) about a hundred pages, and
₅
I'm really enjoying it. I _____ (be) so busy lately that
₆
I _____ (not / have) much time to read, but I hope to finish
₇
it soon.

Right now, I'm writing a paper for my psychology course. I
_____ (write) it for two weeks. It's going to be long. So far,
₈
I _____ (change) the topic four times, but now I'm finally
₉
pleased with it.

What _____ (you / do) during the past few weeks?
₁₀
_____ (you / work) hard? _____ (you / have)
₁₁   ₁₂
any exams yet? I _____ (have) two so far, and I did pretty
₁₃
well on them.

_____ (you / decide) what you're going to do this
₁₄
summer? We really need to make plans soon! Please write!

Love,

Anne

B. Reread the letter in part A. Write a similar letter to a family member or friend. Use the present perfect and the present perfect continuous to tell what you have been doing recently and to ask questions, too.

Work in small groups. Have you ever exaggerated in order to impress someone or to avoid a problem? Choose one of these situations and write a conversation in which one of the characters exaggerates. Use the present perfect and the present perfect continuous. Act out your conversation to the class.

1. A young man is trying to impress some new friends that he has just met. Although he has just begun a low-paying job at a television station, he exaggerates quite a bit about his job.

   New Friend: So what do you do?
   Young Man: I work for XYZ News. I haven't been there long, but I've been working very hard. I've been writing all of the stories for the news show. I've also been on television three times.

2. A young woman is at a job interview for a well-paying job. She is not qualified for this job. She has not finished college. She has only worked in her uncle's law office for a few months where she answers the telephone and runs errands.

3. A man is on the phone with his mother, who will soon be celebrating her 50th birthday. He and his brothers and sisters are planning a surprise birthday celebration. The mother is getting suspicious and asking a lot of questions.

4. A teenager promises that she will make dinner while her parents pick up relatives at the airport. They call from the airport to check on her progress. She assures them that she has been very busy. In fact, she hasn't really started dinner yet.

Beyond the Sentence

Connecting the Past and the Present in Discourse

In longer conversations and in writing, it is often important to relate past and present situations and events. Choose between the simple past, the present perfect, and the present perfect continuous to focus on whether a situation is complete or incomplete, recent or distant, whether it happened once or many times, and how long it lasted.

A: I**'ve been working** here for nine years, and that's how long I**'ve known** Jenny. This is where we **met**.

B: How long **did** you **know** each other before you **got** married?

A: For a year.

B: So you**'ve been married** for eight years. It doesn't seem that long.

A: Well, we just **celebrated** our ninth anniversary. We **spent** the weekend in the mountains. . . .

Complete this conversation by choosing the correct answers in parentheses. In some sentences, either answer is possible.

Daughter: ((I've been going out)/ I went out) with Eric (for / since) last June, but
<u>1</u>   <u>2</u>
we're not ready to get engaged.

Mother: I think you've (had / been having) enough time. In fact, I thought you
<u>3</u>
(were / have been) ready to decide a few months ago.
<u>4</u>

Daughter: Well . . . we've (been having / had) some problems for a few months
<u>5</u>
now . . . and we haven't (gotten / been getting) along so well. It all started
<u>6</u>
last March.

Mother: What (happened / has been happening)?
<u>7</u>

Daughter: Well, at dinner one night, Eric's parents (criticized / have been criticizing)
<u>8</u>
me.

Mother: Criticized you? What exactly (did they say / have they been saying)?
<u>9</u>

Daughter: Oh, I don't remember exactly. It had something to do with the fact that I
have (been applying / applied) to medical schools, and I've already
<u>10</u>
(gotten / been getting) a master's degree.
<u>11</u>

Mother: And what (has Eric said / did Eric say) then?
<u>12</u>

Daughter: Nothing! But since then we've (been talking / talked) and talking about
<u>13</u>
whether I should go to medical school. Unfortunately, we haven't
(reached / been reaching) a conclusion. So (I've been thinking / I thought)
<u>14</u>   <u>15</u>
that maybe we need some time away from each other.

Mother: Have you (said / been saying) that to Eric yet?
<u>16</u>

Daughter: No. I've (been putting it off / put it off), but you're right. I really should
<u>17</u>
talk to him about it so we can make a decision together.

E Combining Form, Meaning, and Use

E1 Thinking About Meaning and Use

Choose the best response to complete each conversation. Then discuss your answers in small groups.

1. **A:** I've been working at this school for 15 years.
   B: **a.** Why did you leave?
   b. Are you going to retire soon?

2. **A:** Andre has been visiting us for three days.
   B: **a.** Is he having a good time?
   b. Did he have a good time?

3. **A:** Cheryl has been going to Vancouver on business.
   B: **a.** How many times has she been there?
   b. Has she gone there more than once?

4. **A:** Excuse me, Miss. I've been waiting for the doctor for an hour.
   B: **a.** How long have you been here?
   b. He had an emergency. He'll be with you soon.

5. **A:** Joanna has been coming to work late.
   B: **a.** It's happened only once. Can't we ignore it?
   b. It's happened more than once. We can't ignore it.

6. **A:** How long have you known about the scandal?
   B: **a.** A few minutes ago.
   b. Since I saw it in the newspaper.

7. **A:** What has Allen been doing?
   B: **a.** Taking a shower.
   b. He's been sleepy.

8. **A:** My mother has been sending me e-mail.
   B: **a.** When did she buy a computer?
   b. Why did she stop?

Find the errors in this paragraph and correct them. Pay close attention to the context of each sentence.

Life expectancy is the average number of years that a person will live. Two thousand years ago, the Romans ~~have been living~~ *lived* only an average of 22 years. In other words, they have been having a life expectancy of 22. Since the beginning of the twentieth century, life expectancy around the world has been rising dramatically in many parts of the world. It will certainly continue to go up well into the twenty-first century. The rise in life expectancy has been being due to the fact that people have been taking much better care of themselves. Each generation has experienced better nutrition and medical care than the one before. In 1900 people in the United States have been living to an average age of 47. All that has changed, however: The life expectancy in 1998 was 77, and it may be even higher today.

Beyond the Classroom

Searching for Authentic Examples

Find examples of English grammar in everyday life. Choose one of the tasks below. Be prepared to discuss your findings.

Look at advertisements in newspapers, in magazines, on bulletin boards, or on the Internet. Write down five examples of the present perfect continuous and bring them to class. What other tenses are common in the advertisements you have looked at?

Speaking

In small groups, express your opinions on the following problem: More and more people have been living to the age of 80 and beyond. Do you think that society is prepared to take care of the elderly? Use the present perfect continuous and the following sets of questions to guide your discussion.

1. What kind of assistance is available for the elderly in your native country? Talk about housing, finances, health, and recreation. You may want to search the Internet or use other reference sources in the library, or you may want to interview friends or relatives.

2. Do you think your country is doing a good job of taking care of the elderly? What kind of assistance do you think elderly people need? What should the role of the government be? To what extent are family members responsible for their loved ones?

3. Prepare a short summary of your group's opinions and report to the class.

The Past Perfect and the Past Perfect Continuous

A Wild Thing

A1 Before You Read

Discuss these questions.

Have you ever wanted to do something different or unusual, such as climbing a mountain or bungee jumping? Name some challenges that you would like to face. Why do some people like to face great challenges?

A2 Read

Read this book excerpt to find out why a young woman wanted to participate in an educational program called Outward Bound.

WILD THING

With the wind biting my face and the rain soaking through my clothes, it didn't seem like July. I watched a puddle form at the foot
5 of my sleeping bag as the 10-foot plastic sheet above me gave way to the wind. I <u>hadn't eaten</u> for almost a day, and a rumble in my stomach demanded to know why I was
10 in the Northern Cascades of Oregon—alone, soaked—in the first place. With two more days alone in the wilds ahead of me, I had plenty of time to think about
15 that question.

I'd always admired people who had been in Outward Bound,

basically because I'd always lumped myself in the I-could-never-do-that category. For one thing, I just assumed I was too small and urban. . . . I also wasn't a big risk-taker. I'd always relied a lot on my family, friends, and boyfriend, and I evaluated myself on how well I met their expectations of me.

Signing up for an Outward Bound course the summer after my junior year in high school was a chance to break away from that. After all, the courses are described as "adventure-based education programs that promote self-discovery through tough outdoor activities." Exactly what I needed; I would be facing challenges away from my usual supporters. As the starting date approached, though, I became increasingly terrified. I'd never attempted mountain climbing, white-water rafting, backpacking, rappelling, or rock climbing, and I was plagued by fears that I would fail at one or all of them. I begged my mother to cancel for me. No such luck. . . .

Adapted from *Chicken Soup for the Teenage Soul*

---

lump: to put many things into one category
plagued: continuously upset or troubled
rappelling: using ropes to climb down a steep mountain

rely on: to depend on
rumble: a deep, rolling sound
wilds: wilderness; a natural area with few people

A3 **After You Read**

Write *T* for true or *F* for false for each statement.

___T___ **1.** The young woman was going to spend two more days alone in the wilderness.

_____ **2.** She came from the city.

_____ **3.** She had always been very self-confident.

_____ **4.** It was summer.

_____ **5.** She was an expert mountain climber.

_____ **6.** Her mother wanted her to stay home.

The Past Perfect and the Past Perfect Continuous

Examining Form

Look back at the book excerpt on page 122 and complete the tasks below.
Then discuss your observations and read the Form charts to check them.

1. An example of the past perfect is underlined. Find four more examples. What is the contracted form of *had* in the past perfect?

2. Look at the following example of the past perfect continuous. Underline the two auxiliaries and circle the main verb. How does it differ from the past perfect?

   She had been searching for a way to challenge herself.

THE PAST PERFECT

Affirmative Statements

SUBJECT	HAD	PAST PARTICIPLE	
I He They	had	hiked	for hours by then.

CONTRACTION			
He'd		hiked	for hours by then.

Negative Statements

SUBJECT	HAD	NOT	PAST PARTICIPLE	
I He They	had	not	hiked	before.

CONTRACTION			
He	hadn't		hiked	before.

THE PAST PERFECT CONTINUOUS

Affirmative Statements

SUBJECT	HAD	BEEN	VERB + -ING	
I He They	had	been	hiking	for hours by then.

CONTRACTION			
He'd		been	hiking	for hours by then.

Negative Statements

SUBJECT	HAD	NOT	BEEN	VERB + -ING	
I He They	had	not	been	hiking	before.

CONTRACTION				
He	hadn't		been	hiking	before.

THE PAST PERFECT

Yes/No Questions

HAD	SUBJECT	VERB	
Had	you he they	**hiked**	before?

Short Answers

YES	SUBJECT	HAD	NO	SUBJECT	HAD + NOT
Yes,	I he they	**had.**	**No,**	I he they	**hadn't.**

Information Questions

WH-WORD	HAD	SUBJECT	PAST PARTICIPLE	
Where	had	you	**hiked**	before?
What		he	**done?**	

WH-WORD	HAD		PAST PARTICIPLE	
What	**had**		**happened?**	

THE PAST PERFECT CONTINUOUS

Yes/No Questions

HAD	SUBJECT	BEEN	VERB + -ING	
Had	you he they	**been**	**hiking**	before?

Short Answers

YES	SUBJECT	HAD	NO	SUBJECT	HAD + NOT
Yes,	I he they	**had.**	**No,**	I he they	**hadn't.**

Information Questions

WH-WORD	HAD	SUBJECT	BEEN	VERB + -ING	
Where	had	you	**been**	**hiking**	before?
What		he		**doing?**	

WH-WORD	HAD		BEEN	VERB + -ING	
What	**had**		**been**	**happening?**	

The Past Perfect

- The past perfect has the same form with all subjects.
- The past participle of regular verbs is the same as the simple past form (verb + -*ed*). See Appendices 4 and 5 for spelling and pronunciation rules for verbs ending in -*ed*.
- Irregular verbs have special past participle forms. See Appendix 6 for irregular verbs and their past participles.
- See Appendix 14 for contractions with *had*.
- Note that the past perfect form of *have* is *had had*. It is an irregular form.

  It was 2:00 P.M. We **had had** a busy day at the store, and I was exhausted.

(Continued on page 126)

B1 **Listening for Form**

🎧 Listen and write the simple past, past perfect, or past perfect continuous verb forms you hear. Use full forms or contractions.

In 1928, Amelia Earhart _____became_____
                                    1
the first woman to fly across the Atlantic. Ten years

before, she _____ as a nurse's aide
                        2

when she _____ an airfield near
                    3

Toronto. She _____ her mind that
                        4

she _____ to fly an airplane right
                5

then. After her trans-Atlantic flight, Ms. Earhart

_____ an instant heroine, although
                6

she really _____ the plane. Her two
                    7

male companions _____ her touch any of the controls. But the
                                8

world _____.
            9

Charles Lindbergh _____ the Atlantic a year earlier, and many
                                    10

aviators _____ to repeat his successful flight since then. Sadly,
                    11

fourteen pilots, including three women, _____ since Lindbergh's
                                                    12

triumph. Because Ms. Earhart _____ embarrassed about her role
                                            13

in her first trans-Atlantic flight, she _____ more determined than
                                            14

ever to fly across the Atlantic alone. And that's exactly what _____
                                                                        15

in 1932 when she finally _____ over the Atlantic by herself.
                                    16

Amelia Earhart

Complete the chart.

	SIMPLE PAST	PAST PERFECT	PAST PERFECT CONTINUOUS
1.	I flew home.	I had flown home.	I had been flying home.
2.		We had gone to school.	
3.			They had been trying hard.
4.	I held his hand.		
5.			You had been having fun.
6.	He made a mess.		
7.		They had thought about it.	
8.			We had been doing nothing.
9.	What happened?		
10.		It had gotten harder.	

B3 Building Sentences

Build as many meaningful sentences as possible. Use an item from each column.
Punctuate your sentences correctly.

Had you been working?

had you	been	working
she	had	left
who	had been	lunch
		sick
		taken a walk

A. Work with a partner. Take turns asking and answering questions using the phrases below and the past perfect. Start your questions with *Before you started this course* and use *ever.* Respond with short answers and an explanation.

1. take any other English courses

   A: *Before you started this course, had you ever taken any other English courses?*
   B: *Yes, I had. I'd studied English for a year in high school.* OR
   No, I hadn't. I'd never taken any English courses.

2. study English grammar

3. speak on the phone in English

4. write any letters in English

5. see any English-language movies

B. Now take turns asking and answering questions using the phrases below and the past perfect continuous. Start your questions with *Before you started this course.* Respond with short answers and an explanation.

1. read any English-language newspapers

   A: *Before you started this course, had you been reading any English-language newspapers?*
   B: *Yes, I had. I'd been reading* The New York Times *almost every day.* OR
   No, I hadn't.

2. learn any songs in English

3. practice English with friends

4. watch any TV programs in English

5. listen to English-language news broadcasts

Change the past perfect continuous to the past perfect. Where possible, change the past perfect to the past perfect continuous. Which sentences cannot change? Why?

1. We had been standing outside for a long time.

   We had stood outside for a long time.

2. I had never had a car with so many problems.

3. She had been limping for the last mile.

4. How long had they known about the accident?

5. Where had everybody been?

6. Had anyone been looking for us?

7. They had been trying to call for help.

8. What had happened?

Informally Speaking

Reduced Forms of *Had*

Did you see Dan and Maria at the party last night?

Dan had already left by the time I got there, but I saw Maria.

Look at the cartoon and listen to the conversation. How is the underlined form in the cartoon different from what you hear?

Especially in fast speech, *had* is usually reduced with subject nouns. *Had* is also reduced with many information question words.

STANDARD	WHAT YOU MIGHT HEAR
Dan had already left.	"/ˈdænəd/ already left."
The **cars had** stopped.	"The /ˈkɑrzəd/ stopped."
Who had already left?	"/hud/ already left?"
What had you been doing?	"/ˈwʌtəd/ you been doing?"

B6 Understanding Informal Speech

Listen and write the standard form of the words you hear.

1. She __had__ never __been__ alone in the woods before.

2. Her family _____ camping when she was young.

3. Her father _____ her the skills she needed.

4. No one _____ her for this experience, though.

5. Why _____ she _____ for this program?

6. Who _____ she _____ to impress?

The Past Perfect

Examining Meaning and Use

Read the sentences and complete the tasks below. Then discuss your observations and read the Meaning and Use Notes to check them.

    a. I called for help because a tree had fallen across my driveway.
    b. She wanted to withdraw from the course after she had enrolled.
    c. He'd been on a mountain climbing expedition before he wrote the article.
    d. Although I'd been terrified, I felt quite brave the next morning.

Think about the two events in each sentence.

1. Underline the clause that expresses the earlier event.

2. What verb form is in the clause that expresses the earlier event?

3. What verb form is in the clause that expresses the later event?

Meaning and Use Notes

> ### Order of Events in the Past
>
> **1A** The past perfect expresses the relationship in time between two past events. It shows that one action or state occurred before another action or state in the past. The past perfect expresses the first (or earlier) event. The simple past often expresses the second (or later) event.
>
> | *Past Perfect (1st Event)* | *Simple Past (2nd Event)* |
> |---|---|
> | I **had** just **completed** the exam. | I **felt** so relieved. |
>
> ---
>
> **1B** The past time can be recent or distant.
>
> *Recent Time*
> Miguel called me <u>this morning</u>, but I wasn't there. I**'d gone** to a meeting.
>
> *Distant Time*
> Miguel wrote me <u>last year</u>, but I never got the letter. I**'d moved** away.

2A The past perfect is often used in sentences containing past time clauses. The past perfect is used to indicate the first event. The simple past is used to indicate the second event. *Before, by the time, when, until,* and *after* introduce the time clause.

Past Perfect (1st Event)	*Simple Past (2nd Event)*
The thief **had escaped**	<u>before</u> I **called** the police.
We **had calmed** down	<u>by the time</u> the police **came**.
He **had been** upstairs	<u>when</u> we **came** home.
We **hadn't noticed**	<u>until</u> we **heard** the footsteps.
<u>After</u> I **had called** the police,	we **realized** the thief was gone.

2B In sentences with *before, after, by the time,* and *until,* the past perfect is sometimes replaced by the simple past with no difference in meaning. This is especially common with *before* and *after.*

Past Perfect and Simple Past		*Simple Past Only*
I'd gone inside before I **took off** my coat.	=	I **went** inside before I **took off** my coat.
After **I'd gone** inside, I **took off** my coat.	=	After I **went** inside, I **took off** my coat.

3A The past perfect is often used with the same adverbs and prepositions that are used with the present perfect: *already, yet, still, ever, never, for, since,* and *just.* These expressions help to clarify the sequence of past events.

By lunchtime, we **had** <u>already</u> **discussed** the new budget and written a report. We **hadn't written** the new vacation policy <u>yet</u>.

I **had lived** in Texas <u>for 12 years</u> before I moved to California.

A: **Had** she <u>ever</u> **eaten** a hot dog before she came to the United States?
B: No, she**'d** <u>never</u> **had** one!

3B *By* + a time can be used with the past perfect to express the later time in the sentence.

We **had finished** <u>by then</u>.
<u>By noon</u>, we **had hiked** two miles.

Listening for Meaning and Use ► Notes 1A, 1B, 2A, 2B, 3B

🎧 Listen to the sentences. For each pair of past events below, choose the event that happened first.

1. **(a.)** The patient's condition improved.
   b. The doctor came.

2. **a.** We got to the airport.
   b. The plane landed.

3. **a.** I entered the building.
   b. I took off my hat.

4. **a.** The emergency crew arrived.
   b. The building collapsed.

5. **a.** I saw Betty.
   b. She heard the news.

6. **a.** He became vice president.
   b. He worked hard.

7. **a.** I called my mother.
   b. I spoke to my sister.

8. **a.** She hurt her wrist.
   b. She went to work.

C2 **Expressing the Order of Past Events** ► Notes 1A, 1B, 2A, 2B

Read the pairs of sentences and order the events. Number the first event with a *1* and the second with a *2*. Then make a sentence with the word(s) in parentheses that includes both events. Use the past perfect and the simple past where appropriate.

1. __2__ The sink overflowed.   __1__ I left the water running.

   (after) _The sink overflowed after I had left the water running._____

2. ____ He graded the exam.   ____ He read the answers carefully.

   (before) _____

3. ____ They were married for five years.   ____ They got divorced.

   (when) _____

4. ____ The car collided with a truck.   ____ Someone called the police.

   (after) _____

5. ____ The doctor said she was very healthy.   ____ She was worried.

   (until) _____

6. ____ She slept for ten hours.   ____ I decided to wake her up.

   (by the time) _____

Work with a partner. Read each situation and look at the picture. Tell what things had been done already and what had not been done yet. Use the expressions in parentheses and the past perfect with *already* and *not . . . yet*.

1. Sonia was hoping to move into her new apartment a few days early. Yesterday she went to see if it was ready yet.
   (paint the apartment)   *They had already painted the apartment.*
   (clean the carpet)   *They hadn't cleaned the carpet yet.*
   (fix the window)
   (repair the lock)

2. Martin checked to see if he had completed the requirements for graduation.
   (complete the English requirement)
   (take the math courses)
   (pass the writing test)

> Requirements for high school graduation:
>
> ✔ 3 Math courses
>
> ✔ 4 English courses
>
>   Writing test

3. Your cousin has been looking for a job for a month. You spoke to her a few days ago.
   (look at the classified ads)
   (go to an employment agency)
   (write her résumé)

HELP WANTED
Attorney for international law firm
Minimum 10 years experience necessary
call 555-6324

EMPLOYMENT AGENCY

Résumé

A. These situations describe new experiences. Use the phrases below and the past perfect with *never* and *before* to describe the things that the people had never done before. Then add one of your own ideas.

1. Brian and Jo Ann have just had their first child.

   a. diaper a baby <u>They had never diapered a baby before.</u>

   b. bathe a baby _____

   c. _____

2. Irina started college last fall.

   a. live on her own _____

   b. sleep in a dormitory _____

   c. _____

3. Dominick got his first summer job at a supermarket.

   a. use an electronic cash register _____

   b. get a paycheck _____
   c. _____

4. Nora took her first driving lesson.

   a. drive a car _____

   b. be so scared _____

   c. _____

B. Think of something you did for the first time. Describe the aspects of the experience that were new to you. Write four sentences using the past perfect and *never*. Then tell your class about your new experience.

New Experience: <u>I decided to have a surprise party for my friend.</u>

1. <u>I had never cooked for 30 people before.</u> _____

2. _____

3. _____

4. _____

D The Past Perfect Continuous

Examining Meaning and Use

Read the sentences and complete the task below. Then discuss your observations and read the Meaning and Use Notes to check them.

Match each illustration to the sentence that best describes it.

a. We arrived at 9:30 P.M. Julia had been eating her dinner. (Dinner was just ending.)
b. We arrived at 9:30 P.M. Julia had eaten her dinner. (Dinner was over.)

Meaning and Use Notes

Order of Events in the Past with Continuing Actions

1A Similar to the past perfect, the past perfect continuous shows that one action occurred before another action or state in the past. However, the past perfect continuous emphasizes that the first event was ongoing, and continued up to or just before the second event.

Past Perfect Continuous (1st Event)	*Simple Past (2nd Event)*
Keiko **had been studying** all night.	She **was** exhausted at breakfast.

1B *For* and *since* show how long a situation lasted before the second past event.

Simple Past (2nd Event)	*Past Perfect Continuous (1st Event)*
Marie **left** her office at 6:00 P.M.	She'**d been working** <u>since 8:00 A.M.</u>

1C The past perfect continuous is often used in sentences containing past time clauses.

Past Perfect Continuous (1st Event)	*Simple Past (2nd Event)*
Marie **had been working** for nine and a half hours	<u>by the time</u> she **left** her office.

(Continued on page 136)

2A Certain common verbs can be used with the past perfect and past perfect continuous with little or no difference in meaning. Remember, though, that using the continuous can show a more intense or emotional situation.

Past Perfect	*Past Perfect Continuous*
Mr. Ortiz **had lived** there since 1960.	Mr. Ortiz **had been living** there since 1960.
I**'d waited** for an hour.	I**'d been waiting** for an hour! I was so angry.

2B The past perfect can express a completed action that may or may not have occurred recently. In contrast, the past perfect continuous suggests that an action was continuing up to or ended just before a specific time in the past.

Past Perfect	*Past Perfect Continuous*
Hiro **had watered** the garden before I arrived. (Hiro may have watered it a few minutes or many hours before I arrived.)	Hiro **had been watering** the garden before I arrived. (Hiro watered the garden a few minutes before I arrived.)

 A sentence with the past perfect continuous usually does not tell how many times an action is repeated.

Past Perfect	*Past Perfect Continuous*
I**'d read** it three times before.	*I**'d been reading** it three times before. (INCORRECT)

3 Both the past perfect continuous and the past perfect are often used to provide background information about earlier events. They are used to give reasons with *because* and express contrasts with *although* or *even though*. They are also used to draw conclusions.

Reasons
She looked very tired   <u>because</u> she **had been studying** all night.
    <u>because</u> she **had studied** all night.

Contrasts
She looked very tired   <u>although</u> she **had been sleeping** for 12 hours.
    <u>even though</u> she **had slept** for 12 hours.

Conclusions
I realized that   he **had been criticizing** my work.
    he **had** just **criticized** my work.

Listen to the two events in each sentence. Check (✓) *Just Before* if the context makes it clear that the first event happened right before the second. Check (✓) *Unclear* if the context does not specify how close together in time the two events were.

	JUST BEFORE	UNCLEAR
1.	✓	
2.		
3.		
4.		
5.		
6.		
7.		
8.		

D2 **Talking About Continuing Past Actions** ► Notes 1A–1C

Write two different sentences that tell how long each situation lasted. Use the past perfect continuous with *for* and *since* and simple past time clauses with *when.*

1. Elena worked from 1992 to 1994. Then she went back to school.

   When Elena went back to school, she had been working for two years.
   When Elena went back to school in 1994, she had been working since 1992.

2. Brigitte began to work at C & M in 1997. Her fiancé joined the company in 1999.

3. The chicken started baking at 5:30. The electricity went off at 5:45.

4. Lisa went to sleep at 11:00 P.M. The phone woke her up at 2:00 A.M.

5. Paulo and Celia started dating in 1998. They got married in 2000.

6. Kate studied from 1996 to 2002. She graduated from medical school in 2002.

7. Carlos lived in Mexico City from 1998 to 2000. He moved to Paris in 2000.

8. Eric started taking piano lessons in January of 2000. He gave his first recital in July of that year.

A. Work with a partner. Complete each sentence with a *because* clause in the past perfect or the past perfect continuous. Then write one more main clause in the simple past and ask your partner to complete it using *because*.

1. He looked very tired *because he had been sleeping poorly.*

2. The student was expelled from school _____

3. She quit her job _____

4. _____

B. Now complete each sentence with a main clause in the simple past. Then write one more *because* clause and ask your partner to complete it with a main clause.

1. *He didn't hear the doorbell*   because he had been taking a shower.

2. _____ because we had been exercising.

3. Because she hadn't listened to her parents, _____

4. _____

A. Complete each sentence with a clause using *although* or *even though* in the past perfect or the past perfect continuous.

1. I passed the exam *although I hadn't studied.*

2. She was able to answer the question _____

3. _____, everyone became sick.

4. _____, he wanted to quit his job.

B. Complete each sentence with a main clause in the simple past.

1. Even though I had been calling for days, *she never called me back.*

2. _____ although I had gone grocery shopping two days before.

3. Although we had been good friends, _____

4. Even though I had been trying as hard as I could, _____

Beyond the Sentence

> ### Adding Background Information in Longer Discourse
>
> Both the past perfect and the past perfect continuous are often used in a story to give details and background information about an earlier past time. These verb forms usually appear near the beginning of the story. Then the story often continues in the simple past.
>
> We finally landed in London at 9:30 a.m. We **had been traveling** for thirteen hours and the whole family was exhausted and cranky, especially me. The seat **had been** uncomfortable, and I **hadn't slept** at all. I tried not to be too unpleasant, but it was difficult because nothing seemed to be going right. When we got to the baggage claim area, two suitcases came through quickly, but the other two were missing. . . .

D5 Adding Background Information

A. Read each introductory statement. Then write two or three past perfect or past perfect continuous sentences that provide background information.

1. I was in my favorite restaurant that Sunday afternoon.

   We had gathered for a family reunion in honor of my parents' 25th wedding anniversary. My brother and I had been planning this event for months.

2. I remember the day I moved here.

3. I'll never forget that afternoon. We were stuck in heavy traffic on a bridge.

4. I entered my apartment and immediately felt that something was strange.

B. Write a paragraph. Choose one of the items in part A as the beginning of your paragraph. Add some background information in the past perfect or the past perfect continuous. Then complete the paragraph using the simple past to explain more about what happened in the first sentence.

   I was in my favorite restaurant that Sunday afternoon. We had gathered for a family reunion in honor of my parents' 25th wedding anniversary. My brother and I had been planning this event for months. We had been e-mailing each other almost daily with plans, menus, and guest lists. As they had been doing for 25 years, my parents arrived exactly on time. When they saw everyone . . .

Combining Form, Meaning, and Use

E1 Thinking About Meaning and Use

Read each sentence and the statements that follow. Write *T* if the statement is true, *F* if it is false, or *?* if you do not have enough information to decide. Then discuss your answers in small groups.

1. After he had eaten a sandwich, he ate a salad.

    __F__ **a.** He ate the salad first. Then he ate the sandwich.

    __F__ **b.** He ate the salad and sandwich together.

2. He had left before the play ended.

    _____ **a.** The play ended. Then he left.

    _____ **b.** He was gone by the end of the play.

3. He had known her for many years when they started to work together.

    _____ **a.** He met her at work.

    _____ **b.** He knew her a long time.

4. Tom didn't lose weight until he went on a diet.

    _____ **a.** Tom didn't lose weight.

    _____ **b.** Tom went on a diet.

5. It was lunchtime. I looked out the window, and I saw that it had rained.

    _____ **a.** It had rained just before I looked out the window.

    _____ **b.** I looked out the window after the rain stopped.

6. He left his job because he had found a better one.

    _____ **a.** He left his job. Then he looked for a better job.

    _____ **b.** He left his job after he found another job.

7. The hospital didn't lose power, although there had been a power failure in the city.

_____ **a.** The hospital had a power failure.

_____ **b.** The city lost power.

8. The two men had been working on a project together when I met them.

_____ **a.** They worked together before I met them.

_____ **b.** They finished the project.

E2 Editing

Find the errors in these paragraphs and correct them, using either the simple past or the present perfect.

In 1953, Edmund Hillary and Tenzing Norkay ~~had been~~ *were* the first climbers to reach the top of Mount Everest. Since then, many people had climbed Mount Everest, especially in recent years. Before 1953, no human had ever stood on top of the world's highest peak, although some had tried. George Mallory and Sandy Irvine, for example, had died almost 30 years earlier on a perilous path along the North Ridge.

Since 1953, many more people had set world records. In 1975, Junko Tabei of Japan had become the first woman on a mountaineering team to reach the top. In 1980, Reinhold Messner of Italy had become the first person to make the climb to the top alone, without other people and without oxygen. In 1995, Alison Hargreaves of Scotland had duplicated Messner's triumph. She became the first woman to climb Mount Everest solo and without oxygen.

Each climber faces frigid winds, storms, avalanches, and most dangerous of all, the serious effects of the high altitude on the heart, lungs, and brain. So why had many hundreds of people tried to climb Mount Everest in recent years? In 1998, for example, 650 people had tried to reach the top, and on one single day, 12 people actually succeeded. The only way to explain these numbers is to understand that the climb up Mount Everest represents the ultimate challenge of reaching the "top of the world."

Beyond the Classroom

Searching for Authentic Examples

Find examples of English grammar in everyday life. Choose one of the tasks below. Be prepared to discuss your findings.

A. Look in a newspaper, in a magazine, or on the Internet. Write down five examples of the past perfect and the past perfect continuous and bring them to class. Why do you think the past perfect or the past perfect continuous was used? Where in the article did you find the examples? Could you substitute the simple past instead?

B. Find examples of the past perfect and the past perfect continuous in a short story and bring them to class. Why do you think the past perfect and the past perfect continuous were used? Where in the story did you find the examples? Could you substitute the simple past instead?

Speaking

In small groups, follow these steps to prepare a description of a famous "mystery person."

1. Think of a famous person in history or sports who accomplished something that had never been done before. You are going to role-play that person by describing yourself and your accomplishment without revealing your identity to your group. You may wish to find out more about this person in the library or on the Internet.

2. Prepare a description of your mystery person using the first person. Give background information using the past perfect, the past perfect continuous, time clauses, and other tenses, where appropriate.

3. Present your description to your group and ask them to guess who you are. The group may wish to ask more questions.

Modals

Modals of Possibility

A Going to the Dogs

A1 Before You Read

Discuss these questions.

Have you ever had a pet? Why are pets important for some people? What are some of the advantages and disadvantages of having a pet?

A2 Read

Read this magazine article to find out what researchers have learned about the benefits of owning a dog.

HEALTH NEWS

Going to the Dogs:
Dog Ownership Linked to Reduced Risk of Second Heart Attack

People have thought for a long time that there <u>must be</u> a positive connection between health and pet ownership. In fact, Lassie might do more than search for and
5 rescue a person in trouble. She might also have something to do with preventing a crisis in the first place. It turns out that ownership of dogs of all breeds is linked to a lower risk of second heart attacks and
10 some other fatal conditions.

When researchers looked at 369 people who had suffered from heart attacks in the previous year, they noticed that people who owned dogs progressed better than people
15 without them.

If dogs really do influence life spans, the researchers think it could be due to their

function as man's best friend. High degrees of social support have been linked to longer life spans, and dogs might strengthen those feelings of support. Dogs may also offer owners long life by requiring exercise. Doing laps with Spot produces all kinds of health benefits: to the heart, mind, lungs, and maybe even the bones.

Of course, before giving your heart and home over to a puppy, understand that dogs take work, says *Prevention* magazine advisor and social-support expert Redford Williams, M.D. You need to walk them and so on, which could be why they're good for you. "It may be a hassle for some people who are not used to it and may add stress," he says. So before you pick out a pup, it might be a good idea to try taking care of someone else's pup for a while.

breed: a group of animals with similar genetic characteristics

doing laps: running or walking around a track

hassle: something annoying

Lassie: a dog on an American TV show

life span: how long you live

pup: (short for *puppy*) a young dog

Spot: a typical name for a dog in the U.S.

A3 After You Read

Choose the answer that best completes each sentence.

1. Researchers think that dog ownership _____ certain serious medical conditions.
   a. causes
   b. prevents
   c. speeds up

2. Heart attack victims recover more _____ if they have a dog.
   a. unwillingly
   b. slowly
   c. quickly

3. It is _____ that dogs influence how long we live.
   a. absolutely certain
   b. possible
   c. very unlikely

4. Health benefits of dog ownership are related to the _____ support dogs provide.
   a. social
   b. nutritional
   c. spiritual

5. Dog owners _____ get exercise.
   a. usually
   b. seldom
   c. never

6. The author advises getting experience with a dog _____ owning one.
   a. after
   b. before
   c. instead of

B Modals of Present and Future Possibility

Examining Form

Look back at the article on page 146 and complete the tasks below. Then discuss your observations and read the Form charts to check them.

1. An example of a modal + main verb is underlined. Find six more examples.

2. Sort your examples into modals followed by:

   a. the main verb *be*   **b.** a different main verb

PRESENT MODALS

Affirmative Statements

SUBJECT	MODAL	MAIN VERB or *BE* (+ VERB + *-ING*)	
He	**may** **might**	**have**	a dog.
She	**could**	**be meeting**	him now.
They	**should** **must**	**be**	home.

Negative Statements

SUBJECT	MODAL + *NOT*	MAIN VERB or *BE* (+ VERB + *-ING*)	
He	**may not** **might not**	**have**	a dog.
She	**couldn't** **can't**	**be meeting**	him now.
They	**shouldn't** **must not**	**be**	home.

FUTURE MODALS

Affirmative Statements

SUBJECT	MODAL	MAIN VERB or *BE* (+ VERB + *-ING*)	
He	**may** **might**	**get**	a dog soon.
She	**could**	**be meeting**	him later.
They	**should** **will**	**be**	home soon.

Negative Statements

SUBJECT	MODAL + *NOT*	MAIN VERB or *BE* (+ VERB + *-ING*)	
He	**may not** **might not**	**get**	a dog soon.
She	**couldn't** **can't**	**be meeting**	him later.
They	**shouldn't** **won't**	**be**	home yet.

Modals of Present Possibility

- Modals have only one form with all subjects.
- *Must not*, *may not*, and *might not* have no contracted forms as modals of possibility.
- ⚠️ Do not confuse the two words *may be* (modal + *be*) with *maybe*, a one-word adverb that often begins a sentence.

  > He **may be** late. **Maybe** he's late.

- *Could* and *can* are used to ask questions about present possibility. *Might* is very uncommon. Use *be* in short answers to questions containing *be*.

  > A: **Could** he **be sleeping**? A: **Can** it **be true**?
  > B: He **might be**. B: It **must not be**.

- See Appendix 14 for contractions with *should, could,* and *can*.

Modals of Future Possibility

- *Must (not)*, *can't*, and *couldn't* are not usually used to express future possibility unless they are combined with the continuous.

  > She **must not be getting** a dog next month.

- *Could* may be used to ask questions about future possibility. Notice the short answers.

  > A: **Could** he **arrive** before we get home?
  > B: Yes, he **might**. / No, he **won't**.

- See Appendix 14 for contractions with *will*.

——— PRESENT PHRASAL MODALS ———

Affirmative Statements

SUBJECT	MODAL	MAIN VERB or *BE* (+ VERB + -*ING*)	
He	**ought to**	**be**	home.
She	**has to** **has got to**	**be walking**	the dog.
They	**have to** **have got to**	**have**	a dog.

CONTRACTIONS			
She**'s** They**'ve**	**got to**	**have**	a dog.

——— FUTURE PHRASAL MODALS ———

Affirmative Statements

SUBJECT	MODAL	MAIN VERB or *BE* (+ VERB + -*ING*)	
He	**ought to**	**be**	home soon.
She	**has to** **has got to**	**be coming**	
They	**have to** **have got to**		

CONTRACTIONS			
She**'s** They**'ve**	**got**	**to be coming**	home soon.

(*Continued on page 150*)

Phrasal Modals of Present Possibility

- The phrasal modal *ought to* has one form with all subjects. The phrasal modals *have to* and *have got to* have different third-person singular forms.
- None of these phrasal modals is used in the negative to express possibility.
- *Have got to* has contracted forms. *Ought to* and *have to* do not.

Phrasal Modals of Future Possibility

- *Have to* and *have got to* are only used to express future possibility with the continuous. They**'ve got to be arriving** soon.

B1 **Listening for Form**

🎧 **Listen to this story and write the modals or phrasal modals you hear. Use contractions if you hear them.**

The Abominable Snowman of the Himalayas and the Loch Ness Monster of Scotland are two creatures that _____ may _____ or _____ may not _____ be real—that depends on your beliefs. If you ask someone about them, they _____ respond, "That _____ be true," or they _____ respond, "That _____ be true." Over the years, it has been difficult to separate fact from fiction as stories about these creatures continue.

The Loch Ness Monster or a hoax?

_____ it be true that an ape-like creature with long hair lives high in the Himalayas? _____ the large footprints found there belong to such a creature? While many scientists say this _____ be a myth, others claim that there _____ be some kind of creature out there. But no one knows for sure.

In Scotland, _____ there really be a mysterious water monster
                    11
with a long neck and a large body like a brontosaurus? Many claim that there

_____ be some truth to this story that's been around since the
        12
fifteenth century. Just ask the two million tourists who visit the area each year, hoping

to see the monster.

B2) Completing Conversations with Modals

**Work with a partner. Complete the conversations with the words in parentheses.
Use contractions when possible. Then practice the conversations.**

Conversation 1

A: That number ____may not be____ (be/not/may) right.
                          1
B: Don't worry. It _____ (be/not/can) wrong. The
                              2
   computer doesn't make mistakes!

Conversation 2

A: They _____ (arrive/should) soon.
                    1
B: I doubt it. They probably _____ (arrive/not/will) until later.
                                          2
A: No, I spoke to them a half hour ago. They _____
                                                            3
   (be/ought to) here in 20 minutes.

Conversation 3

A: This _____ (be/have to) a mistake. My phone bill
                    1
   _____ (be/not/could) $300 for just one month!
            2
B: Don't worry about it. Just call up the phone company. There

   _____ (be/must) an explanation.
            3

Conversation 4

A: Why isn't Sasha home yet? The movie _____
                                                        1
   (be/have got to) over by now.
B: Actually, it just ended. He _____ (be/should) here soon.
                                          2

B3 Using Short Answers with Modals

Work with a partner. Switch roles for each question.

Student A: Ask a question about animal behavior.
Student B: Answer the question with your beliefs. Use positive or negative short answers with *may, might, must,* or *could.* Use *be* where necessary.

1. Do animals have emotions?

   A: Do animals have emotions?
   B: They must. or They couldn't.

2. Are mules really stubborn?

   A: Are mules really stubborn?
   B: They may be. or They might not be.

3. Does a full moon affect animal behavior?

4. Do laboratory rats feel pain?

5. Do dogs understand language?

6. Do pigs predict earthquakes?

7. Do cats and dogs have dreams?

8. Is the Loch Ness monster real?

B4 Building Sentences with Modals

Build as many meaningful sentences as possible. Use an item from each column. Punctuate your sentences correctly.

John must be sleeping.

	must		sleeping
John	might	be	true
it	can't	have	a problem
	has to		broken

B5 Writing Your Own Sentences with Modals

Think about a distant city where you have relatives or friends. Use modals of present possibility to do the tasks below.

1. Write three sentences about the weather in the city you are thinking about.

   It must be raining in Rio.
   It may be cool. . . .

2. Write three sentences describing what you think your friends or relatives are doing right now.

   Carla must be traveling.
   Marco might be teaching a class, or he could be . . .

Modals of Present Possibility

Examining Meaning and Use

Read the sentences and answer the questions below. Then discuss your observations and read the Meaning and Use Notes to check them.

    a. He must be telling the truth. He never lies.
    b. He may be telling the truth. I'm not sure.
    c. He can't be telling the truth. His story doesn't make sense.
    d. He could be telling the truth. It's possible, I guess.
    e. He might be telling the truth. I don't know.
    f. He should be telling the truth. He usually does.

1. In which sentences is the speaker more certain?

2. In which sentences is the speaker less certain?

Meaning and Use Notes

Overview

1 Modals and phrasal modals of possibility are used to express guesses, expectations, or inferences about present situations. The modal you choose shows how certain you are that something is true.

Less Certain		
Less Certain ↑	• could, might, might not	Jim **could be** upstairs, or he **might be** outside.
	• may, may not	He **may not be** awake yet. I'm not sure.
	• should, shouldn't, ought to	Jim **should be** upstairs. I saw him go up a few minutes ago.
	• must, must not, have to, have got to	I don't see Jim. He **must not be feeling** well. He **has to be** upstairs.
More Certain ↓	• can't, couldn't	Jim **couldn't be** upstairs. I saw him go out.

(*Continued on page 154*)

2 Use *could, might (not),* and *may (not)* to guess about a present situation when you don't have much proof. *Could* and *might* sometimes show less certainty than *may,* especially when they express more than one possibility.

More Certain

A: Where's Jim?

B: He **may be** upstairs.

Less Certain

A: Where's Jim?

B: He **could be** upstairs, or he **might be** outside.

3 Use *should(n't)* and *ought to* when you have an expectation about a present situation based on proof or experience.

A: Where's Jim?

B: He **should be** upstairs. I saw him go up a few minutes ago.

 Expectations expressed with *should* and *ought to* may be confused with the meanings of advisability and necessity that are also expressed by these modals. To make the meaning clear, the context must be stated or understood.

Jim **ought to be** in bed. I thought I saw him go upstairs before.
   (*ought to* = expectation)

Jim **ought to be** in bed. He looks very sick. (*ought to* = advisability)

4A Use *must (not), have to,* and *have got to* to draw conclusions when you are certain of something, and you believe there is only one logical explanation.

A: We can't find Jim.

B: He ⎰ **must**
     ⎱ **has to**   **be** upstairs. We've looked everywhere else.
        has got to

4B In conversation, *must be* or *must feel* with an adjective often show understanding of someone's feelings.

A: I hardly slept at all last night. My neighbors had a party.

B: You **must be** very annoyed at them.

C: You **must feel** tired. Do you still want to go out later?

5A Use *can't* and *couldn't* when you are certain something is unlikely or impossible. Notice that in the affirmative, however, *could* expresses less certainty.

A: I think Jim is upstairs.

B: He **couldn't be** upstairs. I saw him go out. (*couldn't* = strong certainty)

A: Well, I **could be** wrong. (*could* = less certainty)

5B *Can't* and *couldn't* sometimes express surprise or disbelief.

A: I heard that you're going to be promoted.

B: That **can't be** true. The boss doesn't like me. (*can't* = disbelief)

C1 **Listening for Meaning and Use** ▶ Notes 1–3, 4A, 4B, 5A, 5B

Listen to each situation. Is the speaker expressing less certainty or more certainty about the situation? Check (✓) the correct column.

	LESS CERTAINTY	MORE CERTAINTY
1.	✓	
2.		
3.		
4.		
5.		
6.		
7.		
8.		

Work with a partner. Read each question and the two responses. Then complete each response with a modal that expresses the appropriate degree of certainty. More than one answer may be possible for each item.

Conversation 1

A: What's wrong with Alice? She has been looking strange ever since class ended.

B: She ___might___ be upset. I don't think she did very well on the exam.
₁

C: She ___must___ be upset. I saw her exam. She got a very low grade.
₂

Conversation 2

A: Are the clothes dry yet?

B: They _____ be dry by now. They usually take 45 minutes to dry,
₁
and they've been in the dryer almost 40 minutes.

C: They _____ be dry by now. They usually take 45 minutes, and
₂
they've been in the dryer for almost an hour.

Conversation 3

A: Do you think they've finished repairing your car by now?

B: It _____ be ready. It's 2:00 P.M., and they said it'd be ready at noon.
₁

C: It _____ be ready. It's noon. They said it would probably be
₂
ready by noon.

Conversation 4

A: Whose black jacket is this? Someone forgot to take it after the party.

B: It _____ be Diane's. I saw her wearing a black jacket earlier.
₁

C: It _____ be Diane's. She wears a lot of black.
₂

Conversation 5

A: It's 10:30 P.M. Who could be calling so late?

B: It _____ be Chris. She said she wanted to talk to me today.
₁

C: It _____ be Chris. She said she was going to call after ten o'clock.
₂

C3 Guessing with *Could, Might,* and *May*

Work in small groups. Describe what you think the people in the pictures are doing. Use *could, might,* and *may* to make as many guesses as you can.

They could be watching a car show.
They might be looking at . . .

C4 Making Guesses and Drawing Conclusions

► Notes 1, 2, 4A

Work in small groups. Write guesses and conclusions about each situation below. Use *could, must, may, might, has to,* and *has got to.* Add one or two more sentences to explain what you mean. Discuss your answers.

1. The teacher is absent today.

   She must be sick. She wasn't feeling well yesterday. OR
   She might be out of town, or she could be sick. Nobody knows. OR
   She might not be feeling well again. She was sick a few weeks ago.

2. The fire alarm is ringing.

3. Your new neighbor never smiles.

4. Everyone's eating chocolate cake for dessert except Tina.

5. You've been sneezing all morning.

6. Your sister has just received a dozen long-stemmed roses with no card.

7. Jenny doesn't answer the telephone.

8. Sam always looks tired.

Work with a partner. Terry is a nurse. Read Terry's work schedule and complete each sentence below. Give your conclusions or expectations using *must be* or *should be* + a continuous verb or a time of day.

```
Day Shift Schedule

  6:45 A.M.    meet with night nurses
  7:15 A.M.    check vital signs of patients
               (temperature, pulse, blood pressure)
  7:45 A.M.    meet with doctors
  8:30 A.M.    give patients medicine
 10:00 A.M.    write notes on charts
 11:00 A.M.    discharge patients
 12:30 P.M.    attend meeting
  1:00 P.M.    admit new patients
  2:45 P.M.    take a break
  4:30 P.M.    go home
```

1. If it's 7:20, <u>Terry must be checking the patients' vital signs.</u>

   OR <u>Terry should be checking the patients' vital signs.</u>

2. If Terry is meeting with the doctors, <u>it must be 7:45.</u> OR <u>it should be 7:45.</u>

3. If it's 1:10, _____

4. If Terry is going home, _____

5. If it's 8:30, _____

6. If it's 11:00, _____

7. If it's 6:50, _____

8. If Terry is writing notes on charts, _____

9. If Terry is taking a break, _____

10. If it's 12:30, _____

Work with a partner. Take turns reading these statements. Answer with *you must be* or *you must feel* + an adjective to show your understanding of each situation.

1. I studied all night for my exam.

   You must be exhausted. OR *You must feel tired.*

2. I didn't eat breakfast or lunch today.

3. Tomorrow is my first job interview.

4. My English teacher canceled our midterm exam.

5. My best friend is going to visit me next week. I haven't seen him for six months.

6. My car broke down again. I just spent $300 on it last week.

7. I didn't get accepted to graduate school.

8. My parents are going to get a divorce.

A. Work with a partner. Write a dialogue in which the speakers express strong certainty and surprise or disbelief about one of the topics below. Use some of these modals: *can't, couldn't, must, have to, have got to.*

1. A teenager is trying to make excuses to his or her parents about not doing well in school.

   Teenager: There's got to be a mistake. My grades can't be that bad.
   Parent: You must be kidding! What about the homework that you didn't do, and the classes that you missed?
   Teenager: Well, . . .

2. Two friends are discussing the surprising behavior of a mutual friend.

3. Two co-workers are discussing some rumors that are going around the office.

4. Two teachers are discussing a student's work, which has suddenly improved.

B. Practice your dialogue. Be prepared to present it to the class.

D Modals of Future Possibility

Examining Meaning and Use

Read the sentences and answer the questions below. Then discuss your observations and read the Meaning and Use Notes to check them.

    a. The plane might be on time. It's not clear yet.
    b. The plane should be on time. It left on time.
    c. The plane could be on time. They sometimes make up time in the air.
    d. The plane will be on time. They just announced it.

1. In which sentences is the speaker less certain?

2. In which sentences is the speaker more certain?

3. Which sentences have about the same meaning?

Meaning and Use Notes

Overview

1 Modals and phrasal modals of possibility are used to make predictions about the future. The modal you choose can make your sentence sound more or less certain.

Less Certain	• could, might, might not	The plane **could arrive** soon.
	• may, may not	The plane **may arrive** soon.
	• should, shouldn't, ought to	The plane **should arrive** soon.
More Certain	• will, won't	The plane **will arrive** soon.

⚠️ *Must (not), can't, couldn't, have to,* and *have got to* are not usually used to express beliefs about the future unless they are combined with the continuous. They are used to express certainty about the present.

They **must be coming** home soon.
*They must not be home later. (INCORRECT)

2   Use *could, might (not),* and *may (not)* to guess about a future situation when you don't have much proof. *Could* and *might* sometimes show less certainty than *may,* especially when they are used to express more than one possibility.

More Certain

A: When is Liz arriving?

B: She **may be arriving** soon.

Less Certain

A: When is Liz arriving?

B: She **could arrive** at 7:30, but she **might be** late.

3   Use *should(n't)* and *ought to* when you have an expectation about a future situation based on proof or experience. *Should* and *ought to* are used to indicate future expectations more frequently than present expectations.

A: When is she coming?

B: She **should be** here at 7:30. That's what she told me yesterday.

   Expectations expressed by *should* and *ought to* can become confused with the meanings of advisability and necessity that are also expressed by these modals. To make the meaning clear, the context must be stated or understood.

Liz **ought to be** here on Friday. She said she's coming. (*ought to* = possibility)

Liz **ought to be** here on Friday. I told her to come. (*ought to* = advisability)

4A   Use *will* and *won't* to express strong certainty about the future.

She**'ll come** soon. I'm not worried. (very likely)

She **won't be coming**. (very unlikely)

4B   *Will* is often weakened with adverbs of possibility such as *maybe, perhaps,* and *probably. Probably* is the strongest of these adverbs, although it still expresses a small amount of doubt.

Maybe she**'ll come**. (= She **might come**.)

Perhaps she**'ll come**. (= She **might come**.)

She**'ll probably come**. (= She **should be coming**.)

D1) Listening for Meaning and Use

🎧 Listen to each situation. Is the speaker expressing less certainty or more certainty about the future situation? Check (✓) the correct column.

	LESS CERTAINTY	MORE CERTAINTY
1.	✓	
2.		
3.		
4.		
5.		
6.		
7.		
8.		

D2) Expressing Degrees of Certainty

Rewrite each sentence using a modal to express the appropriate degree of certainty about the future. More than one answer may be possible for each item.

1. I expect the exam to be easy.

   The exam should be easy.

2. Maybe we'll come later.

3. The flight definitely arrives at 8:10.

4. There's a small chance of rain this afternoon.

5. I don't expect it to be cold tonight.

6. There's a good possibility that he'll get the job.

7. It's possible that genetically engineered dogs and cats will become common.

8. Perhaps he's taking the express train this evening.

9. I'm certain that the class meets on Thursdays next semester.

10. She's probably in Miami for the winter.

Work in small groups. Look at the four-day weather forecast and describe the weather for each day. Use affirmative or negative modals, and adverbs of possibility.

TONIGHT

Travel advisory: definite snowfall, heavy at times, and 5 to 8 inches expected by tomorrow morning.

High: 34°F
Low: 30°F

SATURDAY

80% chance of rain accompanied by strong winds. Partial clearing in the afternoon, but returning clouds in the evening with a 50% chance of rain. Possibility of flooding.

High: 40°F
Low: 35°F

1. <u>There will be heavy snow tonight. We should have five to eight inches by morning.</u> OR <u>There will probably be five to eight inches by morning.</u>

3. _____

TOMORROW

Increasing chance of clouds, 30% chance of sleet in the afternoon. Rain likely overnight.

High: 38°F
Low: 32°F

SUNDAY

Sunshine followed by partly cloudy skies late in the afternoon. A slight chance of snow in the evening. Thickening clouds, but snow very unlikely after midnight.

High: 45°F
Low: 39°F

2. _____

4. _____

A. Complete each sentence with an affirmative or negative modal to make a prediction about your lifetime.

1. During my lifetime, more people _____will_____ live to the age of 100.

2. People _____may not_____ visit other planets.

3. Researchers _____ find a cure for cancer.

4. Astronomers _____ solve the mysteries of the universe.

5. People _____ clone their pets.

6. I _____ ride in a spaceship.

7. Robots _____ do all of our housework.

8. Countries _____ stop producing nuclear weapons.

9. Scientists _____ solve the mysteries of animal behavior.

10. There _____ be another world war.

B. Now write five more predictions about things that *could, might, may,* or *will* happen in your lifetime. Use adverbs of possibility in at least two of your sentences.

In the future, personal computers may be small enough to fit in your hand.
Maybe everyone will be driving electric cars.
My country will probably host the Olympics.

C. Follow these steps to write a paragraph about one of your predictions from parts A or B.

1. Write down some details about the prediction.

2. Use the prediction to write a clear introductory sentence and a paragraph explaining what might or might not happen.

3. Make sure to use various modals and adverbs of possibility, but don't use them in every sentence.

    During my lifetime, people may not visit other planets, but unmanned space vehicles will certainly continue to visit them. People might be able to . . .

Combining Form, Meaning, and Use

E1 Thinking About Meaning and Use

Work with a partner. Read each situation. Choose the sentence that is the most certain.

1. The key is missing.
   a. It may be on the table.
   b. It must be on the table.
   c. It ought to be on the table.

2. Ken is eating lunch with an older woman.
   a. She may be his mother.
   b. She could be his mother.
   c. She's got to be his mother.

3. A letter has just arrived.
   a. It can't be from Mary.
   b. It must not be from Mary.
   c. It might not be from Mary.

4. Thomas is doing his homework.
   a. He might finish by four o'clock.
   b. He could finish by four o'clock.
   c. He won't finish by four o'clock.

5. The answer is 25.
   a. That may not be right.
   b. That couldn't be right.
   c. That might not be right.

6. The doorbell is ringing.
   a. It has to be the mail carrier.
   b. It should be the mail carrier.
   c. It ought to be the mail carrier.

7. I'm worried about Jeanne.
   a. She might be ill.
   b. She must be ill.
   c. She could be ill.

8. My car is at the service station.
   a. It won't be ready soon.
   b. It will probably be ready soon.
   c. It ought to be ready soon.

E2 Editing

Find the errors in this paragraph and correct them.

Epilepsy is an illness that causes people to have brain seizures. ~~Might~~ *Could* a dog help
a person with epilepsy? Scientists believe that dogs should warn their owners
before a seizure, and researchers think there maybe an explanation. They believe
that a dog may smelling the chemical changes that usually happen in a person's
body before a seizure. Some dogs have success rates of over 90 percent. Since this
rate is higher than chance, researchers think there's to be something going on.

Beyond the Classroom

Searching for Authentic Examples

Find examples of English grammar in everyday life. Choose one of the tasks below. Be prepared to discuss your findings.

A. Look in a newspaper, in a magazine, or on the Internet. Write down five examples of modals that express beliefs about the present, and bring them to class. Which modals did you find? Which ones were you unable to find?

B. Listen to weather reports on the radio or television. Write down five examples of future possibility modals and bring them to class. What other expressions of possibility are used besides modals?

Writing

Follow these steps to write an article for a tabloid newspaper (a popular newspaper filled with unusual, sensational, or impossible stories instead of news).

1. Make up a story about someone who claims to have seen the Loch Ness Monster, the Abominable Snowman, or some other unusual creature.

2. Make notes about who saw the incident and what happened. Where, when, and how did the incident happen? Describe the reactions of other people to the story. Do they believe it? Were there other witnesses?

3. Use your notes to write a first draft of your article. Try to include modals and adverbs to describe people's opinions and beliefs about the story. Think of an attention-getting headline.

4. Read over your work carefully and circle grammar, spelling, and punctuation errors. Work with a partner to decide how to fix the errors. Then rewrite your draft with the changes that you and your partner have discussed.

Past Modals

The Really Early Birds

A1 Before You Read

Discuss these questions.

Have you ever thought about how birds are able to fly? Do you know what makes it possible? Have you ever dreamed or wished you could fly?

A2 Read

Read this magazine article to find out what new evidence has been found about how birds first learned to fly.

The Really Early Birds

Anew theory explains how the first feathered creatures to fly <u>may have gotten</u> off the ground. Researchers believe that a prehistoric bird that descended 5 from dinosaurs, archaeopteryx (pronounced "ar-kee-op-te-riks"), had a good wingspan for a half-pound bird—more than 20 inches. That has to have been enough to enable the crow-sized bird to fly, or at 10 least glide, through the Jurassic skies. But the toughest part of flying is the takeoff. And the first birds and their dinosaur ancestors just didn't have the same specialized muscle power for liftoff that 15 their modern descendants do. It's a question that scientists have been arguing about for more than 200 years: How did the first fliers get into the air? A study in the journal *Nature* shows how it could 20 have happened.

Fly or die? According to this popular theory, a tree-dwelling prehistoric bird could have launched itself—or could have fallen—from its perch and managed to 25 stay up by flapping its wings. That solves the gravity issue, but Luis Chiappe, a paleontologist at the Natural History Museum of Los Angeles County, points out a problem. "We don't know of any bird ancestors that lived in trees."

A running start? This could have helped a bird like archaeopteryx into the air, but the ancient bird's estimated speed wasn't fast enough for liftoff. Chiappe worked with an expert in aerodynamics, Phillip Burgers, to simulate the takeoff of the archaeopteryx. They found that the bird's wings were able to rotate in a way that may have provided the extra burst of speed needed to outrun a hungry predator or catch a quick-running lizard. And, the new calculations show, the wing flapping could have generated sufficient speed for takeoff. During the early phase of liftoff, archaeopteryx's wings must have acted more like an airplane's engines, providing extra speed. Then, when the archaeopteryx was in the air, it must have rotated its wings back to horizontal position, to maintain altitude.

Modern birds do exactly the same thing, so why hasn't anyone noticed until now? Experts have been fascinated by lift, probably because it's something humans can't do. Chiappe and Burgers have shown that the archaeopteryx could have taken off from the ground, but whether or not it actually did may never be known. According to the researchers, the answer to this question is not really important. Rather, the importance of their discovery is that the wings could have helped the archaeopteryx gain speed. Flying might have developed as the archaeopteryx ran faster and faster while flapping its wings, not by falling out of trees. Perhaps flying is just the continuation of running by other means.

Adapted from *Newsweek*

aerodynamics: the science that studies forces that act on things moving through air
altitude: height in the air
Jurassic: the time period when dinosaurs and the earliest birds lived

paleontologist: a scientist who studies fossils to learn about the history of life on earth
predator: an animal that lives by killing and eating other animals
wingspan: measurement across the wings when the wings are extended

A3 **After You Read**

Check (✓) the facts that scientists who study prehistoric birds are certain about.

___✓___ **1.** They had feathers.

_____ **2.** They descended from dinosaurs.

_____ **3.** They had wings.

_____ **4.** They were much smaller than modern birds.

_____ **5.** They could fly.

_____ **6.** They lived in trees.

B Past Modals

Examining Form

Look back at the article on page 168 and complete the tasks below. Then discuss your observations and read the Form charts to check them.

1. An example of a past modal is underlined. Find six more examples.

2. Find two past modals with singular subjects and two with plural subjects. Is there any difference in form between them?

3. What auxiliary follows the modals? What is the form of the main verbs?

PAST MODALS

Affirmative Statements				
SUBJECT	MODAL	*HAVE*	PAST PARTICIPLE	
I	may might could should must	have	passed	the test.

Negative Statements				
SUBJECT	MODAL + *NOT*	*HAVE*	PAST PARTICIPLE	
I	may not might not couldn't can't shouldn't must not	have	passed	the test.

- Past modals have only one form with all subjects.
- Past modals have two auxiliary verbs: a modal and *have*. Only the modal forms contractions.
- *May not have, might not have,* and *must not have* have no contracted forms as past modals.
- *Could have* and *should have* may be used to ask questions with past modals. Notice that short answers contain modal + *have* and optional main verb *be* if appropriate.

  A: **Could** they **have called**?   A: **Should** she **have been** at the meeting?
  B: No, they **must not have**.   B: Yes, she **should have been**.

- See Appendix 14 for contractions with *can, could,* and *should*.
- See Appendix 6 for irregular verbs and their past participles.

PAST PHRASAL MODALS

Affirmative Statements

SUBJECT	MODAL	*HAVE*	PAST PARTICIPLE
He	**ought to**	**have**	**come.**
She	**has to** **has got to**	**have**	**known.**
You	**have to** **have got to**		

CONTRACTIONS			
She**'s** You**'ve**	got to	have	known.

Negative Statements

SUBJECT	MODAL + *NOT*	*HAVE*	PAST PARTICIPLE
He	**ought not to**	**have**	**come.**

- *Ought to have* has only one form. *Have to have* and *have got to have* have different third-person singular forms.
- *Ought to have* can be used in the affirmative or negative. *Have to have* and *have got to have* are used only in the affirmative.
- *Have got to have* has contracted forms. *Have to have* and *ought to have* do not.
- *Had to have* + past participle can often replace *have to have* + past participle.

    You $\begin{cases} \textbf{have to have} \\ \textbf{had to have} \end{cases}$ known the answer.

Listen to this news story and write the past modals you hear.

According to a recent poll, many people believe that aliens ____must have____ visited the earth at some time in the past. They believe that experts and government officials _____ ignored the sightings of unusual flying objects and strange lights that people have reported over the years. In fact, a group of experts has conducted the first scholarly investigation of

unidentified flying objects (UFOs) in 30 years. According to the experts, by ignoring reports of UFOs, we _____ overlooked important information that _____ led us to new discoveries. They point out how scientists in the past ignored reports of meteorites by saying that these objects _____ fallen from outer space. Looking back now, experts agree that it was inappropriate to assume that those reports were lies or dreams.

UFO believers are delighted with this news. According to one believer, "It's about time. The scientific community _____ done this a long time ago. But it's also sad. They _____ ignored hundreds, or maybe thousands, of good pieces of scientific data. They _____ been so naïve."

Work with a partner. Complete these conversations using the past modal form of the words in parentheses. Then practice the conversations using contractions where appropriate.

Conversation 1

A: I ___could have gone___ (could/go) to the movies with you, but I decided
to study instead.

B: You didn't miss anything. You _____ (might/not/like) it anyway.
There _____ (must/be) ten different violent scenes!

Conversation 2

A: I _____ (should/not/drive) to work this morning.
There was so much traffic.

B: You _____ (should/take) the bus. It was empty.

Conversation 3

A: She _____ (could/not/leave) yet. We're not that late.

B: But she _____ (might/forget) to wait for us.

Conversation 4

A: You _____ (must/have) a great time last night. I heard
you come in at 2:00 A.M.

B: It was great. You _____ (should/stop by) after you left the
library. You _____ (could/hear) the new band.

Conversation 5

A: I lost my keys last night. I _____ (might/leave) them at
your house.

B: No, you _____ (could/not). You drove home with them.

A: That's right. Then I _____ (must/drop) them after I parked
the car.

B: You _____ (might/lock) them in your car. Have you checked?

Work with a partner. Switch roles for each question.

Student A: Ask a question about prehistoric birds. Use the words below with *could have.*

Student B: Answer the question in your own opinion. Use short answers with modals.

1. have feathers

    A: Could prehistoric birds have had feathers?
    B: Yes, they could have. OR *They must have.*

2. descend from dinosaurs

    A: Could prehistoric birds have descended from dinosaurs?
    B: No, they couldn't have.

3. have wings

4. jump from trees

5. run fast

6. live on the ground

7. eat smaller animals

8. eat seeds

Rewrite these sentences. Change the modals to past modals.

1. The researchers might be wrong. There may be some data they ignored.

    The researchers might have been wrong. There may have been some data they ignored.

2. The report should be available on April 12.

3. He ought to study more for the test.

4. I could work harder.

5. She has to be home.

6. I should do things differently. I should exercise more. I know I could find the time.

7. I should relax more. Perhaps I could learn yoga.

8. I shouldn't worry so much. Worrying couldn't be good for my health.

Informally Speaking

Reducing Past Modals

Look at the cartoon and listen to the conversation. How is each underlined form in the cartoon different from what you hear?

This traffic is terrible. We <u>should have</u> stayed in the office!

Yeah. We <u>could have</u> left after rush hour.

In informal speech, affirmative and negative past modals are often reduced. *Have* may sound like /əv/. If it is reduced even more, it sounds like /ə/.

STANDARD FORM	WHAT YOU MIGHT HEAR		
I **could have** come.	"I /ˈkʊdəv/ come."	OR	"I /ˈkʊdə/ come."
They **must have** come.	"They /ˈmʌstəv/ come."	OR	"They /ˈmʌstə/ come."
He **may not have** come.	"He /ˈmeɪnɑtəv/ come."	OR	"He /ˈmeɪnɑdə/ come."
We **should not have** come.	"We /ˈʃʊdntəv/ come."	OR	"We /ˈʃʊdndə/ come."

B5 Understanding Informal Speech

Listen and write the standard form of the words you hear.

A: I'm sorry I'm late. I ___*should have*___ called you. Then you _____
₁   ₂
met me downtown.

B: That _____ worked anyway. I didn't get out of work until six. And
              ₃
then there _____ been fifty people waiting for the elevator. It took
                       ₄
me ten minutes to get out of the building.

A: So where's Linda? She _____ been here by now.
                                            ₅
She _____ forgotten.
          ₆

B: I doubt that. She _____ gotten stuck in traffic, or she
                                   ₇
_____ left work late, too. Let's sit down over there and wait for her.
        ₈

Modals of Past Possibility

Examining Meaning and Use

Read the sentences and answer the questions below. Then discuss your observations and read the Meaning and Use Notes to check them.

   a. Prehistoric birds **must have been** able to fly. They had wings.
   b. Prehistoric birds **could have been** able to fly. They were small.
   c. Prehistoric birds **might have been** able to fly. They were light enough.
   d. Prehistoric birds **couldn't have been** able to fly. They had no way of getting into the air.

1. In which sentences is the speaker more certain?

2. In which sentences is the speaker less certain?

Meaning and Use Notes

> ### Overview
>
> **1** Modals of past possibility are used to make guesses or inferences about the past. The modal you choose shows how certain you are that something was true in the past.
>
> *Less Certain* • might have, might not have, could have
>
> • may have, may not have
>
> • must have, must not have, have to have, have got to have
>
> *More Certain* • can't have, couldn't have
>
> A: Where was Jim this morning?
> B: He **might have been** outside. I'm not sure.
> C: He **may not have been** awake yet.
> D: He **must have been** in bed. He never gets up before noon.
> E: He **can't have been** upstairs. He wasn't home.

> ### Guessing with *May Have, Might Have,* and *Could Have*
>
> **2** Use *may (not) have, might (not) have,* and *could have* to guess about a past situation when you don't have much proof.
>
> Dinosaurs **may have perished** because of a climate change, or they **might have perished** because of disease. Some people think they **could have perished** because a large meteor hit the earth.

3 Use *must (not) have, have to have,* and *have got to have* to draw conclusions about the past when you are certain of something, and you believe there is only one logical explanation.

Problem: Someone stole the money from the drawer. No one was in the room except Sally.

Conclusion: Sally **must have taken** it.

Sally **has (got) to have taken** it.

4A Use *can't have* and *couldn't have* when you are certain something was unlikely or impossible.

No one believes him. He **can't have been** home at the time of the crime. The police have evidence that he was at the crime scene.

4B *Can't have* and *couldn't have* sometimes express surprise or disbelief about the past.

A: You got an A on the exam.

B: I **couldn't have gotten** an A! That's impossible. Didn't I get the last question wrong?

C1 Listening for Meaning and Use ▶ Notes 1–3, 4A, 4B

🎧 Listen to the different opinions among archaeologists about Neanderthals. Is each speaker expressing less certainty or more certainty? Check (✓) the correct column.

	LESS CERTAINTY	MORE CERTAINTY
1.	✓	
2.		
3.		
4.		
5.		
6.		
7.		
8.		

Understanding Degrees of Certainty

► Notes 1–3, 4A

Work with a partner. Read what two different archaeologists (A and B) have said about the "Iceman," a 5,000-year-old frozen mummy that was discovered in 1991 in the Alps. Rewrite their opinions with modals of possibility.

1. **A:** Maybe the Iceman was a shepherd.

   B: We don't believe he was a shepherd.

   A: The Iceman may have been a shepherd.
   B: He couldn't have been a shepherd.

2. **A:** It was impossible for him to build a fire.

   B: Perhaps he built a fire.

3. **A:** It is possible he froze to death.

   B: He almost certainly froze to death.

4. **A:** We can conclude that he lived in a valley.

   B: It's not likely he lived in a valley.

5. **A:** Perhaps he wasn't older than 25.

   B: We can assume he wasn't older than 25.

 Making Guesses and Drawing Conclusions

► Notes 1–3, 4A

Work in small groups. Read this description of a mysterious incident and discuss what you think happened. Use different affirmative and negative past modals to express possibility.

The aircraft may have been on a secret mission.
There couldn't have been any space aliens.

In July of 1947, something crashed in the desert near a town called Roswell, New Mexico. On July 8, an army officer announced to the press that the U.S. government had found a "flying disk" that had crashed. News of flying saucers and aliens from outer space spread quickly around the world. A few hours later, however, another army officer said that after further examination, they concluded that the wreckage was a U.S. government weather balloon.

Over the years, people have continued to wonder about the incident and there have been many rumors. Was there more than one crash? Is it likely that the U.S. government found space aliens and kept it a secret? Did they actually find a flying saucer? Is it possible that the incident was really part of a secret government project? Were the "space aliens" really chimpanzees used for testing special secret aircraft?

Expressing Impossibility and Disbelief ► Notes 4A, 4B

Work with a partner. Switch roles for each statement.

Student A: Read a statement.
Student B: Express disbelief with *couldn't have*. Give a reason for your disbelief.

1. You just won the lottery.

   A: You just won the lottery.
   B: I couldn't have won the lottery. I didn't even buy a ticket.

2. Your great-great-grandfather sent you a letter.

3. Your Rolls Royce ran out of gas.

4. You grew three inches taller this week.

5. You lost a million dollars yesterday.

6. You swam the English Channel last week.

C5 **Writing About Impossibility and Disbelief** ► Notes 4A, 4B

A. Do you believe everything you read in the news? Make a list of events or situations that you have read about that seem unbelievable. Why do you think they are unbelievable?

B. Choose one of your events or situations from part A. Write a paragraph expressing your disbelief. Tell why you think the incident couldn't have happened the way it was described. Describe what you think must have happened instead.

There was another article about UFOs in the newspaper yesterday. This time people in northern Canada saw strange lights in the sky. The lights couldn't have come from alien space crafts. They must have . . .

D Other Functions of Past Modals

Examining Meaning and Use

Read the sentences and answer the questions below. Then discuss your observations and read the Meaning and Use Notes to check them.

a. Paul lived near his office. He could walk there every morning.
He liked the exercise.

b. Paul lived near his office. He could have walked there every morning, but he broke his leg.

c. Paul lived near his office. He should have walked there every morning, but he was too lazy.

1. Which sentences suggest that Paul didn't walk to work every day?

2. Which one suggests that he did?

3. Which sentence expresses the speaker's opinion and advice about a past situation?

Meaning and Use Notes

> ### Past Ability and Opportunity
>
> **1** *Could have* suggests that a person had the ability or opportunity to do something in the past but <u>did not</u> do it. *Could* suggests that a person had the ability or opportunity to do something and <u>was able to</u> or <u>did</u> do it.
>
> Could Have *(Did Not Do It)*
> I **could have walked** to school, but I got a ride instead. (I didn't walk to school.)
> You **could have spoken** French with her, but you were too shy. (You didn't speak French with her.)
>
> Could *(Did It)*
> I lived near the school, so I **could walk** there. (I walked to school.)
> You **could speak** French at an early age. (You spoke French at an early age.)

2A *Should(n't) have* expresses advice about past situations. *Should(n't) have* and *ought (not) to have* express past obligations (what you were or were not supposed to do). Compare the actions that the speakers actually <u>did</u> do and the actions that the speakers <u>did not</u> do.

Did Not Do It

You **should have asked** for help. (Asking for help was a good idea, but you <u>didn't</u> do it.)

She **ought to have registered** on Monday. (She was supposed to register on Monday, but she <u>didn't</u>.)

He **should have visited** his aunt in the hospital. (Visiting his aunt was the right thing to do, but he <u>didn't</u> do it.)

Did It

You **shouldn't have driven** in bad weather. (It was a bad idea to drive, but you <u>did</u> it anyway.)

He **shouldn't have taken** the money. It's illegal. (He wasn't allowed to take the money, but he <u>did</u> it anyway.)

2B In the first person, *should(n't) have* shows regret. It means that you think that something you did or did not do was a mistake.

Did Not Do It

I **should have accepted** the job offer. (I didn't accept the job. Now I am sorry.)

Did It

I **shouldn't have lost** my temper. (I lost my temper. It was a mistake.)

---

3 *May (not)* for expressing permission and *must* for expressing necessity do not have past modal forms. Several different past expressions are used instead.

Present Modals	*Past Expressions*		
Seniors **may have** cars.	Seniors	were permitted to / were allowed to	**have** cars.
Freshmen **may not have** cars.	Freshmen	were not permitted to / were not allowed to	**have** cars.
All visitors **must register**.	All visitors	were required to / were supposed to / had to	**register**.

D1 **Listening for Meaning and Use**

🎧 **Listen to the statements. Choose the sentence that best expresses the meaning of the situation that you hear.**

1. **(a.)** John should have applied for the scholarship.

   b. John must have applied for the scholarship.

2. **a.** John could have left early.

   b. John should have left early.

3. **a.** John shouldn't have asked for help.

   b. John ought to have asked for help.

4. **a.** John must have taken two English courses.

   b. John had to take two English courses.

5. **a.** John may have registered late.

   b. John was permitted to register late.

6. **a.** John shouldn't have called his parents yesterday.

   b. John was supposed to call his parents yesterday.

7. **a.** John had to work in a department store.

   b. John could have worked in a bank.

8. **a.** I should have called John last night.

   b. I shouldn't have called John last night.

D2 **Contrasting *Could* and *Could Have*** ► Note 1

Read each situation. Choose *could* + verb or *could have* + verb.

1. When I worked downtown, I ((could buy)/ could have bought) fresh coffee on my way to the office, so I never made any at home in the morning.

2. I (could ride / could have ridden) my bicycle to school every day, but I never did because I was afraid of the traffic.

3. We always knew when my father got off the bus because we (could see / could have seen) the bus stop from our window.

4. Why didn't anyone tell me? I (could take / could have taken) my vacation last week.

5. You (could call / could have called) me when the car broke down. Why did you leave the car on the side of the road instead?

A. Work with a partner. Make up sentences about each situation using *could have* and the expressions that follow to express the different opportunities that were available to the person. Then think of one more opportunity for each situation.

Situation 1
Paul went to college. He majored in biology and education. He became a teacher, but there were other possibilities that he considered.

1. work in a lab

   He could have worked in a lab.

2. go to medical school

3. teach science in a high school

Situation 2
Lee went to cooking school. He became a chef on a cruise ship after he considered several other careers.

1. become a cook in a restaurant

2. open a restaurant

3. work in a hotel

Situation 3
Ella majored in English. She became an editor after she considered some other choices.

1. be a fiction writer

2. go to law school

3. work for a newspaper

Situation 4
Ed majored in art. He thought about other careers before he decided to paint on his own.

1. become an art teacher

2. get a job in advertising

3. do graphic design

B. On your own, think about some opportunities you had for jobs, schools, or places to live. What did you decide to do? Write four sentences describing what you could have done and a description of what you decided to do instead.

I could have lived in London, but I decided to move to New York instead.

C. Tell the class about one of your opportunities.

D4

Work in small groups. Ask questions about each situation using *should have* and the possibilities that follow. Then give short answers with *should have* or *shouldn't have*. You can also use *could have* to express other possibilities. Explain your answers and discuss any differences in opinion you may have.

Situation 1
Ko is a foreign student who recently arrived in the United States. Last night he was invited to an American friend's house for dinner. He didn't know what to bring.

1. flowers

A: *Should he have brought flowers?*
B: *Yes, he should have. It's polite.* OR *He could have. Flowers are always nice.*

2. an expensive gift

3. a bottle of wine

4. five friends with him

Situation 2
At the dinner table, he started eating before the host sat down. Then he ate his food quickly and he was still hungry.

1. wait for the host

2. eat more slowly

3. ask for more

4. wait for someone to offer him more

Situation 3
In a restaurant a few days later, Ko wanted to speak to his waiter. He didn't know how to get the waiter's attention.

1. whistle

2. snap his fingers

3. clap loudly

4. raise his hand when the waiter was looking at him

Situation 4
There was a mistake on Ko's bill at the restaurant. He didn't know what to do.

1. ignore it

2. tell the waiter

3. call the manager immediately

4. shout at the waiter

D5 Expressing Regret

Work with a partner. Imagine that you each made these mistakes. Take turns making sentences using *should have* and *shouldn't have* to express your regret.

1. You didn't go to the party. Everyone else had a great time.

   I should have gone to the party.
   I shouldn't have stayed home last night.

2. You cooked the rice too long. It burned.

3. You left your car windows open during a rainstorm.

4. You were in a hurry at the post office. You sent an expensive birthday gift to your aunt. She never received it, and you did not insure it.

5. You didn't apply for a summer job. Now it's too late.

6. You drove over the speed limit. You got a traffic ticket.

D6 Writing About Regrets

A. Work in small groups. Read this list of the top ten regrets that women have. Discuss whether you think that men have the same regrets. Do you agree with the list? What other regrets would you add to the list?

B. Make a list of your biggest regrets. Then write a paragraph describing a few things you think you should have done differently and tell why you feel that way. Remember to begin your paragraph with a clear topic sentence.

   My biggest regrets are all related to the fact that I moved so far away from my family. Because of the distance, I often missed holiday gatherings and last-minute lunches I could have had with my sisters. I should have stayed closer to home, and I should have visited more often. I shouldn't have . . .

Top Ten Regrets of Women

1. Not enough education
2. Wrong career, wrong job, wrong work situation
3. Marrying; marrying too early or too late; marrying the wrong person
4. Having children too early or not at all
5. Not being assertive enough
6. Not being self-disciplined
7. Not taking risks
8. Not getting along better with parents, brothers, or sisters
9. Not spending enough time with parents or not appreciating them enough
10. Not being more active in neighborhood or community affairs

from *Prevention* Magazine

E Combining Form, Meaning, and Use

E1 Thinking About Meaning and Use

Work with a partner. Read each sentence and the statements that follow. Write *T* if the statement is true or *F* if it is false. Then discuss your answers in small groups.

1. I shouldn't have gone to the movies.

   _F_   **a.** I didn't go to the movies.

   _T_   **b.** I am sorry that I went to the movies.

2. He couldn't have been at work.

   _____   **a.** I don't believe that he was at work.

   _____   **b.** It's very unlikely that he was at work.

3. She ought to have called first.

   _____   **a.** She called first.

   _____   **b.** She should have called first.

4. Students may not chew gum in class.

   _____   **a.** Students are not allowed to chew gum in class.

   _____   **b.** Students were allowed to chew gum in class.

5. I should have told you.

   _____   **a.** I think I made a mistake.

   _____   **b.** I'm sorry that I didn't tell you.

6. There is only one flight from Centerville per day. They have got to be on that plane.

   _____   **a.** They can't be on the plane.

   _____   **b.** They must be on the plane.

7. I couldn't have passed my driver's test. I didn't practice at all!

_____ **a.** I'm surprised that I passed.

_____ **b.** I didn't pass.

8. I could go to the beach every day when I lived in Florida.

_____ **a.** I wanted to go to the beach, but I didn't do it.

_____ **b.** I went to the beach a lot.

E2 Editing

Find the errors in these sentences and correct them.

1. They ~~mayn't~~ *may not* have called yet.

2. When he could have called?

3. He might a been late.

4. I ought to visited him at the hospital.

5. May he have taken the train instead of the bus?

6. She must have a cold yesterday.

7. I should have asked him. I'm sorry that I did.

8. He should have taking the exam.

9. You could of called me. I was home.

10. She have to have arrived yesterday.

11. The letter might arrived this afternoon.

12. He must had a cold yesterday.

Beyond the Classroom

Searching for Authentic Examples

Find examples of English grammar in everyday life. Choose one of the tasks below. Be prepared to discuss your findings.

A. Look for articles about unsolved crimes or other mysterious happenings. Write down examples of past modals and bring them to class. Which examples express possibilities? assumptions? conclusions? How do you know?

B. Look for articles about scientific discoveries. Write down examples of past modals and bring them to class. Which examples express more certainty? less certainty? How do you know?

C. Read some advice columns. Write down examples of past modals and bring them to class. Which examples express suggestions? regrets? obligations?

Writing

Follow these steps to write a review of a movie, a TV show, or a short story.

1. First make a list of the important events. Then list what you liked and disliked.

2. Use your list to help you write a first draft. In the first paragraph, give a brief summary of the story using the simple past and other past tenses. In the second paragraph, tell what you liked about the story. In the third paragraph, tell what you did not like. What do you think could have or should have happened differently? What should the characters/author/producer have done differently?

3. Read over your work carefully and circle grammar, spelling, and punctuation errors. Work with a partner to decide how to fix your errors. Then rewrite your draft with the changes that you and your partner discussed.

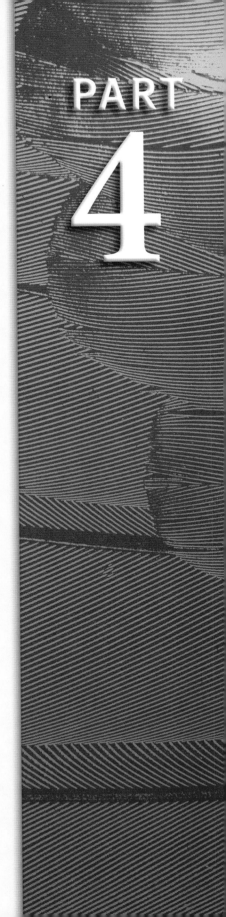

The Passive, Gerunds, and Infinitives

Passive Sentences (Part 1)

A The Expression of Emotions

Discuss these questions.

Look at the photographs below. Discuss what emotion you think each person is expressing. Do you agree with your classmates?

 Read this excerpt from a psychology textbook to find out if the expression of emotions is universal.

The Expression of Emotions

  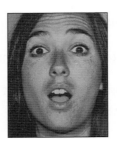 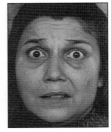

The four basic emotions

Joy and sadness <u>are found</u> in diverse cultures around the world, but how can we tell when other people are happy or despondent? It turns out that the expression of many emotions may be universal (Rinn 1991). Smiling is apparently a universal sign of friendliness and approval. Baring the teeth (was noted) by Charles Darwin (1872) as a
5 possible universal sign of anger. As the originator of the theory of evolution, Darwin believed that the universal recognition of facial expressions would have survival value. For example, facial expressions could signal the approach of enemies (or friends) in the absence of language.

Most investigators (e.g., Brown 1991, Buss 1992, etc.) agree that certain facial
10 expressions suggest the same emotions in all people. Moreover, people in diverse cultures recognize the emotions that are signaled by the facial expressions. In classic research, Paul Ekman (1980) took photographs of people exhibiting the emotions of anger, disgust, fear, happiness, sadness, and surprise. He then asked people around the world to indicate what emotions were being shown in the photos. Ekman's results suggested that the expression
15 of several basic emotions such as happiness, anger, surprise, and fear is universally

recognized. The subjects of the study ranged from European college students to members of the Fore, a New Guinea highlands tribe that had had almost no contact with Western culture. It was found that all groups, including the Fore, agreed on the emotions the pictures expressed.

20   Ekman and his colleagues obtained similar results in a study of ten different cultures. In this study, the participants were permitted to report whether they thought that more than one emotion was shown by a facial expression. The participants generally agreed on which two emotions were being expressed and which emotion was the most intense.

Emotions are also being studied from other perspectives. For example, although it is 25 generally recognized that facial expressions reflect emotional states, it is not unreasonable to ask whether feelings must always come before facial expressions. Are positive feelings ever produced by smiling? Is anger ever produced by frowning? Psychological research has shown in experiments that when participants are induced to smile first, they rate cartoons as funnier. When they are induced to frown first, they rate cartoons as more 30 aggressive. Psychologists have a number of complicated explanations for these results, but not surprisingly, they have also concluded that none of the theories of emotion apply to all people in all situations. Our emotions are not quite as easily understood as some theories have suggested.

Adapted from *Essentials of Psychology*

baring the teeth: holding the lips up to reveal the teeth
despondent: sad and without hope
diverse: different from each other

evolution: the gradual development of plants and animals
induce: to make someone do something
perspective: view; a way of judging something

A3 After You Read

Choose the answer that best completes each sentence.

1. The expression of many of our emotions appears to be _____.
   a. universal
   b. limited by culture

2. Psychologists would be surprised to find a culture with people who _____.
   a. never smile
   b. frown

3. Darwin was interested in emotions and their relationship to _____.
   a. love
   b. survival

4. Ekman showed _____ to people around the world.
   a. photos
   b. reports

5. The reactions of the Fore are important because _____.
   a. they show Western influence
   b. they suggest similarity across cultures

6. Other research has shown that _____ may produce _____.
   a. facial expressions; emotions
   b. emotions; facial expressions

B The Present and Past Passive

Examining Form

Look back at the excerpt on page 192 and complete the tasks below. Then discuss your observations and read the Form charts to check them.

1. An example of the simple present passive is underlined. Find three more examples. Sort them into singular and plural.

2. An example of the simple past passive is circled. Find three more examples. Sort them into singular and plural.

3. Look at the examples of the present continuous and past continuous passives below. Find one example of each of these forms in the text.

   a. A great deal of research **is being done**.

   b. A great deal of research **was being done**.

THE PRESENT PASSIVE	THE PAST PASSIVE
Simple Present Passive	**Simple Past Passive**
AM/IS/ARE + PAST PARTICIPLE (+ *BY* + NOUN)	*WAS/WERE* + PAST PARTICIPLE (+ *BY* + NOUN)
The directions **are explained (by the teacher)**.	The directions **were explained (by the teacher)**.
The answer **isn't explained**.	The answer **wasn't explained**.

Is the study **published** yet?
    Yes, it **is**. / **No**, it **isn't**.
	Was the study **published**?
	    Yes, it **was**. / **No**, it **wasn't**.

When are the results **announced**?	**Where were** the results **announced**?

THE PRESENT PASSIVE

Present Continuous Passive
AM/IS/ARE + *BEING* + PAST PARTICIPLE (+ *BY* + NOUN)
The directions **are being explained (by the teacher)**. The answer **isn't being explained**. **Is** the study **being published**?   **Yes**, it **is**. / **No**, it **isn't**. **How are** the results **being announced**?

THE PAST PASSIVE

Past Continuous Passive
WAS/WERE + *BEING* + PAST PARTICIPLE (+ *BY* + NOUN)
The directions **were being explained (by the teacher)**. The answer **wasn't being explained**. **Was** the study **being published**?   **Yes**, it **was**. / **No**, it **wasn't**. **Why were** the results **being announced**?

- Only transitive verbs can be in the passive. A transitive verb is a verb that is followed by an object. For example: **give** an exam, **throw** a baseball, **cook** a meal.
- *By* + a noun phrase is optional at the end of passive sentences.
    The directions **were explained (by the teacher)**.
    The study **is being published (by *Psychology Today*)**.
- See Appendices 4 and 5 for spelling and pronunciation rules for verbs ending in *-ed*.
- See Appendix 6 for irregular verbs and their past participles.

B1 Listening for Form

Listen to this information about facial expressions and write the passive forms you hear.

1. Last year some research __was being done__ on smiling across cultures.

2. I _____ to join the study after it began.

3. A number of questions _____ at the same time.

4. For example, _____ the general meaning of a smile always _____?

5. Why _____ the mouth _____ in some cultures?

6. Is it true that smiles _____ for friends and family in some cultures?

7. The results of this research _____ at a psychology conference.

8. The results _____ also _____ in a popular psychology magazine.

Asking and Answering Questions with Simple Present Passives

Work with a partner. Complete this conversation with the words in parentheses and the simple present passive. Then practice the conversation.

A: When _____is the trash collected_____ (the trash/collect) in your neighborhood?
                              1

B: It _____ (pick up) on Mondays, but we don't have much
                 2

trash anymore. Almost everything we use _____ (recycle).
                                                        3

A: And _____ (the recycled items/collect) too?
               4

B: Some of them _____ (collect). Newspapers, glass, and
                          5

cans _____ (take away) by a private recycling company.
         6

A: And then what _____ (do) with all of that stuff?
                          7

B: It _____ (sell) to other companies for further recycling.
           8

Working on Simple Past Passives

Work with a partner. Complete this paragraph about how glass was made in the picture. Use the words in parentheses and the simple past passive.

When the glass _____was made_____ (make),
                          1
certain materials _____ (melt)
                           2
together and then they _____ (cool).
                                3
The materials _____ (heat) in large
                       4
furnaces that _____ (build) of ceramic
                       5
blocks. When the bubbles _____
                                     6
(remove) from the hot mixture, the hot liquid

_____ (pour) into molds, and it
           7
_____ (form) into different shapes.
           8

A. Complete this paragraph with the words in parentheses and the present continuous passive.

The building where I work _____is being renovated_____ (renovate) right
now, and a number of changes _____ (make). For
example, all of the offices _____ (paint), and the
carpeting _____ (replace). New shelves
_____ (build), and the computer system
_____ (upgrade). Finally, a new kitchen
_____ (add) for the staff. A refrigerator, microwave,
and sink _____ (install) in the new kitchen.

B. Now rewrite the paragraph in the past continuous passive.

The building where I work was being renovated last month, and a
number of changes . . .

A. Imagine you are interviewing the director of the computer lab at your school
about changes that are taking place. For items 1–4 write information questions
with the present continuous passive. For items 5–8 write *Yes/No* questions with
the present continuous passive.

1. what kind of computers/buy
   What kind of computers are being bought?

2. how many computers/not replace

3. which software program/install

4. how much money/spend

5. more employees/hire

6. new furniture/purchase

7. the old equipment/throw away

8. the hours of operation/expand

B. Change questions 1–4 to the past continuous passive.

What kind of computers were being bought?

C. Change questions 5–8 to the simple past passive. End each question with *last
semester.*

Were more employees hired last semester?

Changing Focus from Active to Passive

Examining Meaning and Use

Read the sentences and answer the questions below. Then discuss your observations and read the Meaning and Use Notes to check them.

> **1a.** High winds damaged the bridge.
> **1b.** The bridge was damaged by high winds.
>
> **2a.** The state inspects the bridge once a year.
> **2b.** The bridge is inspected by the state once a year.

1. Do the sentences in each pair have about the same meaning or different meanings?

2. Which sentences focus more on a noun that is performing an action or causing something to happen?

3. Which sentences focus more on a noun that receives an action?

Meaning and Use Notes

```
┌─────────────────────────────────────────────────────────────────────┐
│        Contrasting Active and Passive Sentences                     │
```

1A   The passive form changes the usual order of the subject and object of an active sentence. The object of an active sentence becomes the subject of a passive sentence.

> *Active Sentence:* <u>Jonah</u>   **sent**   <u>the letter</u>.
>
> *Passive Sentence:* <u>The letter</u> **was sent** by <u>Jonah</u>.

1B   In active sentences, the agent (the noun that is performing the action) is in subject position. In passive sentences, the receiver (the noun that receives or is the result of an action) is in the subject position. Passive sentences very often do not mention the agent at all.

	Agent		*Receiver*
Active Sentence:	Jonah	**sent**	the letter.

	Receiver		*Agent*
Passive Sentence:	The letter	**was sent**	by Jonah.
	The letter	**was sent**.	

2 Choosing the active or the passive form of a sentence does not change the meaning, but it does affect the way you think about the information in the sentence. Use an active sentence to focus on who or what performs the action. Use a passive sentence to focus on the receiver or the result of an action.

Active Sentence

We **tried** to get help during the storm, but we **couldn't get through** on the phone, so we **waited** until the next morning.

(The focus is on us—the speakers—and what we did during the storm.)

Passive Sentence

The next morning, our roof **was damaged** and the basement **was flooded**. Next door, the porch **was ruined** and several windows **were broken**.

(The focus is on the results of the storm. The sentences describe the damage caused by the storm.)

C1 **Listening for Meaning and Use**   ► Notes 1A, 1B

Listen to this description of a research study. Check (✓) whether each sentence is active or passive.

	ACTIVE	PASSIVE
1.		✓
2.		
3.		
4.		
5.		
6.		
7.		
8.		

Create meaningful active or passive sentences in the simple past. Use the words given. The first words in each item must be the subject of your sentence.

1. the medicine/take/the patient <u>The medicine was taken by the patient.</u>

2. the patient/take/the medicine <u>The patient took the medicine.</u>

3. the window/break/the child _____

4. the concert/attend/many people _____

5. she/make/the cake _____

6. we/cancel/the appointment _____

7. the car/repair/two mechanics _____

Work with a partner. Use the words in parentheses and the past continuous passive to tell what was happening. Then add another idea of your own.

1. Your friend's wedding reception started at 2:00 P.M. When you arrived at 2:15,

   a. (the guests/greet) <u>The guests were being greeted.</u>

   b. (the bride and groom/photograph) _____

   c. (drinks/serve) _____

   d. _____

2. When your dinner guests arrived, you were still getting ready and

   a. (the wine/chill) _____

   b. (the salad/made) _____

   c. (the table/set) _____

   d. _____

3. When you arrived at the scene of the accident,

   a. (one person/lift into an ambulance) _____

   b. (a man/give oxygen) _____

   c. (two witnesses/question) _____

   d. _____

Vocabulary Notes

Verbs with No Passive Forms

Intransitive Verbs Verbs that cannot be followed by objects are called intransitive verbs. They have no passive forms. Here are some common intransitive verbs:

appear	come	die	go	look	rain	stay
arrive	cry	emerge	happen	occur	sleep	walk

See Appendix 7 for a list of more intransitive verbs.

Transitive Nonpassive Verbs Verbs that can be followed by objects are called transitive verbs. Most transitive verbs have passive forms, but some do not. Notice how the passive form of *fit* does not make sense in English.

ACTIVE	PASSIVE
The dress fits Valerie.	*Valerie is fit by the dress. (INCORRECT)

Here are some more transitive verbs that have no passive forms:

Ben **has** a CD player.	Jenny **resembles** Bob.	She **became** a doctor.
He **weighs** 150 pounds.	The test **consists of** two parts.	The book **costs** ten dollars.
Two cups **equal** a pint.	The dress **suits** her.	We **lack** funds.

Verbs That Are Intransitive or Transitive Some verbs can be transitive or intransitive. When they are intransitive they do not have passive forms. Here are some examples:

begin	break	close	end	freeze	open	start	stop

C4 Choosing Verbs with Active or Passive Forms

Change these active sentences to passive sentences if possible. Some of the sentences cannot be changed. Explain why some of the sentences have no passive form.

1. A graduate student is gathering data for a study on emotions.

   Data is being gathered by a graduate student for a study on emotions.

2. A psychologist proposed a new theory about facial expressions.

3. Some interesting results are emerging from cross-cultural data.

4. The research team was considering the new theory.

5. They already have 75 participants for the study.

6. The psychology department is paying each participant.

7. Some new equipment for the project arrived yesterday.

8. The researchers still need more equipment for data analysis.

Reasons for Using the Passive

Examining Meaning and Use

Read the sentences and answer the questions below. Then discuss your observations and read the Meaning and Use Notes to check them.

A radio broadcast
1a. A former employee robbed the C&R bank at about 8:00 P.M. last night.
1b. The C&R bank was robbed at about 8:00 P.M. last night.

A sign in a doctor's office
2a. Patients are requested to pay before leaving.
2b. Dr. Lewis requests that patients pay before leaving.

1. In which sentence is the agent probably unknown?

2. In sentences 2a and 2b, which sign is more impersonal and indirect?

Meaning and Use Notes

Focus on Results or Processes

1 Use the passive when the receiver or result of an action is more important than the agent. The passive is often used in descriptions of results or processes involving things rather than people.

Many homes **were damaged** by the flood. (The result is more important than the agent.)

The mixture **is boiled** before it **is poured** into the bowl. (The focus is on the process.)

Omitting the Agent

2A Passive sentences that do not mention the agent are called agentless passives. They are used when the agent is unimportant, unknown, or obvious.

Unimportant Agent
Supercomputers **were developed** to solve complex problems.

Unknown Agent
This package **was left** on my desk. Do you know who left it?

Obvious Agent
The mail **is delivered** at noon. (It is obvious that a mail carrier delivers the mail.)

2B The agentless passive is used to avoid very general subjects such as *people,* *someone, we, one,* and impersonal *you* and *they.* The passive often sounds more indirect or impersonal.

Agentless Passive

ID photos **are being taken** today.

Calcium **is needed** for strong bones.

Reservations **are required**.

Parsley is an herb that **is used** as a garnish.

Active

<u>They</u> are taking ID photos today.

<u>People</u> need calcium for strong bones.

<u>We</u> require reservations.

Parsley is an herb that <u>one</u> uses as a garnish.

2C Sometimes the agentless passive is used to avoid taking responsibility for an action or to avoid blaming another person.

A Boss Speaking to His Employees

A serious error **was made** in the payroll.
(The boss deliberately doesn't say who made the error.)

D1 **Listening for Meaning and Use**

► Notes 1, 2A, 2B

Listen to each situation. Check (✓) the sentence that has approximately the same meaning as the passive sentence you hear.

1. _____ **a.** You can smoke in this building.

   __✓__ **b.** We ask visitors not to smoke in this building.

2. _____ **a.** They speak French in Quebec.

   _____ **b.** Nobody speaks French in Quebec.

3. _____ **a.** We permitted Julie to speak.

   _____ **b.** They permitted Julie to speak.

4. _____ **a.** A falling tree injured several people.

   _____ **b.** Several people injured a tree.

5. _____ **a.** The author wrote the book in 1966.

   _____ **b.** My friend wrote the book in 1966.

6. _____ **a.** You appreciate our assistance.

   _____ **b.** We appreciate your assistance.

Work with a partner. Describe the results of the situations below by completing each sentence with the simple past passive. Try to use a different verb in each sentence.

1. An earthquake rocked a small town in Southern California last night.

   a. No major power lines _were knocked down._

   b. One major road _____

   c. Twelve people _____

   d. A person _____

   e. One building _____

   f. Many windows _____

2. A serious flu epidemic spread through the area last month.

   a. One school _____

   b. A rock concert _____

   c. Many flu shots _____

   d. Dozens of people _____

3. John was surprised to see that his roommate had cleaned their apartment.

   a. The dishes _____

   b. The carpets _____

   c. The furniture _____

   d. The windows _____

   e. The kitchen floor _____

Work with a partner. Change each sentence to the agentless passive. Choose a reason for omitting the agent. Is it (a) unknown, (b) unimportant or obvious, (c) a general subject, or (d) not used to avoid blame?

1. Some painters were painting the office yesterday.

   The office was being painted yesterday. (b)

2. The vendors are always reducing the prices at the farmer's market.

3. They're accepting applications for summer employment at the supermarket.

4. When a pipe burst in our house, the water ruined our new carpet.

5. I lost the report sometime during the week.

6. At that moment, somebody was unlocking the door.

7. Attention, please. We are now selling tickets for the 5:00 P.M. show.

8. Authors are writing many books about health and nutrition.

9. Last year, the university required undergraduates to take a minimum of four courses per semester.

10. In Brazil people speak Portuguese and a number of other languages.

A. Work with a partner. Use the words in parentheses and your own words to write definitions for these terms. Use the passive in your definition.

1. Caffeine (stimulant/find) _Caffeine is a stimulant that is found in coffee._

2. Labor Day (an American holiday/celebrate) _____

3. The tuxedo (garment/wear) _____

4. Farsi (language/speak) _____

5. Wine (alcoholic beverage/make) _____

6. Rice (food/eat) _____

B. Now make a list of six nouns. Exchange papers with your partner and write definitions like those above for any three nouns on the list your partner gives you.

Beyond the Sentence

> ## Keeping the Focus
>
> You can choose between an active or passive sentence in order to keep the focus on a noun that was mentioned in a previous sentence. To keep the focus, make the noun the subject of the next sentence. Sometimes you will need an active sentence to do this; sometimes you will need a passive sentence. It is easier to follow ideas from sentence to sentence when the focus is understood.
>
> *Active Sentence Followed by Passive Sentence*
>
> Yesterday, the old man lost his <u>wallet</u>. Fortunately, <u>it</u> **was found** by a police officer a few hours later.
>
> *Active Sentence Followed by Active Sentence*
>
> Yesterday, the old man lost his <u>wallet</u>. Fortunately, <u>it</u> **had** no money inside.

D5 Keeping the Focus

A. Choose the active or passive sentence that best completes each item. Your answer will depend on the underlined focus.

1. <u>Charlotte</u> opened the door,

   (a.) and she was greeted by a strange dog.

   b. and a strange dog greeted her.

2. When <u>we</u> lived in that house,

   a. a garden was never planted.

   b. we never planted a garden.

3. <u>Golf</u> is one of the most popular sports in the United States.

   a. It is played by people of all ages.

   b. People of all ages play it.

4. My uncle got <u>a new car</u>.

   a. It was purchased in New Jersey.

   b. He bought it in New Jersey.

5. In 1994, <u>she</u> wrote a best-selling novel.

   a. After that, many offers were received to write more fiction.

   b. After that, she received many offers to write more fiction.

6. Tibet and Nepal have many <u>mountains</u>.

    a. In those countries, transportation is difficult.

    b. They make transportation difficult in those countries.

7. <u>The Great Lakes</u> are the largest group of freshwater lakes in the world.

    a. They were formed by glaciers about 250,000 years ago.

    b. Glaciers formed them about 250,000 years ago.

8. As soon as <u>the robber</u> tried to leave the bank,

    a. he was arrested by a detective waiting outside.

    b. a detective waiting outside arrested him.

B. **Each of these sentences has an underlined noun indicating the focus. For each noun, write an appropriate active or passive sentence that gives additional information about the focus. Use nouns or pronouns.**

1. <u>Sushi</u> is a rice delicacy in Japan. <u>It is often filled or topped with raw fish.</u>

    Sushi is a rice <u>delicacy</u> in Japan. <u>Another popular delicacy is sashimi.</u>

2. <u>Antibiotics</u> kill certain bacteria. _____

    Antibiotics kill <u>certain bacteria</u>. _____

3. <u>French</u> is a Romance language. _____

    French is a <u>Romance language</u>. _____

4. <u>Music</u> used to be recorded on vinyl records. _____

    Music used to be recorded on <u>vinyl records</u>. _____

5. <u>Psychologists</u> are interested in facial expressions. _____

    Psychologists are interested in <u>facial expressions</u>. _____

6. <u>Rice</u> is a staple in many countries around the world. _____

    Rice is a <u>staple</u> in many countries around the world. _____

C. **Choose one of the sentences from part B and expand it into a short paragraph of four or five sentences. Work on maintaining the focus between sentence pairs. Use active or passive sentences where appropriate.**

    Sushi is a rice delicacy in Japan. Another popular delicacy is sashimi. While both delicacies are made from very thinly sliced raw fish, sushi is served with . . .

E Combining Form, Meaning, and Use

E1 Thinking About Meaning and Use

Read each sentence and the statements that follow. Choose the statement that best explains the meaning of the sentence. Then discuss your answers in small groups.

1. Students are required to take the final exam.
   a. The students require the final exam.
   b. The professor requires the final exam.

2. Student photos are being taken in the gym.
   a. Students are taking pictures.
   b. Students are being photographed.

3. He has been called a liar by the mayor.
   a. The mayor has called him a liar.
   b. He has called the mayor a liar.

4. Laser beams are used in surgery.
   a. Laser beams use surgery.
   b. Surgeons use laser beams.

5. He was asked to resign by the board of directors.
   a. He asked the board of directors to resign.
   b. The board of directors asked him to resign.

6. It is believed that she will run for president.
   a. It is certain that she will run for president.
   b. People think that she will run for president.

7. The letter was sent to all patients by the doctor.
   a. The patients sent the letter.
   b. The doctor sent the letter.

8. He is not being hired for the job.
   a. He is not going to get the job.
   b. He is not hiring us for the job.

Find the errors in these paragraphs and correct them.

It is ~~claiming~~ *claimed* by psychologists that everyone lies at some time or other. Moreover, many people can lie without showing it in their facial expressions or body language. For this reason, lie detector tests are frequently use in police investigations. The use of such tests to detect lies is many hundreds of years old.

For example, it is believe that in China suspected liars were forced to chew rice powder and then spit it out. If the powder was dry, the suspect is considered guilty. In Spain, another variation for lie detection used. The suspect was being required to swallow a slice of bread and cheese. It was believed that if the bread stuck inside the suspect's mouth, then he or she was lying. Psychologists report that these strange methods actually show a basic principle that is know about lying: Anxiety that is related to lying is linked to lack of saliva, or dry mouth.

Modern lie detectors, which are calling polygraphs, are used to indicate changes in heart rate, blood pressure, breathing rate, and perspiration while a person is be examined. Questions about the validity of the polygraph, however, are frequently raising. Consequently, results from polygraphs are often thrown out in legal cases.

Beyond the Classroom

Searching for Authentic Examples

Find examples of English grammar in everyday life. Choose one of the tasks below. Be prepared to discuss your findings.

A. Look in a newspaper or on the Internet or listen to a news broadcast. Write down four examples of the agentless passive and four examples of the passive used with an agent. Bring your examples to class. Which examples were easier to find?

B. Look in a textbook for examples of the passive. Write down four examples of the agentless passive and four examples of the passive used with an agent. Bring your examples to class. Which examples were easier to find?

C. Look at some public signs. Write down five examples of the passive and bring them to class. Did you find any examples with agents? Can you guess the agent in the agentless examples?

Speaking

Follow these steps for making a short presentation to the class about body language.

1. Make a list of gestures and facial expressions that are typical in your culture.

2. Interview a native English speaker or a speaker of another foreign language to find out about his or her use of body language. Write down any interesting facts that you discover. How does it compare with body language in your own culture?

3. In small groups, discuss your findings and compare the differences that you have found. Prepare a short presentation for the class in which different members of your group demonstrate various gestures and facial expressions. Use the passive to describe those gestures and expressions.

4. With the class, discuss any differences and similarities that you have found among cultures.

Passive Sentences (Part 2)

A Should Parents Be Punished for Their Children's Crimes?

A1 Before You Read

Discuss these questions.

Do children ever commit crimes in your country? How are they punished? Are their parents ever punished, too? Can parents stop children from committing crimes?

A2 Read

Read this newspaper article to find out what lawmakers in the U.S. are doing about children's crimes.

Should Parents Be Punished for Their Children's Crimes?

A number of widely publicized school shootings and other violent crimes by children in recent years have resulted in a growing trend that says parents 5 must be held responsible for their children's crimes. At least 38 states in the United States have laws in which parents of juvenile offenders can be punished under certain conditions, and similar 10 laws will be introduced in many state legislatures in the future. At the national level, proposals have been made to mandate prison sentences of three to ten years and $10,000 fines for adults, 15 including parents, who "knowingly or recklessly" allow children to have guns.

Parental responsibility laws in various states make parents accountable for children's criminal actions. Many of these

20 laws involve fines ranging from $25 to $2,500, although in Maryland, parents can be ordered to pay up to $10,000 for a single criminal incident. In Oklahoma, parents may be required to pay a fine or
25 perform community service if their child possesses a firearm on school property, and in Arizona, parents have been required to pay for some of the costs involved in caring for their child in jail.
30 In other states, like Louisiana and California, parents can be imprisoned. Supporters of these laws believe that parents will be more attentive to their children if they know they could be fined
35 or jailed for their crimes.

Critics say many parental responsibility laws have been enacted out of hysteria. Some of the laws will be considered unconstitutional and will not be enforced.
40 In addition, many people are concerned about imposing impossible standards on parents. They have mixed feelings about such laws: What about the parents who try very hard to bring up their child right,
45 but the child still turns out wrong?

---

accountable: responsible
fines: money paid as punishment for crimes
hysteria: uncontrolled excitement or panic
juvenile offenders: children who commit crimes

knowingly: with knowledge of the result or effect
mandate: to require
recklessly: irresponsibly, without caring about the results

A3) After You Read

Choose all the words or phrases that correctly complete each statement.

1. Parental responsibility laws are becoming more common because of increases in _____.

   a. adult crime
   b. juvenile crime
   c. school shootings
   d. children with guns

2. Currently, punishment for parents of juvenile offenders in various states includes _____.

   a. fines
   b. loss of job
   c. imprisonment
   d. community service

3. Critics say that parental responsibility laws are _____.

   a. overreactions
   b. unconstitutional
   c. outdated
   d. too gentle

B The Future, Present Perfect, and Modal Passive

Examining Form

Look back at the article on page 212 and complete the tasks below. Then discuss your observations and read the Form charts to check them.

1. An example of a modal passive is underlined. Find five more examples. What are the three parts of each modal passive?

2. An example of the future passive is circled. Find two more examples. What are the three parts of the future passive? Can you think of another way to form it?

3. Look at this example sentence. What are the three parts of the present perfect passive?

   Proposals have been made to mandate prison sentences.

THE FUTURE PASSIVE

Future Passive with *Will*
WILL + *BE* + PAST PARTICIPLE (+ *BY* + NOUN)
TV violence **will be limited.**
The child **won't be punished.**
Will the parents **be blamed**?   **Yes,** they **will.** / **No,** they **won't.**
Why will the parents **be punished**?

Future Passive with *Be Going To*
BE GOING TO + *BE* + PAST PARTICIPLE (+ *BY* + NOUN)
TV violence **is going to be limited.**
The child **isn't going to be punished.**
Are the parents **going to be blamed**?   **Yes,** they **are.** / **No,** they **aren't.**
Why are the parents **going to be punished**?

THE PRESENT PERFECT PASSIVE

Present Perfect Passive
HAS/HAVE + *BEEN* + PAST PARTICIPLE (+ *BY* + NOUN)
TV violence **has been limited.**
The child **hasn't been punished.**
Have the parents **been blamed**?   **Yes,** they **have.** / **No,** they **haven't.**
Why have the parents **been punished**?

Modal Passive

MODAL + *BE* + PAST PARTICIPLE (+ *BY* + NOUN)

TV violence **must be limited.**

The child **should not be punished.**

Could the parents **be blamed?**
   Yes, they **could be.** / **No,** they **couldn't be.**

Why should the parents **be punished?**

Phrasal Modal Passive

MODAL + *BE* + PAST PARTICIPLE (+ *BY* + NOUN)

TV violence **has (got) to be limited.**

The child **ought to be punished.**

Do the parents **have to be blamed?**
   Yes, they **do.** / **No,** they **don't.**

Why do the parents **have to be punished?**

Future, Present Perfect, and Modal Passive

- In passives with more than one auxiliary verb (*will be punished, is going to be punished, has been punished, should be punished*), only the first auxiliary changes position or combines with *not* in questions and negative sentences.
  Isn't he going to be punished for his crimes?
  He **isn't** going to be punished for his crimes.

Phrasal Modal Passive

- The negative and question forms of *have to* and *need to* use *do*.
  He **doesn't** have to be punished.
  Does he have to be punished?

- *Have got to* is not used with negatives or questions.

B1   **Listening for Form**

Listen to each sentence. Is it active or passive? Check (✓) the correct column.

	ACTIVE	PASSIVE
1.		✓
2.		
3.		
4.		
5.		
6.		
7.		
8.		

A. Complete these sentences with the words in parentheses and the future passive with *will*.

Community Center Policies

1. New courses _____will be offered_____ (offer) every six weeks.

2. Instructor schedules _____ (post) at the front desk.

3. Schedule changes _____ (not/announce) until the first day of classes.

4. Classes with fewer than five participants _____ (cancel).

Mail-Order Information

1. Your order _____ (ship) within 48 hours.

2. Postage and handling _____ (add) to all orders.

3. Refunds for credit card purchases _____ (credit) to your account.

4. Check or money order purchases _____ (refund) within ten days of receipt.

B. Complete these sentences with the words in parentheses and a modal passive.

Product Instructions

1. This product __should be refrigerated__ (should/refrigerate) after opening.

2. This prescription _____ (can/not/refill).

3. This product _____ (should/keep) out of the reach of children.

4. After opening, this product _____ (may/store) for up to three months in a cool, dry place.

Mail-Order Information

1. Each item _____ (need to/list) separately.

2. Any damage _____ (have to/report) within two weeks.

3. Each return _____ (must/accompany) by a receipt.

4. Mail orders _____ (should/send) to the address below.

Working on Present Perfect Passives

Complete each sentence with the words in parentheses and the present perfect passive.

1. The exam _has been canceled by the teacher._
   (cancel/the teacher)

2. These products _____
   (manufacture/the company/for three years)

3. This book _____
   (translate/into many languages)

4. The senator _____
   (call/dishonest)

5. The recipes _____
   (create/a famous chef)

6. A new prescription _____
   (recommend/the doctor)

Asking and Answering Passive Questions

A. Work in small groups. Take turns asking and answering questions using the words below and the modal *should*. Then make up two more questions to ask the class.

1. smoking/permit/in public places

   A: *Should smoking be permitted in public places?*
   B: *Yes, it should.* OR *No, it shouldn't.*

2. bicyclists/allow/on busy streets

3. violent scenes/ban/from television

4. guns/sell/in stores

5. men/give/parental leave for childcare

6. women/pay/the same wages as men

7. parents/punish/for their children's crimes

8. animals/use/for medical research

B. Which issues did your group agree on? Which ones didn't you agree on?

The Role of the Agent

Examining Meaning and Use

Read the sentences and complete the tasks below. Then discuss your observations and read the Meaning and Use Notes to check them.

1a. The course will be given by the instructor on Mondays.
1b. The course will be given by a team of experts via satellite on Mondays.

2a. The article was written by Gregory Marks in one day.
2b. The article was written by the author in one day.

1. Underline the agent in each sentence.

2. Which agents give important or unexpected information? Which ones seem unnecessary?

Meaning and Use Notes

Including the Agent

1A Passives are often used without agents if the agent is unimportant, unknown, or obvious. However, the agent is necessary when it is surprising or unexpected.

Agentless Passive	*Passive with an Agent*
The mail **has been delivered**.	The mail **has been delivered** <u>by an experimental robot</u>. (The agent is surprising.)
We **were given** six pages of homework.	We **were given** six pages of homework <u>by a substitute teacher</u>. (The agent is unexpected.)

1B An agent is used to provide additional or new information.

Agentless Passive	*Passive with an Agent*
You **will be notified** about the exam date.	You **will be notified** about the exam date <u>by e-mail</u>.

1C An agent is used to complete the meaning of the sentence or to add important information—especially a proper noun, such as the name of an author, artist, composer, inventor, or designer.

Agentless Passive	*Passive with an Agent*
Washington, D.C. **was designed**.	Washington, D.C. **was designed** <u>by Pierre L'Enfant</u>.

🎧 Listen to each sentence. Does the agent complete the meaning and/or provide necessary information? Check (✓) whether the agent is necessary or unnecessary.

	NECESSARY AGENT	UNNECESSARY AGENT
1.		✓
2.		
3.		
4.		
5.		
6.		
7.		
8.		

Work with a partner. Change each sentence to the passive. Decide whether to keep or omit the agent. Be prepared to explain your decision.

1. Next week a painter will paint our house.

   Next week our house will be painted.
   (The agent is omitted because it is obvious.)

2. Pablo Picasso painted *The Three Musicians*.

   The Three Musicians *was painted by Pablo Picasso. (The agent is included because it adds important information.)*

3. Drunk drivers have caused many car accidents in this community.

4. Parents shouldn't allow children to watch too much television.

5. Lawmakers will pass a gun control law soon.

6. Winston Churchill led the British government during World War II.

7. Will the courts punish the parents of juvenile offenders?

8. A young child has written this incredible story.

Rewrite these active descriptions using the future passive. Then work in small groups and discuss whether or not you needed to use the agent in any of your sentences. What is the difference between the active and passive descriptions?

At the Hospital

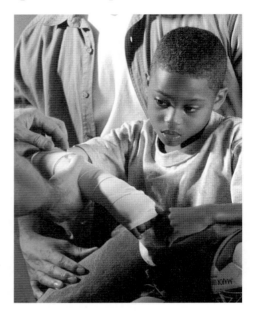

1. When Derek arrives at the emergency room, they are going to examine his arm.

   When Derek arrives at the emergency room, his arm is going to be examined.

2. Then they will send him for an X ray.

   Then he'll be sent for an X ray.

3. They will tell him whether it is broken.

4. If his arm is broken, they will send him back to the emergency room.

5. First they will put his arm in the proper position.

6. Then they will put a cotton sleeve over his arm, and they will wrap it with wet bandages.

7. After it sets, they will tell him how to care for the cast.

At School

1. Please listen carefully. The teacher is going to read the instructions only once.

2. He will give each student a test booklet and a pencil.

3. He will ask the students to turn to the first page.

4. Then he will show them a set of pictures.

5. He will tell them to check the correct answer in the booklet.

6. After the last picture, he will collect the booklets.

7. Finally, he will dismiss the students.

D The Passive in Academic and Public Discourse

Examining Meaning and Use

Read the sentences and complete the tasks below. Then discuss your observations and read the Meaning and Use Notes to check them.

    a. Sulfur dioxide is used to produce sulfuric acid.
    b. As a special benefit to on-line customers, orders will be shipped free of charge.
    c. Your vehicle must be insured. Proof of insurance must be presented.

1. Change each sentence to an active sentence.

2. Think about the differences between the active and passive sentences. Which type of sentence sounds more formal and impersonal? Why?

3. In what context would you expect to find each of the passive sentences?

Meaning and Use Notes

Common Uses of the Passive in Academic Discourse

1 Academic discourse, such as textbooks and other factual materials, tends to focus on objects, processes, and results. Such materials try to present an objective and impersonal perspective to convey a sense of authority. To express this tone, writers often use passive expressions with *it*-subjects (e.g., *It is expected that*) as well as other passive constructions.

Psychology Text
It **is** generally **agreed** that people can learn something much more
    rapidly the second time.

Encyclopedia
Dams **may be built** on main streams or their branches. They **are** usually **built** at a
    spot where the river becomes narrow.

Computer Programming Book
Subprograms **are defined** between SUB and END SUB statements.

(Continued on page 222)

Common Uses of the Passive in Public Discourse

2 In public discourse, such as newspaper headlines, public announcements, and signs, the passive is used to convey an objective or impersonal tone. The passive often sounds more formal, factual, or authoritative. Note that newspaper headlines and signs often omit forms of *be*.

Newspaper Headlines
Over 100 People **Injured** by Aftershocks

News Report
More than a hundred people **have been injured** by the aftershocks.

Sign
No Pets **Allowed**

Telephone Recording
Please continue to hold. Your call **will be answered** by the next available agent.

Rules at a Health Club
Handball courts **may be reserved** one week in advance.

Announcement on an Airplane
Passengers **are requested** to remain seated.

D1 Listening for Meaning and Use ► Notes 1, 2

A. 🎧 Listen to each example. Is it from academic discourse (e.g., college lectures), public discourse (e.g., ads, announcements, TV broadcasts), or personal discourse (e.g., conversations between friends)? Check (✓) the correct column.

	ACADEMIC DISCOURSE	PUBLIC DISCOURSE	PERSONAL DISCOURSE
1.		✓	
2.			
3.			
4.			
5.			
6.			
7.			
8.			

B. Work in groups. Listen to each example again. Discuss what specific features of each announcement influenced your choice.

A. Change each newspaper headline into two full sentences, one using the present perfect passive and one using the simple past passive. If necessary, add articles and other missing words.

Two Children Injured in Train Accident

Site Selected for Recycling Plant

1. <u>Two children have been injured in a train accident.</u> OR <u>Two children were injured in a train accident.</u>

4. _____

_____

_____

New Cancer Treatment Discovered

Restaurant Closed by Health Department

2. _____

_____

_____

5. _____

_____

_____

Presidents's Trip Delayed by Weather

Golfer Struck by Lightning

3. _____

_____

_____

6. _____

_____

_____

B. Think about the active forms of each of the headlines. Why do you think the passive was used instead? Why was the agent used in certain headlines?

Informally Speaking

Using Passives with *Get*

 Look at the cartoon and listen to the conversation. How is the underlined form in the cartoon different from what you hear?

Guess what? I'm going to <u>be promoted</u> to district manager.

Congratulations!

Get commonly replaces *be* in informal conversation. *Get* passives are often more dynamic and emotional than *be* passives. Sentences with *get* passives are usually about people rather than objects and especially about situations people can't control.

STANDARD FORM

Tran **was accepted** by several colleges, but his best friend **was rejected** by the same ones.

WHAT YOU MIGHT HEAR

"Tran got accepted by several colleges, but his best friend got rejected by the same ones."

D3 Understanding Informal Speech

Listen and write the standard form of the words you hear.

1. Do you think you *'ll be sent*_____ to the convention in Hawaii?

2. I _____ soon.

3. John _____ to the Boston office.

4. He _____ by Harvard Business School.

5. Liz _____ breaking the rules.

6. She _____ .

7. Steve finally _____ for all of his extra work.

8. He _____ for a special award yesterday.

A. Change the rules on the first sign to a more formal, impersonal style by using passive instead of active sentences. Write your rules on the second sign.

SWIMMING POOL RULES

1 Members must show their membership passes at the gate.
2 Members can purchase guest passes at the main office.
3 We may limit the number of guests on weekends.
4 We do not admit children under 12 unless an adult accompanies them.
5 You must supervise small children at all times.
6 You must take a shower before entering the pool.
7 You must obey the lifeguard at all times.
8 We permit diving in designated areas only.
9 We prohibit smoking, gum chewing, and glass bottles.
10 You may eat food in the picnic area only.

SWIMMING POOL RULES

1 Membership passes must be shown at the gate.
2 _____
3 _____
4 _____
5 _____
6 _____
7 _____
8 _____
9 _____
10 _____

B. Now write a set of rules for one of these topics or a topic of your choice: (a) course requirements at your school, (b) rules for using books and other materials at the library, (c) rules for living in an apartment building, or (d) rules for members of a health club. Use the passive to give your rules a more formal, impersonal tone.

Combining Form, Meaning, and Use

E1 Thinking About Meaning and Use

Read each sentence. Check (✓) the sentences that have approximately the same meaning. Then discuss your answers in small groups.

1. Your order should be accompanied by a check.

   ✓   **a.** A check should accompany your order.

   _____ **b.** Someone should accompany your order.

2. The problem could be solved.

   _____ **a.** The problem will be solved.

   _____ **b.** Someone might solve the problem.

3. He got robbed twice last year.

   _____ **a.** He has robbed two people.

   _____ **b.** On two different occasions, someone robbed him.

4. All reservations must be accompanied by a cash deposit.

   _____ **a.** Deposit some money in the bank in order to make a reservation.

   _____ **b.** Customers need to leave a cash deposit when they make a reservation.

5. No one will be hired by the company.

   _____ **a.** No one will get fired by the company.

   _____ **b.** The company won't be hiring anyone.

6. Your prescription can be refilled three times.

   _____ **a.** You will be able to get three refills.

   _____ **b.** You must get three refills.

7. Passengers have been requested to check in at the gate.

_____ a. Passengers have requested to check in at the gate.

_____ b. We have requested that passengers check in at the gate.

8. Several factors need to be considered by the judge.

_____ a. The judge needs to consider several factors.

_____ b. We need to consider several factors.

E2 Editing

Find the errors in these sentences and correct them.

1. These pills should be ~~take~~ *taken* every four hours.

2. The letter ought to delivered in the afternoon.

3. The bell will be rang several times.

4. A young man has put in prison for 20 years. That's terrible!

5. The mail has sent to the wrong address.

6. Will a new road build soon, or will the old one be repaired?

7. It will be not needed any longer.

8. All applications must get accompanied by a check.

▶ Beyond the Classroom

Searching for Authentic Examples

Find examples of English grammar in everyday life. Choose one of the tasks below. Be prepared to discuss your findings.

A. Look in textbooks or other printed material and write down four examples of the passive with agents. Bring your examples to class. Why was the agent needed in each sentence?

B. Listen for four or five examples of the *get* passive in spoken English on TV or on the radio. Write down the examples and try to explain the context. Bring your examples to class. Why do you think the *get* passive was used instead of the *be* passive?

Speaking

In groups of four, follow these steps to prepare a short debate presenting both sides of an argument.

1. Choose one of the topics below or one from Exercise B4 on page 217:

   a. Violence should be limited on television and in the newspapers.

   b. Guns should not be sold without strict limitations.

   c. The Internet and video games can be blamed for violence by children.

2. Brainstorm the various arguments for and against your group's topic. Write down the different arguments.

3. Now work with one person in your group. You and your partner will take the same side in the debate. Work together to develop your arguments. Try to use passives where appropriate in your discussion.

4. Present your debate to the class. Encourage your classmates to share their opinions.

Contrasting Gerunds and Infinitives

A Become a Less Aggressive Driver

A1 Before You Read

Discuss these questions.

Driving aggressively means driving in an unsafe and angry manner. How safe do you feel on the road? Do you ever see angry drivers? What do you do?

A2 Read

Read this book excerpt to find out what psychologist Richard Carlson has suggested for aggressive drivers.

Become a Less Aggressive Driver

Where do you get the most uptight? If you're like most people, driving in traffic is probably high on your list. Most major highways these days are more like racetracks than like roadways.

There are three major reasons for becoming a less aggressive driver. First, when
5 you are aggressive, you put yourself and everyone around you in extreme danger. Second, driving aggressively is extremely stressful. Your blood pressure goes up, your grip on the wheel tightens, your eyes are strained, and your thoughts are spinning out of control. Finally, you end up saving no time at all.

Recently, I was driving south from Oakland to San Jose. Traffic was heavy, but it
10 was moving. I noticed an extremely aggressive and angry driver who kept weaving in and out of his lane. He was constantly speeding up and slowing down. Clearly, he was in a hurry. For the most part, I remained in the same lane for the entire 40-mile journey. I was listening to a new audio tape and daydreaming along the way. I enjoyed the trip a great deal because driving gives me a chance to be alone. As I was
15 exiting off the highway, the aggressive driver came up behind me and raced on by. His weaving, rapid acceleration, and putting families at risk had earned him nothing except perhaps some high blood pressure. On average, he and I had driven at the same speed.

The same principle applies when you see drivers who are speeding past you in
20 order to beat you to the next stoplight. It simply doesn't pay to speed.

When you make the conscious decision to become a less aggressive driver, you begin using your time in the car to loosen up. Instead of tensing your muscles, try to relax them. I even have a few audio tapes that are specifically for muscular relaxation. Sometimes I put one in and listen. By the time I reach my destination, I feel more relaxed than I did before getting into the car. During the course of your lifetime, you'll probably spend a great deal of time driving. You can spend those moments being frustrated, or you can use them wisely. If you do the latter, you'll be a more relaxed person.

Adapted from *Don't Sweat the Small Stuff . . . And It's All Small Stuff*

grip: a strong hold or grasp
it doesn't pay: it's not worth doing
latter: the second of two things just mentioned
sweat: (informal) to worry about something

uptight: (informal) tense
weave: to move around things and change directions quickly

A3 **After You Read**

Write *T* for true and *F* for false for each statement about the author.

___F___ **1.** He is always in a hurry.

_____ **2.** He gets angry at other drivers when they pass him.

_____ **3.** He sees a direct relationship between stress and driving.

_____ **4.** He tries to find ways to relax in the car.

_____ **5.** He probably follows and honks at aggressive drivers.

_____ **6.** He probably allows himself extra time in order to get to places on time.

B Gerunds and Infinitives

Examining Form

Look back at the excerpt on page 230 and complete the tasks below. Then discuss your observations and read the Form charts to check them.

1. A gerund can act as the subject of a sentence. An example is circled. Find another example.

2. A gerund can directly follow a verb. An example is underlined. Find another example.

3. Look in the last paragraph. Find an infinitive that directly follows a verb.

4. Look at the example sentence below. The infinitive appears at the end of the sentence. What word is in subject position?

> It simply doesn't pay to speed.

OVERVIEW

Affirmative and Negative Gerunds	
	GERUND
I hate	driving. driving slowly. driving in traffic. driving a big car.
I prefer	not driving.

Affirmative and Negative Infinitives	
	INFINITIVE
I hate	to drive. to drive slowly. to drive in traffic. to drive a big car.
I prefer	not to drive.

GERUNDS

Gerunds as Subjects	
GERUND	VERB PHRASE
Owning a car	costs a lot. is expensive.

Gerunds After Verbs		
SUBJECT	VERB	GERUND
Drivers	should consider	slowing down.
Experts	suggest	driving slowly.

INFINITIVES

It Subject . . . + Infinitive

IT	VERB + NOUN	INFINITIVE
It	costs a lot	**to own a car.**

IT	VERB + ADJECTIVE	INFINITIVE
It	is expensive	**to own a car.**

Infinitives After Verbs

	VERB	INFINITIVE	
Drivers	agree	**to slow down.**	

	VERB	OBJECT	INFINITIVE
Experts	warn	people	**to drive slowly.**

	VERB	(OBJECT)	INFINITIVE
I	want		**to drive carefully.**
I	want	him	**to drive carefully.**

Overview
- All verbs, except modal auxiliaries, have gerund and infinitive forms.
- A gerund can be one word (*driving*) or part of a longer phrase, with an adverb (*driving slowly*), a prepositional phrase (*driving in traffic*), or an object (*driving a big car*).
- All verbs, except modal auxiliaries, have infinitive forms.
- An infinitive can be two words (*to drive*) or part of a longer phrase with an adverb (*to drive slowly*), a prepositional phrase (*to drive in traffic*), or an object (*to drive a big car*).

Gerunds as Subjects
- A gerund can function as the subject of a sentence. Gerunds function as singular nouns and take singular verbs. A gerund can be replaced by the pronoun *it*.

    Owning a car costs a lot.   (**It** costs a lot.)

Gerunds After Verbs
- Here are some examples of verbs followed by gerunds (see Appendix 8 for a list of more verbs):

advise	delay	enjoy	mind	practice
avoid	deny	finish	miss	recommend
consider	dislike	go	postpone	suggest

It Subject . . . + Infinitive
- Although an infinitive can function as the subject of a sentence (*To own a car is expensive*), this is not common. Instead, the pronoun *it* begins the sentence. *It* has the same meaning as the infinitive it replaces.

    It costs a lot **to own a car.** (It = to own a car)

- *It* is followed by *be* or one of a limited group of verbs. For example:

appear	be	cost	look	pay	seem	take

(Continued on page 234)

> **Infinitives After Verbs**
>
> • Infinitives after verbs appear in one of three patterns:
>
> VERB + INFINITIVE
>
> | | | | | |
> |---|---|---|---|---|
> | agree | decide | learn | plan | refuse |
> | appear | hope | offer | seem | wait |
>
> VERB + OBJECT + INFINITIVE
>
> | | | | | | |
> |---|---|---|---|---|---|
> | advise | force | invite | remind | teach | urge |
> | cause | get | order | require | tell | warn |
>
> VERB + (OBJECT) + INFINITIVE
>
> (These verbs can be followed by the infinitive with or without an object.)
>
> | | | | |
> |---|---|---|---|
> | ask | expect | need | promise | wish |
> | choose | help | pay | want | would like |
>
> • See Appendix 9 for a list of more verbs followed by infinitives.

B1 Listening for Form

🎧 Listen to each sentence. Do you hear an infinitive or a gerund? Check (✓) the correct column.

	GERUND	INFINITIVE
1.		✓
2.		
3.		
4.		
5.		
6.		

B2 Rephrasing Subject Gerunds as *It* . . . + Infinitive

Rewrite each of these opinions. Change the subject to *It* and the gerund to an infinitive. Remember to put the infinitive at the end of the sentence.

1. Raising children is not easy.　　　　*It's not easy to raise children.*

2. Studying all night is not a good idea.　　_____

3. Walking to work takes too much time.　_____

4. Getting exercise is important.　　　　　_____

5. Owning a house costs a lot of money.　_____

6. Knowing a foreign language can be useful.　_____

A. Work with a partner. Choose one of the topics below and make a list of five common problems related to that topic. Use affirmative and negative gerunds.

Living in a big city   Owning a car
Having a pet   Living in a foreign country

Problems with living in a big city: parking, making friends, not having a garden, . . .

B. Write two sentences about each of the problems you listed, one with a subject gerund and one with *it* + an infinitive.

Parking is difficult in a big city.
It is difficult to park in a big city.

Build as many meaningful sentences as possible. Use an item from each column, or from the first and third columns only. Punctuate your sentences correctly.

He told me to go more slowly.

he told		to go more slowly
she expects		to speak Spanish
he learned	me	leaving
they advised		taking a driving class
don't delay		

Imagine that some people are discussing a controversial new movie. Complete each sentence with *seeing it* or *to see it*.

1. I'm planning _to see it._

2. Do you recommend _____

3. You should consider _____

4. I've decided _____

5. I suggest _____

6. Don't expect me _____

7. He refuses _____

8. I warn you not _____

9. You should avoid _____

10. I urge you _____

Vocabulary Notes

Short Answers to Questions with Infinitives

Short answers in response to questions with infinitives can contain the main verb + *to*.

Do you plan to take a vacation soon? Yes, **I plan to.** / No, **I don't expect to.**

If you begin a short answer with an infinitive, *to* is omitted.

What do you want to do later? **Take a walk.**

When you join two or more infinitives with *and* or *or,* *to* appears only with the first infinitive.

Do you want **to eat out** or **make dinner at home?**

B6 **Using Short Answers to Questions with Infinitives**

Take turns asking and answering questions. Use the verbs in parentheses to form affirmative or negative short answers with infinitives.

1. **A:** Are you going to graduate in June?

   B: Yes, <u>I hope to</u>. (hope)

2. **A:** Are your parents taking a vacation this summer?

   B: No, they _____. (expect)

3. **A:** Do you think you'll come to the party?

   B: Yes, we _____. (would like)

4. **A:** Is she interested in going with us?

   B: No. She _____. (want)

5. **A:** Are you going to get married?

   B: Yes, we _____ soon. (plan)

6. **A:** Please ask him not to leave so early.

   B: I'm sorry, but he really _____. (need)

Asking Information Questions with Gerunds and Infinitives

A. Work with a partner. Ask questions using *What* and these words and phrases + the verb *do* as a gerund or an infinitive. Answer the questions and then ask *What about you?*

1. expect/this weekend

   A: What do you expect to do this weekend?
   B: Sleep late. What about you?
   A: I expect to study most of the time.

2. enjoy/on Sundays

3. suggest/after dinner

4. would like/on your birthday

5. want/during your vacation

6. avoid/on the weekend

7. hope/next summer

8. dislike/in the morning

B. Now write three sentences that compare your partner's answers with yours. Use the appropriate verbs or phrases with gerunds or infinitives.

   Anna expects to sleep late this weekend, but I expect to study most of the time.

B8 **Asking *Yes/No* Questions with Gerunds and Infinitives**

Work with a partner. Take turns asking and answering questions with gerunds or infinitives.

1. expect/travel/stay home/next summer

   A: Do you expect to travel or stay home next summer?
   B: Stay home.

2. suggest/stay home/go out/tonight

3. hope/live in a big city/a small town

4. need/study a lot/a little

5. recommend/eat breakfast/skip breakfast

6. want/stay in your apartment/find a new apartment

C Verbs Used with Gerunds and Infinitives

Examining Meaning and Use

Read the sentences and answer the questions below. Then discuss your observations and read the Meaning and Use Notes to check them.

1a. I stopped to shop at London's Bakery. It's so inexpensive.
1b. I stopped shopping at London's Bakery. It's so expensive.

2a. He started to talk as soon as he saw me. He's not shy.
2b. He started talking as soon as he saw me. He's very friendly.

Which pair has the same meaning? Which pair has a different meaning?

Meaning and Use Notes

Same Meanings with *Begin, Start,* and *Continue*

Some verbs are used with both infinitives and gerunds. See Appendix 10 for a list of these verbs.

1 After *begin, start,* and *continue,* the infinitive and the gerund have the same meaning. If the main verb is in the continuous, use the infinitive, not the gerund.

Infinitive	*Gerund*
He <u>started</u> **to laugh**.	He <u>started</u> **laughing**.
We <u>continued</u> **to read**.	We <u>continued</u> **reading**.
It <u>began</u> **to snow**.	It <u>began</u> **snowing**.
It <u>was beginning</u> **to snow**.	*It <u>was beginning</u> snowing. (INCORRECT)

Similar Meanings with *Like, Love, Hate,* and *Prefer*

2 After *like, love, hate,* and *prefer,* the infinitive and the gerund are similar in meaning. However, sometimes it is more common to use an infinitive to talk about an activity at a specific time, and a gerund to talk about an activity in general.

Infinitive	*Gerund*
I <u>like</u> **to swim** early in the morning.	I <u>like</u> **swimming** and **boating**.
Would you <u>prefer</u> **to play tennis** or **swim** today?	Do you <u>prefer</u> **playing tennis** or **swimming**?

3A After *try*, the infinitive and the gerund are similar in meaning.

Infinitive

<u>Try</u> **to relax** more.

Gerund

<u>Try</u> **relaxing** more.

3B When *try* is in the past, the infinitive often implies that an action did not occur. The gerund implies that an action occurred but may or may not have been successful.

Infinitive (Didn't Occur)

I <u>tried</u> **to take some aspirin** for the pain, but I couldn't open the bottle.
(I didn't take any aspirin.)

Gerund (Did Occur)

I <u>tried</u> **taking some aspirin** for the pain, but it didn't help.
(I took some aspirin.)

4A After *remember, stop, forget,* and *regret,* the infinitive refers to an action that happens after the action of the main verb. The gerund refers to an action that happened before the action of the main verb.

Infinitive Action Happens After Verb

I <u>remembered</u> **to mail the letter**.
(I remembered the letter. Then I mailed it.)

I <u>stopped</u> **to smoke**.
(I stopped what I was doing. Then I smoked.)

Gerund Action Happened Before Verb

I <u>remembered</u> **mailing the letter**.
(I mailed the letter. Later I remembered doing it.)

I <u>stopped</u> **smoking**.
(I was a smoker. Then I stopped doing it.)

4B *Forget* is more commonly used with an infinitive. With a gerund, it occurs mostly in sentences with *will never*.

Infinitive Action Happens After Verb

I <u>forgot</u> **to pay my telephone bill**.
(I forgot, so then I didn't pay the bill.)

Gerund Action Happened Before Verb

I <u>will never forget</u> **living in Ecuador**.
(I lived there. Now I'll never forget it.)

4C *Regret* can take either an infinitive or a gerund with verbs such as *inform, tell, say,* and *announce*. With all other verbs, *regret* takes a gerund.

Infinitive Action Happens After Verb

I <u>regret</u> **to inform you** that I'm leaving.
(I feel regret. Then I inform you.)

* I <u>regret</u> to leave. (INCORRECT)

Gerund Action Happened Before Verb

I <u>regret</u> **informing you** that I'm leaving.
(I informed you. Now I regret it.)

I <u>regret</u> **leaving**.

Listening for Meaning and Use ▶ Notes 3A, 3B, 4A, 4B

Listen to each situation. Choose the sentence that is more likely to follow it.

1. **(a.)** He was rude to me.
   b. He was so grateful to me.

2. **a.** It's a good thing I did, though.
   b. That was a terrible mistake.

3. **a.** But I couldn't stand the smell.
   b. It really helped me feel better.

4. **a.** But I had no choice.
   b. But I have no choice.

5. **a.** I like the editorials.
   b. It's not well written.

6. **a.** It's on my calendar for tomorrow.
   b. It was so exciting.

C2 **Rephrasing Gerunds and Infinitives** ▶ Notes 1, 2

Work with a partner. Change each gerund to an infinitive, and each infinitive to a gerund. Then practice the conversations.

1. **A:** I love skiing. What about you?

   B: I like skiing, but I prefer staying indoors in the winter.

   A: I love to ski. What about you?

   B: I like to ski, but I prefer to stay indoors in the winter.

2. **A:** I hate to drive in traffic.

   B: Then you should continue to take the bus home.

   A: _____

   B: _____

3. A: It started to rain a few minutes ago.

   B: Then let's wait here for a while. I don't like to walk in the rain.

   A: _____

   B: _____

4. A: I hate waiting in line.

   B: So do I. That's why I prefer to shop late at night.

   A: _____

   B: _____

C3 **Making Suggestions** ▶ Notes 3A, 4A, 4B

Work in small groups. Choose one of the topics below. Make suggestions by completing each sentence with a gerund or infinitive. Then read your suggestions to the class without mentioning your topic. The class guesses what topic the advice is for.

Reducing stress
Cleaning your apartment
Studying for a test
Finding a job
Improving your English
Making more friends

Suggestions for reducing stress

1. Try _to get more sleep._

2. Consider _taking a yoga class._

3. Avoid _____

4. Don't forget _____

5. Plan _____

6. Don't delay _____

7. Aim _____

8. Volunteer _____

A. Work with a partner. Jay is visiting his cousin Joe in Chicago. Complete these conversations with the words in parentheses and gerunds or infinitives. In some cases, you may use either one.

1. **Joe:** Another beautiful day! I love <u>getting up/to get up</u> (get up) in the
   1

   morning.

   Jay: You're kidding! I really dislike _____ (get up) in the
   2

   morning. I immediately start _____ (worry) about
   3

   all of the things I need _____ (do).
   4

2. **Joe:** Let's go _____ (shop). I like _____
   1   2

   (watch) the crowds, and I'd like _____ (buy) some gifts.
   3

   Jay: Do we have to? I don't like _____ (fight) my way
   4

   through crowds.

   Joe: Well, would you like _____ (go) to the top of the
   5

   Sears Tower? The view is great. You can see the lake from there.

   Jay: I remember _____ (go) up there once. It was
   6

   terrible. I prefer _____ (have) both of my feet on
   7

   the ground.

3. **Joe:** I'm beginning _____ (feel) hungry. Let's try
   1

   _____ (find) a good restaurant.
   2

   Jay: I try _____ (avoid) eating out. You wouldn't mind
   3

   _____ (cook) something at home, would you?
   4

B. Now work on your own and write a paragraph about a person that you know. Use gerunds and infinitives to discuss the person's feelings and likes or dislikes.

My friend Alex loves to meet new people. He's very sociable and prefers going to big parties instead of small gatherings. That's fine, except that he always wants me to go with him, and he refuses to listen to my objections. He considers . . .

D

More About Gerunds and Infinitives

Examining Form

Read the sentences and complete the tasks below. Then discuss your observations and read the Form charts to check them.

a. Instead of <u>tensing your muscles</u>, try to relax them.
b. During your lifetime, you'll probably spend a lot of time <u>driving on the highway</u>.
c. You end up <u>saving no time at all</u>.
d. Some drivers are too anxious <u>to reach their destinations</u>.

1. Write the letter of the sentence that contains one of these forms before a gerund:

_____ a verb phrase ending in a noun   _____ a phrasal verb (verb + particle)

_____ a preposition or prepositional phrase

2. Which sentence has a phrase containing an infinitive? What part of speech does it follow?

GERUNDS

Verb Phrase + Gerund

	VERB PHRASE	GERUND
She	is busy	**talking.**
He	spent some time	**relaxing.**

Preposition + Gerund

PREPOSITION	GERUND	
Without	**realizing it,**	drivers speed.
In addition to	**swimming,**	we played tennis.

	PREPOSITION	GERUND
Drivers speed	without	**realizing it.**

Verb + Preposition + Gerund

VERB + PREPOSITION	GERUND
Think about	**slowing down.**

	PHRASAL VERB	GERUND
We	ended up	**waiting an hour.**

Be + Adjective + Preposition + Gerund

	BE + ADJECTIVE + PREPOSITION	GERUND
We	were afraid of	**driving in the snow.**

(Continued on page 244)

- Some common verb phrases that end in adjectives or nouns can be followed by gerunds:

be busy	have a good time	it's no use	spend an hour	waste time
have fun	have trouble	it's (not) worth	spend time	

- Examples of one-word prepositions and longer phrases followed by gerunds:

after	besides	in	instead of
before	by	in addition to	without

- Examples of verb + preposition combinations followed by gerunds:

approve of	depend on	insist on	talk about	work on
believe in	disapprove of	look forward to	think about	worry about

- Examples of *be* + adjective + preposition combinations followed by gerunds:

be accustomed to	be good at	be surprised at	be used to
be afraid of	be interested in	be tired of	be worried about

- Phrasal verbs (*end up, call off*) can be followed by gerunds.
- See Appendix 8 for a list of more combinations with prepositions followed by gerunds.
- See Appendix 15 for a list of common phrasal verbs.

INFINITIVES

Adjective + Infinitive

	VERB	ADJECTIVE	INFINITIVE
She	was	ready	**to talk.**

***In Order* + Infinitive**

	(*IN ORDER* +) INFINITIVE
Put on some music	(in order) **to relax.**

IN ORDER + NOT + INFINITIVE	
In order not **to panic,**	take a deep breath.

- Many adjectives can be followed by infinitives.

afraid	eager	excited	hesitant	sorry
determined	embarrassed	happy	ready	surprised

- See Appendix 9 for a list of more adjectives followed by infinitives.
- Infinitives do not directly follow prepositions.
- Infinitives may follow the expression *in order*. They are called purpose infinitives.
- In affirmative purpose infinitives, *in order* may be omitted. In negative purpose infinitives, *in order* is necessary.
- ⚠ Do not confuse expressions ending in the preposition *to* followed by gerunds with verbs followed directly by the infinitive.

  I <u>look forward to</u> **leaving** soon.   I <u>expect</u> **to leave** soon.

Listen to this conversation. Write the gerunds or infinitives you hear.

A: You should consider ___taking___ a vacation. You could spend some time
     1

_____.
     2

B: I can't. I'm busy _____ on a project that's due soon. My boss has told me
     3

_____ it as quickly as possible.
     4

A: I know. That's the point. Aren't you sick of _____?
     5

B: Well, instead of _____ a long vacation, I might be interested in
     6

_____ away for a weekend. But I'd have trouble _____ before
     7   8

noon on Saturday. I save Saturday morning for _____ on my office
     9

e-mail.

A: Didn't you promise _____ more?
     10

Complete each prepositional phrase with the gerund form of the expressions
below. Then complete each sentence.

| clean your apartment | do the laundry | look for an apartment | take a trip |
| cook dinner | find a job | reduce stress | use a computer |

1. Before _taking a trip, check your car carefully._____

2. After _____

3. Instead of _____

4. Besides _____

5. By _____

6. In addition to _____

7. Before _____

8. After _____

Choosing Between Gerunds and Infinitives

A. Work with a partner. Switch roles for each question.

Student A: Ask a *What* question using the phrase and the verb *do* as a gerund or an infinitive.

Student B: Answer and then ask *What about you?*

1. be hesitant

    A: What are you hesitant to do?
    B: I'm hesitant to take too many classes.
       What about you?
    A: I'm hesitant to look for a part-time job.

2. be good at

3. be eager

4. be afraid of

5. be ready/right now

6. be accustomed to

7. be determined/before you are 50

8. look forward to/next year

B. Report three of your partner's answers to the class using full sentences with gerunds or infinitives.

Leroy is hesitant to take too many classes.

D4 **Working on Purpose Infinitives**

A. Complete these sentences about errands with affirmative purpose infinitives. Use your own ideas. You can omit *in order.*

1. First I went to the bank <u>to get some money.</u>

2. Then I stopped at the dry cleaners _____

3. Next I went to the drugstore near my home _____

4. After that I stopped by the library _____

5. On the way home, I stopped at the gas station _____

B. Work with a partner. Choose two items from the suggested topics below and write simple instructions for each. Use affirmative and negative purpose infinitives.

How to open a jar of jelly, a can of beans, a box of crackers, or a bottle of wine
How to operate your VCR or computer
How to start your car, drive safely in traffic, fix a flat tire, or fill your car with gas

To open a jar of jelly, grip the jar tightly and twist the lid.
In order to loosen the top, run it under hot water.

Interpreting Gerunds and Infinitives

Examining Meaning and Use

Read the sentences and answer the questions below. Then discuss your observations and read the Meaning and Use Notes to check them.

1a. Tom worries about Jane's driving at night.
1b. Tom worries about driving at night.

2a. Susan wants Sam to come early.
2b. Susan wants to come early.

1. Compare 1a and 1b. In each sentence, who is driving?

2. Compare 2a and 2b. In each sentence, who might come early?

Meaning and Use Notes

The Performer of Gerund Actions

1A Like other actions, the actions expressed by gerunds are performed by someone. Sometimes the performer of the gerund action is the sentence subject. Sometimes the performer of the gerund action is not the subject. In these cases, a possessive adjective is used to indicate the performer.

Gerund Only	*Possessive Adjective + Gerund*
We were surprised at **passing the exam.** (We passed the exam.)	We were surprised at Tim's/his **passing the exam.** (Tim passed the exam.)

1B When a gerund occurs after a verb, an object pronoun can replace the possessive adjective. Sentences with object pronouns convey a less formal tone than those with possessive adjectives.

Verb + Object Pronoun + Gerund
We were surprised at him **passing the exam.**

(Continued on page 248)

The Performer of Infinitive Actions

2A Like other actions, the actions expressed by infinitives are performed by someone. When an infinitive directly follows a verb, the performer of the infinitive action is the sentence subject. When an infinitive follows an object, the performer of the infinitive action is the object.

Verb + Infinitive Only	*Verb + Object + Infinitive*
I <u>want</u> **to take a different route.**	I <u>want</u> him **to take a different route.**
(I may take a different route.)	(He may take a different route.)

2B *Help* + object can be followed by an infinitive or a base form with no change in meaning. The verbs *make, have,* and *let* + object are followed by the base form of a verb, but not the infinitive. Like all objects before infinitives, the objects of these verbs perform the action expressed by the base form.

Verb + Object + Base Form of Verb	*Verb + Object + Infinitive*
He <u>helped me</u> **get** there safely.	He <u>helped me</u> **to get** there safely.
He <u>made me</u> **get** some rest.	
He <u>had me</u> **call** the doctor.	
He <u>let me</u> **call** the hospital.	

E1 **Listening for Meaning and Use**   ▶ **Notes 1A, 1B, 2B**

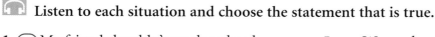

Listen to each situation and choose the statement that is true.

1. **a.** My friend shouldn't work so hard.
   b. The doctor shouldn't work so hard.

2. **a.** I recommended some exercises.
   b. The doctor recommended some exercises.

3. **a.** She called a health club.
   b. We called a health club.

4. **a.** We called in the evening.
   b. They called us in the evening.

5. **a.** We made arrangements.
   b. The manager made arrangements.

6. **a.** We invited him.
   b. He invited us.

7. **a.** He drove in the rain.
   b. I drove in the rain.

8. **a.** The manager left a deposit.
   b. We left a deposit.

E2 **Expressing Intentions and Desires**

Choose either Situation A or B and complete the sentences that you might say. Use sentences with appropriate infinitives or gerunds. Add an object before infinitives or a possessive adjective before gerunds, if possible.

Situation A: You are going to run for president.
Situation B: You are going to resign from your position because of a scandal.

1. I have decided _to run for president._

2. I appreciate _your encouraging me so much._

3. I expect _____

4. I invite _____

5. I'm concerned about _____

6. I urge _____

7. I want _____

8. I don't mind _____

E3 **Talking About Teaching**

A. In small groups, discuss the best way to teach someone to do something. Choose one of the suggested topics below. Use the verbs *make, let, help,* and *have* followed by an infinitive or base form where possible.

Teaching a foreign friend how to speak your language
Teaching a friend how to drive
Teaching a child how to cook

A: *To teach a foreign friend your language, you need to be very patient.*
B: *It is important to practice as much as possible.*
C: *Yes. Also, let him make mistakes. That's how you help him make progress.*

B. Write a summary of your discussion and read it to the class. Find out whether the class agrees with your methods.

F Combining Form, Meaning, and Use

F1 Thinking About Meaning and Use

Read each sentence and the statement that follows. Write *T* if the statement is true and *F* if it is false. Then discuss your answers in small groups.

1. I forgot to mail the letter.

   __F__ I mailed the letter.

2. I didn't remember to take out the dog.

   _____ I took out the dog.

3. I'll never forget opening that letter.

   _____ I opened the letter.

4. I always avoid eating sweets.

   _____ I eat sweets.

5. They permitted me to leave.

   _____ I left.

6. She stopped to eat lunch.

   _____ She didn't eat lunch.

7. I tried soaking my ankle, but it still hurts.

   _____ I soaked my ankle.

8. I heard about his winning the race.

   _____ He won the race.

9. He was surprised at my failing the exam.

   _____ I failed the exam.

10. I had him complain to the manager.

    _____ I complained to the manager.

Find the errors in these paragraphs and correct them.

Unfortunately, it is very common ˄encounter aggressive drivers every day. They are
usually trying to getting somewhere in a hurry. Them speeding can cause them follow
too closely or change lanes frequently without signaling.

In order avoid becoming an aggressive driver, there are a number of rules
following. First, allow enough time to reaching your destination. Second, change your
schedule to keep from drive during rush hours. Third, call ahead for explain if you are
going to be late. Then you can relax.

If you see an aggressive driver, try get out of the way safely. Never challenge an
aggressive driver by speed up or attempting to hold your position in your lane. Don't
let others make you driving dangerously. You need be in control at all times.

Beyond the Classroom

Searching for Authentic Examples

Find examples of English grammar in everyday life. Choose one of the tasks below. Be prepared to discuss your findings.

A. Look for four or five examples of instructions with purpose infinitives on signs or packages and bring them to class. Write down examples with and without *in order*. Which phrase do you find more often?

B. Look in newspapers or magazines for affirmative and negative gerunds. Find four examples of each and bring them to class. Can you change any of the gerunds to infinitives without changing the meaning?

Speaking

In small groups, follow these steps to prepare for a class discussion on stress reduction.

1. Make a list of different ways to reduce stress—for example, relaxation techniques or other activities, eating various foods, using herbs, and so on. Discuss the effectiveness of each of the stress reducers on your list. You may want to use the Internet or the public library to find out more information.

2. Choose three or four of the most effective methods of stress reduction. Discuss why you think they are successful. Summarize your discussion by writing tips for reducing stress to present to the class. Use gerunds and infinitives in your tips. Be prepared to share your summary with the class.

3. Do you agree with your classmates' tips for stress reduction? Ask questions and make comments.

Modifying Nouns

Indefinite and Definite Articles; Review of Nouns

A Chicken Soup, Always Chicken Soup

A1 Before You Read

Discuss these questions.

What do you do when you have a cold? Do you take medicine? vitamins? herbs?
What special treatments are used in your family? Do they work?

A2 Read

Read this book excerpt to find out about the special medicinal properties of
old-fashioned chicken soup.

Chicken Soup,
Always Chicken Soup

Have you ever wondered why chicken
soup is such a popular remedy for the
common cold? The first authority to
recommend chicken soup was the
5 distinguished twelfth-century physician Moses
Maimonides. According to the story, when
Sultan Saladin, a powerful Muslim military
leader, begged Maimonides for a cure for his
son's asthma, Maimonides prescribed chicken
10 soup. The prescription was probably effective
because chicken soup is now known to have
medicinal properties.

Scientific research has begun to explain
why age-old food remedies, passed down for
15 centuries by medical sages and grandmothers,
have been effective against respiratory problems
such as colds and the flu. The doctor who
knows most about this is Irwin Ziment,
M.D., a lung specialist at the University of

20 California at Los Angeles. Dr. Ziment has
concluded from a study of early medical
literature that foods used to fight diseases for
centuries are very similar to many of the drugs
we now use. Chicken, for example, contains a
25 certain chemical which is released when you

make the soup. This substance is remarkably similar to a common drug for bronchitis and respiratory infections. In fact, the drug was originally made from chicken feathers and
30 skin. The substance in chicken soup has been shown to help clear the lungs of congestion in much the same way as certain drugs.

Marvin Sackner, M.D., a lung specialist at Mount Sinai Medical Center in Miami Beach,
35 agrees. "There's an aromatic substance in chicken soup . . . that helps clear your airways." Dr. Sackner is the author of the famous chicken soup study, published in 1978. Dr. Sackner did not believe that chicken
40 soup, often called "grandma's penicillin," fought cold symptoms any better than hot water. In his study, 15 healthy men and women sipped hot chicken soup, hot water, or cold water. Five minutes and 30 minutes later,
45 he measured the rate at which substances passed through the subjects' nasal passages.

To Dr. Sackner's surprise, chicken soup was better at fighting congestion than hot or cold water. Furthermore, even the chicken soup
50 vapors were superior to those of hot water. Dr. Sackner even thinks that cold chicken soup "will help clear the 'cold in your nose,' and if the chicken soup is hot and steamy, it will work even faster and more efficiently."

55 And for a super-congestion-fighting dose of grandma's penicillin, Dr. Ziment advises adding lots of garlic, onions, pepper, and hot spices like curry or hot chilies. He calls such soup "the best cold remedy there is." To avoid
60 or fight colds and the flu, a bowl of spicy chicken soup every day is Dr. Ziment's prescription. One last thing: It's better to sip chicken soup slowly rather than drink it, in order to get the maximum therapeutic effect.
65 So sit back, relax, and enjoy your chicken soup. Grandma was right after all!

Adapted from *Food—Your Miracle Medicine*

aromatic: having a pleasant smell
congestion: blockage
medicinal: having the curing properties of medicine
remedy: something that helps an illness; a cure

respiratory: related to breathing
sage: a very wise person, usually old and highly respected
therapeutic: able to heal or cure

A3 After You Read

Write *T* for true or *F* for false for each statement. Change the false statements to true ones.

__T__ 1. Chicken soup has been used for centuries as a cold remedy.

_____ 2. Chicken soup makes you feel better emotionally, but not physically.

_____ 3. There is a chemical in chicken that fights colds.

_____ 4. Dr. Sacker showed that hot water was most effective.

_____ 5. Chicken soup is good for colds, but when ill you should avoid spices.

_____ 6. For maximum health benefit, you shouldn't eat chicken soup too fast.

FORM

B Indefinite and Definite Articles; Review of Nouns

Examining Form

Look back at the book excerpt on page 256 and complete the tasks below. Then discuss your observations and read the Form charts to check them.

1. Look at the third, fourth, and fifth sentences in the second paragraph (lines 20–28). Then find these common nouns:

   literature   drugs   chemical   drug

   centuries   chicken   soup

2. Which nouns have adjectives before them? Which have articles? Which have both adjectives and articles? What are those adjectives and articles?

3. Which nouns do not have adjectives or articles before them?

4. Which nouns are singular? Which are plural?

NOUNS

Count Nouns	
SINGULAR	PLURAL
(one) **banana**	(two) **bananas**
(one) **physician**	(two) **physicians**

Noncount Nouns
SINGULAR
soup
research

INDEFINITE ARTICLES

Singular Count Nouns
A/AN + SINGULAR COUNT NOUN
I ate **a banana**.
Did you eat **an apple**?

Plural Count Nouns
Ø + PLURAL COUNT NOUN
I ate **Ø bananas**.
Did you eat **Ø apples**?
SOME/ANY + PLURAL COUNT NOUN
I ate **some bananas**.
Did you eat **any apples**?

Noncount Nouns
Ø + NONCOUNT NOUN
I didn't eat **Ø fruit**.
Did you eat **Ø fruit**?
SOME/ANY + NONCOUNT NOUN
I didn't eat **any fruit**.
Did you eat **some fruit**?

DEFINITE ARTICLES

Singular Count Nouns	Plural Count Nouns	Noncount Nouns
THE + SINGULAR COUNT NOUN	*THE* + PLURAL COUNT NOUN	*THE* + NONCOUNT NOUN
I ate **the banana**.	I ate **the bananas**.	I didn't eat **the fruit**.
Did you eat **the apple**?	Did you eat **the apples**?	Did you eat **the fruit**?

Nouns
- Common nouns can be count or noncount.
- Count nouns can be used with numbers. They have both singular and plural forms.
- Noncount nouns cannot be used with numbers. They do not have plural forms.
- Common nouns that occur with an indefinite article or no article (Ø) are indefinite nouns.
- Common nouns that occur with a definite article are definite nouns.

Indefinite Articles with Singular Count Nouns
- Indefinite articles can occur before a singular count noun (*an apple*) or before an adjective + singular count noun (*a green apple*).
- Use *an* before words that begin with a vowel sound; use *a* before all others.

  If a noun begins with the letter *h*, use *an* if the *h* is not pronounced. Use *a* if the *h* is pronounced.

      an hour   **an** honor   **a** house   **a** human

  If a noun begins with the letter *u*, use *an* if the *u* is a short vowel. Use *a* if the *u* is pronounced like the *y* in *yellow*.

      an umbrella   **an** understanding   **a** unit   **a** utensil

Indefinite Articles with Plural Count and Noncount Nouns
- Do not use indefinite articles before plural count nouns or noncount nouns.
- *Some* and *any* often act like indefinite articles with plural count nouns or noncount nouns. We often use *some* in affirmative sentences and questions and *any* in negative sentences and questions.
- Indefinite articles, *some*, and *any* do not have to be repeated when nouns are combined with *and*.

      a banana and **(an)** apple   **some** fruit and **(some)** cereal

Definite Articles with Count and Noncount Nouns
- The definite article *the* can be used before all common nouns—singular and plural count nouns and noncount nouns.
- Definite articles can occur before a noun (*the apple*) or before an adjective + noun (*the green apple*).
- Definite articles do not have to be repeated when nouns are combined with *and*.

      the bananas and **(the)** apples

Listening for Form

🎧 Listen to these facts about the common cold. Write the articles you hear. Write Ø if there is no article. After you finish, check the capitalization.

Although ___the___ common cold is generally not serious, it causes _____
        1   2
people to be absent from _____ work and go to _____ doctor more often
                                        .3   4
than _____ other illnesses. _____ majority of colds come from _____
            5   6   7
contact with _____ surfaces that _____ people touch frequently. People
                        8   9
transmit _____ cold viruses on these surfaces to their eyes, noses, and mouths.
                10
Once _____ symptoms appear, there are many treatments for relieving _____
            11   12
discomfort. Whatever _____ person does, unfortunately, _____ cold will
                                    13   14
probably still last from six to ten days.

B2 **Identifying Indefinite and Definite Articles**

Read the passage and underline all the common nouns, along with their articles and adjectives. Then write *D* for definite or *I* for indefinite to indicate whether the noun is used definitely or indefinitely in its context.

                    I
Have you ever eaten <u>coconut</u>? You probably have, but
you may not be very familiar with coco palms. Coconuts
come from coco palms, which are trees that grow in
tropical regions. Coco palms are very unusual because
all of the parts of the tree have a commercial value. For
example, coconuts are an important food in tropical
regions, and coconut milk, which comes from inside
the coconut, is a nutritious drink. Coconut oil, the most
valuable product of all, also comes from coconuts. Some
of the other parts of the tree that are eaten include the

buds and young stems. Besides food, the tree is also used for manufacturing
commercial products. The leaves are used for making fans and baskets, and the
fibers from the husks and trunks are made into mats, cord, and rope. Even the
hard shells and the husks are used to make fuel, and the trunks are used for timber.

Build as many meaningful sentences as possible. Use an item from each column. Punctuate your sentences correctly.

I ate some rice.

I ate they had	a an some Ø the	pencil rice fun vegetables idea

B4 Transforming Sentences

A. Change the underlined singular nouns to plural nouns, and the underlined plural nouns to singular nouns. You may also need to change pronouns and verbs.

1. I took <u>a book</u> and <u>a pen</u> with me.

   I took books and pens with me. OR *I took some books and pens with me.*

2. Take a <u>peach</u>.

3. Those are <u>herbs</u>.

4. <u>Children</u> get more colds than <u>adults</u>.

5. We need <u>some magazines</u> with more information.

6. I watched <u>a movie</u> last night.

B. Change the underlined definite articles to indefinite articles, and the indefinite articles to definite articles.

1. I went to <u>a</u> bank and took out <u>some</u> money.

   I went to the bank and took out the money.

2. Take <u>the</u> sheet of paper and <u>the</u> pen.

3. Did you eat <u>some</u> cookies or <u>Ø</u> cake?

4. I'm taking <u>the</u> medication and eating <u>the</u> yogurt twice a day.

5. Did you see <u>a</u> movie last week?

6. I went to <u>a</u> store yesterday.

The Indefinite Article

Examining Meaning and Use

Read the sentences and answer the questions below. Then discuss your observations and read the Meaning and Use Notes to check them.

1a. My friend wants to marry <u>a millionaire</u>. She met him last year.

1b. My friend wants to marry <u>a millionaire</u>. She hasn't found one yet.

2a. <u>Bananas</u> are tropical fruits.

2b. Please buy <u>some bananas</u> on your way home.

1. Compare the meanings of 1a and 1b. In which sentence does the speaker have a specific mental picture of the underlined noun?

2. Compare the meanings of 2a and 2b. Which sentence refers to a small quantity of the underlined noun? Which sentence describes or classifies the underlined noun?

Meaning and Use Notes

> ### Introducing Nouns with Indefinite Articles
>
> **1A** Use *a/an* or no article (Ø) to introduce a common noun when it is first mentioned.
>
> *First Mentioned*
> A: What did you do last night?
> B: I watched **a movie**. What did you do?
> A: I had **Ø friends** over and made **Ø dinner**.
>
> ---
>
> **1B** Usually when a common noun is introduced, it is specific for the speaker, but not specific for the listener. This means that the speaker has an idea or a mental picture of the noun, but the listener does not. Sometimes the noun is not specific for the speaker or the listener.
>
> | *Specific for the Speaker Only* | *Not Specific for the Speaker or Listener* |
> |---|---|
> | Jill: I bought **a new coat** yesterday. | Joe: I need **new shirts**. |
> | (Jill has a specific coat in mind, but the listener doesn't.) | (Joe doesn't have any specific shirts in mind, and the listener doesn't either.) |

1C When introducing singular count nouns, *a* and *an* often express the quantity "one." When introducing plural count and noncount nouns, *some* and *any* are often used to express a small quantity.

Singular Count Nouns

Would you like **a cookie**?

I'd like to order **a drink,** please.

Plural Count and Noncount Nouns

Would you like **some cookies**?

I'd like to order **some drinks,** please.

Do you have **any information** about this medicine?

Classifying and Describing Nouns

2 Common nouns with *a, an,* and Ø are often used in sentences with *be* to classify or describe nouns. *Some* and *any* are not used this way.

My father is **a teacher**.

What are those? They're **vitamins**.   * They're some vitamins. (INCORRECT)

C1 **Listening for Meaning and Use**   ▶ Notes 1A–1C

Listen to each situation. Is the noun specific or not specific for the speaker? Check (✓) the correct column.

		SPECIFIC	NOT SPECIFIC
1.	orange juice	✓	
2.	apples		
3.	a new doctor		
4.	a friend		
5.	some soup		
6.	an appointment		
7.	a book		
8.	cough medicine		

C2 Introducing New Information

Complete these conversations with a sentence that introduces new information with three indefinite nouns. Use *a/an, some,* or Ø.

1. **A:** What did you do last night?

   B: I read a book, watched a movie, and took a bath.

2. **A:** What did you buy at the supermarket?

   B: _____

3. **A:** What do you take on a trip?

   B: _____

4. **A:** What do you want for your birthday?

   B: _____

5. **A:** What do you keep in your pockets?

   B: _____

6. **A:** What can you buy at a hardware store?

   B: _____

C3 Classifying Nouns

A. Make a list of all the foods you have eaten in the last two days. Do not list specific quantities. Use *a/an, some,* or Ø next to each noun that you list. Then sort the nouns into three categories: Healthy, Unhealthy, or Not Sure.

HEALTHY	UNHEALTHY	NOT SURE
an apple	potato chips	eggs
milk	a candy bar	
cereal		

B. Share your list with a partner. Discuss whether you agree with the way your partner has classified each item. What foods are you not sure about? Why?

A: Do you think eggs are healthy or unhealthy?
B: I think they're healthy.

D The Definite Article

Examining Meaning and Use

Read the sentences and answer the questions below. Then discuss your observations and read the Meaning and Use Notes to check them.

  a. Did you hear what <u>the mayor</u> said this morning on <u>the news</u>?
  b. I bought a sweater and a shirt but <u>the sweater</u> was too small.
  c. Please pass the <u>salt</u>.

1. In which sentence does the speaker mention the underlined noun more than once?

2. In which sentence are the speaker and the listener from the same geographic area?

3. In which sentence can the listener see the underlined noun?

Meaning and Use Notes

Identifying Nouns with the Definite Article

The is used with a common noun when it is specific for both the speaker and the listener because of information they share. Following are some different ways that speakers and listeners share information about a noun.

1A The listener can identify the noun if it has already been mentioned in a conversation or text. When it is mentioned again, the speaker uses *the*. Notice that the exact words do not have to be repeated.

First Mentioned	*Mentioned Again*
I ordered <u>a steak</u> and <u>a salad</u> for lunch.	**The steak** was great, but **the salad** was awful.
<u>A dog</u> was hit by a car near my apartment.	**The poor creature** howled in pain.

1B The listener can identify the noun if he or she can see or hear it.

Visual Context
Mother: Watch out! Don't shake **the table**. You'll spill **the milk**.
Son: OK. Could you please pass **the rice**?

(Continued on page 266)

1C The listener can identify the noun from the situation or from general knowledge.

General Knowledge

I went to <u>an unusual wedding</u>. **The bride** and **groom** wore jogging clothes.
   (The listener knows that a wedding has a bride and a groom.)

1D The listener can identify the noun if the listener and speaker share geographic or social information.

Shared Information

A: Do you think **the secretaries** make enough money?

B: Yes. I think they do.
   (The listener assumes that this means the secretaries who work with them.)

1E Certain names of places and things that are very familiar to the speaker almost always use *the*. The listener may not know the specific identity of the noun but assumes that it refers to a place that the speaker habitually goes to, an object the speaker habitually uses, and so on.

Familiar Nouns

the bank	the doctor	the library	the office	the radio
the beach	the gym	the mall	the park	the store
the dentist	the hospital	the movies	the post office	the TV

When you go to **the store,** could you buy some milk? And turn off **the TV** before you go.

1F The listener can identify the noun if the noun is unique (there is only one).

Unique Nouns

I took my guests to **the best restaurant** in town, and they chose **the most expensive item** on the menu.

The earth rotates around **the sun** once every 365 days.

Please look at **the top** of this page.

1G The listener can identify the noun with the help of modifiers in the noun phrase.

Noun Modifiers

The book <u>that's on sale</u> is on the counter. (*that's on sale* tells which book)

The <u>red</u> **book** is mine. (*red* tells which book)

🎧 Listen to each sentence. Would the sentence that follows use a definite or indefinite article? Choose the sentence that is more likely to follow.

1. **a.** I bought a blue shirt.
   b. I bought the blue shirt.

2. **a.** The poor child lost all the money.
   b. A poor child lost all the money.

3. **a.** Does anyone know a writer?
   b. Does anyone know the writer?

4. **a.** Did the bride wear a long gown?
   b. Did a bride wear the long gown?

5. **a.** A steering wheel.
   b. The steering wheel.

6. **a.** Not anymore. I lent the CD to Joan.
   b. Not anymore. I lent a CD to Joan.

7. **a.** A doorbell is ringing.
   b. The doorbell is ringing.

8. **a.** Should I send a new one?
   b. Should I send the new one?

Work with a partner. Read each situation and decide whether to use *a, an,* or *the*. Then discuss the reasons why you chose your answers.

1. If there are no chairs left in this classroom, you'll have to sit on __the__ floor.
   1
   Or maybe you should go next door and ask if you can borrow _____ chair
   2
   from that classroom.

2. _____ apartment that I live in now is too small. I have to start looking for
   1
   _____ new one. I'd really like to find _____ apartment with _____
   2   3   4
   garden.

3. There's _____ interesting exercise in your textbook. Please look at _____
   1   2
   bottom of page 10.

4. Did you read _____ magazine that I sent you last week? It had _____
   1   2
   interesting story about _____ mayor of Philadelphia.
   3

5. Would you answer _____ telephone, please? I'm trying to diaper _____
   1   2
   baby.

Vocabulary Notes

Another vs. The Other

Another is indefinite like *a/an*. It means "one more" or "a different one."

There are several cookies on a plate. Your friend asks:
Do you want **another** cookie?

The other is definite. It refers to a specific alternative when you are choosing between two things.

There are only two cookies on a plate. Your friend takes one and asks:
Do you want **the other** cookie?

D3 Using *Another* and *The Other*

Work with a partner. Make up two short conversations for each of these contexts. Use *another* in one conversation and *the other* in the second conversation.

1. at a party

   Conversation 1
   A: *There are a few cookies left. Would you like another one?*
   B: *No thanks. I've already had several.*

   Conversation 2
   A: *Can you please carry that tray into the dining room for me?*
   B: *Do you mean the one with the cookies on it?*
   C: *No, the other one.*

2. at the supermarket   4. at a restaurant

3. at school   5. at a department store

D4 Making Inferences Based on General Knowledge   ► Note 1C

Read each sentence and then write a related sentence with a definite noun that you can identify based on the context. Use these nouns:

the author	the mechanic	the teller
the driver	the receptionist	the waiter

1. Last summer I took a bus ride through a terrible storm.

   The driver was excellent, and we reached our destination safely.

2. I had lunch at the Pinewood Restaurant yesterday.

   _____

3. My car began vibrating, so I took it to a garage.

_____

4. I went to deposit some money at the bank this morning.

_____

5. I read a great book during my vacation.

_____

6. I called my doctor's office yesterday afternoon.

_____

Beyond the Sentence

Connecting Information

Like pronouns, articles help make sentences clear and connect ideas in a paragraph or conversation. Indefinite nouns are used to introduce new information. Definite nouns are used to refer to old information, which is more specific.

> We've just bought **a new puppy**. We brought **her** home last week, and **she's** doing fine. **My son** is so in love with **the puppy** that **he** insisted on sleeping in the kitchen with **her** for the first few nights. But now that **he** is convinced that **the puppy** can stay alone, **he** has gone back to **his own bedroom** to sleep. It probably won't be long, however, before **the puppy** finds **her way** to **his room** for company.

D5 Connecting Information

A. Work with a partner. Number these sentences to make a meaningful paragraph. Pay attention to the articles and pronouns to help you decide on the order.

_____ He cut the wire and jumped from the window into a creek.

_____ No one knows exactly where he found the ladder.

__1__ Another prisoner has escaped from the local prison.

_____ He was able to reach a high window covered with wire.

_____ He swam across the creek, climbed over a wall, stole a car, and drove away.

_____ Sometime during the night, the prisoner climbed up a ladder.

B. Read the story aloud to see if it sounds right. Be ready to explain your choices.

D6) Talking About Familiar Nouns ▶ Note 1E

Work with a partner. Take turns saying each of these sentences. Add a specific identity for each underlined noun. Do any of the nouns have different identities for you and your partner? Why?

1. I went to <u>the supermarket</u> last night.

   I went to the A & P supermarket near my house last night.

2. I went to <u>the bank</u> before I came to class.

3. I bought <u>the newspaper</u> before I came to class.

4. <u>The mayor</u> is going to speak on television tonight.

5. I didn't feel well yesterday, so I went to <u>the doctor</u>.

D7) Understanding Shared Information ▶ Notes 1A–1D, 1G

A. Work in small groups. Imagine that you overhear the conversations below. Think about each situation and try to figure out what information the speaker and listener(s) share. Use your imagination.

1. Two women are talking. One of them says, "Did you order <u>the flowers</u> yet?"

   The women are sisters. They're sending a gift to their mother. OR
   The women are friends. One of them is getting married soon and they're discussing the wedding.

2. Two young men are talking. One says, "<u>The car</u> costs $2,500." The other says, "I don't know how I'll be able to afford it."

3. A woman approaches a man and says, "I got <u>the money</u>."

4. Three women are talking. One asks, "Did you bring <u>the photographs</u>?"

5. A woman is talking to a man. The woman says, "How could you forget to pay <u>the bill</u>?"

6. Two men are talking. One says, "Oh, by the way, I got <u>the tickets</u>."

B. Choose one of the situations from part A. Make a list of details about the situation. Then write a paragraph about it. Begin with a clear topic sentence.

   Two sisters are talking about a gift that they have planned to send their mother for her birthday. The gift is a large bouquet of her favorite flowers. After the flowers arrive, they are going to take their mother to an elegant restaurant for a dinner party. She doesn't know that all of her friends will be at the party.

Article Use with Generic Nouns

Examining Meaning and Use

Read the sentences and answer the questions below. Then discuss your observations and read the Meaning and Use Notes to check them.

1a. Unfortunately, my children have <u>snakes</u> for pets.
1b. <u>Snakes</u> frighten people.

2a. <u>Garlic</u> can help fight certain diseases.
2b. I put <u>garlic</u> in the soup.

3a. I have <u>a mango</u> in the refrigerator.
3b. <u>A mango</u> is a sweet-tasting fruit.

4a. <u>The typewriter</u> is not used much anymore in most offices.
4b. I put <u>the typewriter</u> away because we never use it.

1. Which underlined noun in each pair refers to a whole class or group of nouns?

2. Which underlined noun in each pair refers to a specific noun or nouns?

Meaning and Use Notes

> ### Overview of Generic Nouns
>
> **1** We don't always use a noun to refer to a specific object, event, or concept. Sometimes we use the noun to refer to a whole class or group of objects, events, or concepts. This noun is called a generic noun, and statements about a generic noun are called generic statements.
>
> *Ø*
> **Flies** are insects.
> I like **rice**.
>
> *A/An*
> **A bird** can fly, but **a reptile** can't.
>
> *The*
> **The laser** has become an important tool in surgery.

(Continued on page 272)

2 Plural count nouns and noncount nouns are the most common type of generic nouns. No articles are used with them. They are often used in generic statements to classify nouns, express likes or dislikes, and give opinions.

Classification	*Likes and Dislikes*	*Opinions*
Flies are insects.	I don't like **rice**.	**Dogs** make good pets.

3 Singular count nouns with *a/an* can also be used as generic nouns to represent all members of a class. The nouns are often used in definitions and in sentences expressing general factual information.

Definitions
A locksmith is **a person** who makes and repairs locks and keys.
A penguin is **a black and white bird** that lives in the Antarctic.

Factual Information
A bird can fly.
A child has six to ten colds per year. **An adult** has two colds per year.

4A The use of generic nouns with *the* is less common than the use of other types of generic nouns. Definite generic nouns express a more formal tone and are used more often in scientific and technical writing. They usually refer to plants, animals, mechanical objects, and other scientific phenomena.

More Formal Writing	*Less Formal Writing*
The mosquito can spread malaria.	Mosquitoes can spread malaria.
The computer has changed our lives.	Computers have changed our lives.

 Remember that *the* with a plural noun is not used generically. It refers to specific plural nouns.

The computers that we bought last year have helped our business.

4B Musical instruments are often referred to generically with the definite article.

I used to play **the piano** and **the violin**.

Listen to each situation. Check (✓) *Generic* if the noun refers to a class of things or *Specific* if the noun refers to a particular thing.

		GENERIC	SPECIFIC
1.	the carrot		✓
2.	almonds		
3.	garlic		
4.	food		
5.	the onion		
6.	a cold		
7.	vitamins		
8.	a headache		

E2 Defining Nouns with *A/An* ▶ Notes 1, 3

Work with a partner. Make up a simple generic statement that defines each noun below. Use singular count nouns with *a/an*. You may need a dictionary.

A spatula is a cooking utensil.

spatula   iris   elm   pineapple

crib   octopus   calculator   screwdriver

E3 Rephrasing Formal Generic Sentences

A. Rewrite this paragraph as a less formal version. Use plural generic nouns instead of definite generic nouns. Change pronouns and verbs when necessary. Start your paragraph with *Kangaroos are* . . .

> The kangaroo is an Australian animal with very distinctive physical features. It has large back legs that are used for hopping very fast, and it has a very large tail that helps it maintain its balance. The female kangaroo carries her young around in a special pocket of skin on her stomach that is called a pouch.

B. Read these statements. Rewrite one of them as a less formal sentence and use it to introduce a short, informal explanation that you will present to the class.

> The computer doesn't always make life easier.
> The trumpet is important in orchestras as well as jazz bands.
> The human heart is like a machine.
> The unicorn is an imaginary creature with one horn.

> Computers don't always make life easier. Sometimes they actually make life more frustrating when they break down. For example, last week at the bank . . .

Beyond the Sentence

Indefinite Generic Nouns in Discourse

An indefinite generic noun (with *a, an, Ø*) can remain indefinite throughout a paragraph or conversation as long as it continues to refer to a whole class or group of nouns instead of to a specific noun.

> **An onion** is a small white vegetable with a strong smell and a strong taste. Researchers have found that it is actually the strong taste that makes **an onion** good for your blood. Unfortunately, sweet or mild **onions** do not have this effect on your blood. Someday, according to researchers, **an onion** will taste sweet and benefit your health at the same time.

E4 Choosing Between Generic and Specific Nouns

A. In these following sentences, some nouns are used generically with no article, and others are used to refer to a specific thing. Distinguish between these generic and specific uses by writing *a, an, the,* or *Ø*.

1. I don't really like ___Ø___ dogs, but my neighbor has _____ dog that I'm
   ₁   ₂
   very fond of.

2. _____ cell phone is useful in an emergency. However, in many places, it is

    ¹

unlawful to use _____ cell phone while driving.

    ²

3. It's hard to find _____ inexpensive clothing. _____ clothing in the

    ¹   ²

stores is so expensive these days.

4. I eat _____ rice at almost every meal. _____ rice that I buy is usually on

    ¹   ²

sale downtown. It's _____ very flavorful kind of rice.

    ³

5. _____ camels are animals with long necks and humps on their back. In

    ¹

desert countries, people ride on _____ camels and use them for

    ²

transportation.

6. He's allergic to _____ cats. When he goes near _____ cat, he starts to

    ¹   ²

sneeze.

B. Choose one of these sentences as the introduction to a paragraph. Write a description
that continues to refer to the underlined generic noun.

I don't usually like <u>dinner parties</u>.

<u>A vacation</u> isn't always relaxing.

<u>Teachers</u> have to be patient.

<u>A laptop computer</u> is useful in college.

I don't usually like dinner parties. Sometimes they have good food, but most of the time it's not what I like. Dinner parties are typically too long and boring. They often last for several hours. The worst thing about dinner parties, however, is sitting next to a person I really don't want to talk to.

F Combining Form, Meaning, and Use

F1 Thinking About Meaning and Use

Read each sentence and the statements that follow. Write *T* if the statement is true or *F* if it is false. Then discuss your answers in small groups.

1. I bought a tennis racket last night.

   __T__ **a.** The speaker has a specific tennis racket in mind.

   __F__ **b.** The listener has a specific tennis racket in mind.

2. I looked at an apartment last night, but the kitchen was too small.

   _____ **a.** The listener has seen the kitchen.

   _____ **b.** The listener has just heard about this apartment.

3. Please take the other cookie.

   _____ **a.** The speaker is referring to the last cookie.

   _____ **b.** Someone already took a cookie.

4. I'd like some cheese, please.

   _____ **a.** The speaker is referring to a small quantity of cheese.

   _____ **b.** The listener knows exactly which cheese the speaker wants.

5. Open a window, please.

   _____ **a.** The speaker wants a particular window to be opened.

   _____ **b.** There are at least two windows.

6. **Mother:** Wear the dress to school.
   Daughter: No, not today.

   _____ **a.** The mother has a specific dress in mind.

   _____ **b.** The daughter has a specific dress in mind.

7. I saw Maria at the post office yesterday.

_____ **a.** The speaker usually goes to that post office.

_____ **b.** The listener may not know that post office.

8. The snake is frightening that little girl.

_____ **a.** The speaker is referring to a particular snake.

_____ **b.** The sentence is about all snakes.

F2 **Editing**

Some of these sentences have errors. Find the errors and correct them.

1. I need *a* ∧ new coat. Please help me find one.

2. When you get to my house, you don't have to ring doorbell. Just walk in.

3. We have plenty of sandwiches. Please take the another one.

4. My grandparents were some immigrants. They came to this country in 1920.

5. She graduated with a major in the mathematics and physics.

6. The life is not always easy.

7. Calcium is mineral.

8. Please pass the rice and the salt.

9. Book I bought was on sale.

10. Let's sit in a last row so that we can leave quickly when the play is over.

Beyond the Classroom

Searching for Authentic Examples

Find examples of English grammar in everyday life. Choose one of the tasks below. Be prepared to discuss your findings.

A. Look for newspaper headlines, signs, and other contexts where indefinite and definite articles are missing. Write down your examples and then insert all of the articles that you think are missing. Bring your examples to class. Why did you insert the definite or indefinite article in each particular context?

B. Look in a science textbook or a magazine about health or food. Write down examples of generic nouns with Ø, *a/an*, or *the,* and bring them to class. Why was each of the generic nouns used? Pay attention to the contexts that the nouns are used in.

Writing

Follow these steps to write the first page of a "Healthy Eating" pamphlet that you might find at a doctor's office.

1. Make a list of various foods that are important for good health, and then discuss these questions: What particular health benefits do they offer? Is there any scientific evidence? How often should people eat these foods? How much should they eat? Are there any restrictions or problems with certain foods? What foods should be avoided? Why? You may want to search the Internet or use the public library.

2. Use your list and your notes to write a first draft of your pamphlet. Start with an introduction that makes some generalizations about food and health. Give examples of foods that should be eaten and tell why. Then give advice about foods that should be avoided. Pay attention to your use of articles.

3. Read over your work carefully and circle grammar, spelling, and punctuation errors. Work with a partner to decide how to fix the errors. Then rewrite your draft with the changes that you and your partner discussed.

Relative Clauses with Subject Relative Pronouns

A Formal Wear Gives Company New Attitude

A1 Before You Read

Discuss these questions.

What kind of clothes do you wear to work or school? Would you like to dress more casually or less casually? How do you feel when you wear more formal clothes?

A2 Read

Read this newspaper article to find out why one business decided that its employees should dress formally.

Formal Wear Gives Company New Attitude

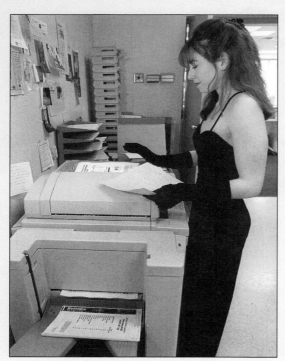

A man wearing a tuxedo looks over some papers. A woman wearing an evening gown sits in a chair nearby. She is talking on the phone.

5   A wedding reception, perhaps, or a party? No, it's just Friday at the Pollak Agency, which is a marketing and public relations firm. There, dressing up—not down—has become a fashion statement
10 that is also good for business.

They call it Formal Fridays.

"We get the strangest looks when we go into the deli for lunch," said art director Charlene DePrizio. She was dressed in a
15 black velvet floor-length gown.

Formal Fridays was the idea of Alison Pollak, who is the director of media. She was tired of dressing in business wear for client presentations while others wore
20 jeans. She suggested that all ten employees

at the firm try dressing up very elegantly one Friday.

"I thought she was crazy, but everyone on the staff liked the idea," said Alan Pollak, 25 chairman of the company and Alison Pollak's father. He was wearing a tuxedo.

That one Friday led to another, and another. Some clients have joined in, and the company even got a new 30 account—advertising pâté—from a person that had read about Formal Fridays.

"Anyone who wears gowns and tuxedos knows pâté," said the new client.

According to the Pollaks, Formal Fridays 35 are also a statement against a business world that has gotten too casual. Casual clothing at work used to mean not wearing a tie. Then it became jeans. Now employers have to counsel employees about appropriate clothing.

40 At the Pollak Agency, Formal Fridays have had a remarkable effect on employee attitude.

"I find people are a little more clear in their diction," said executive vice president 45 Sal Giacchi, who was dressed in a tuxedo.

Production manager Betty Uhler, who was wearing a glittery black dress, said, "I'm wearing three-inch heels. I'm walking a little slower, a little nicer. When you dress up, 50 you sit up straight, act a little more elegant."

Still, Formal Fridays can be a little confusing to outsiders. Alan Pollak remembered one day in a restaurant when his group was heading toward a table. As 55 they walked by, a female customer tapped a Pollak employee who was wearing a tuxedo.

"Waiter," she asked, "can I have a glass of water?"

Adapted from *The Ithaca Journal*

diction: clarity of speech
dress down: to put on casual, less formal clothes
dress up: to put on more formal clothes

firm: a business company
pâté (French): a food similar to a paste or spread, often made of ground liver

 A3 **After You Read**

Write *T* for true or *F* for false for each statement. Then change the false statements to true ones.

__F__ **1.** Employees at the Pollak Agency sell formal clothing.

Employees at the Pollak Agency sometimes wear formal clothing.

_____ **2.** Some of the agency's clients like the idea of dressing up.

_____ **3.** The agency got a new contract advertising formal wear.

_____ **4.** The Pollaks think that the business world is not casual enough.

_____ **5.** The agency has found that clothing influences people's attitudes at work.

_____ **6.** Outsiders always understand "Formal Fridays."

B Relative Clauses with Subject Relative Pronouns

Examining Form

Look back at the article on page 280 and complete the tasks below. Then discuss your observations and read the Form charts to check them.

1. Three examples of relative clauses are underlined. Find six more examples.

2. Circle the subject relative pronoun (*who, which,* or *that*) in each relative clause. Circle the noun or noun phrase it refers to.

3. Nonrestrictive relative clauses are surrounded by commas. Restrictive relative clauses are not. Sort your examples into nonrestrictive and restrictive relative clauses.

RESTRICTIVE RELATIVE CLAUSES

Relative Clauses After the Main Clause				
MAIN CLAUSE		RELATIVE CLAUSE		
	NOUN	SUBJECT RELATIVE PRONOUN	VERB	
I know	a woman	who that	works	at Jones & Roe.
They have	rules	which that	require	business suits.

Relative Clauses Inside the Main Clause				
MAIN CLAUSE				
	RELATIVE CLAUSE			
NOUN	SUBJECT RELATIVE PRONOUN	VERB		
A woman	who that	works	there	won't wear a suit.
The rules	which that	require	suits	are strictly enforced.

NONRESTRICTIVE RELATIVE CLAUSES

Relative Clauses After the Main Clause

MAIN CLAUSE		RELATIVE CLAUSE		
	NOUN	SUBJECT RELATIVE PRONOUN	VERB	
I know	Sue Dunn,	**who**	**works**	**at Jones & Roe.**
No one likes	the rules,	**which**	**are**	**strictly enforced.**

Relative Clauses Inside the Main Clause

MAIN CLAUSE				
	RELATIVE CLAUSE			
NOUN	SUBJECT RELATIVE PRONOUN	VERB		
Sue Dunn,	**who**	**works**	**at Jones & Roe,**	won't wear a suit.
The rules,	**which**	**are**	**strictly enforced,**	require business suits.

Restrictive and Nonrestrictive Relative Clauses
- Relative clauses (also called adjective clauses) modify nouns (or noun phrases). There are two types of relative clauses: restrictive and nonrestrictive.
- Restrictive relative clauses distinguish one noun from another.
  > I know <u>the woman</u> **who works at Jones & Roe**. I don't know <u>the woman</u> **who works at Transco.**
- Nonrestrictive relative clauses give extra information about a noun and are separated from that noun by commas. (In speech, a pause signals the commas.)
  > <u>Sue Dunn</u>, **who works at Jones & Roe,** won't wear a suit.
- As with all clauses, relative clauses have a subject and verb. They are dependent clauses. They cannot stand alone as complete sentences. They must be attached to a main clause.
- A relative clause can occur anywhere in a sentence but it must follow the noun it refers to.
  > I know <u>a woman</u> **who works at Jones & Roe.**
  > <u>A woman</u> **who works at Jones & Roe** won't wear a suit.

Subject Relative Pronouns
- When *who, which,* or *that* is the subject of a relative clause, it is a subject relative pronoun.
- In restrictive clauses, *who* and *that* are used for people. *Which* and *that* are used for things and animals.
- In nonrestrictive clauses, *who* is used for people and *which* is used for things.

(Continued on page 284)

- A subject relative pronoun is followed by a verb. The verb agrees with the noun that the subject relative pronoun refers to.

  I know a man **who works** at **Jones & Roe.**   I know two men **who work** at **Jones & Roe.**

- A subject relative pronoun always has the same form, whether or not it refers to a singular noun (a man) or a plural noun (men).

- Sentences with subject relative pronouns can be thought of as a combination of two sentences.

  I know a woman. She works there. = I know a woman **who** works there.

- Do not repeat the noun or pronoun in the relative clause.

  *I know a woman who she works there. (INCORRECT)

B1) Listening for Form

Listen to these comments about dress codes. Choose the main clause or relative clause that you hear. (Not every sentence contains a relative clause.)

1. **a.** clothes that express my individuality

   b. clothes express my individuality

2. **a.** the dress code, which is very casual

   b. the dress code is very casual

3. **a.** Ms. Chang, who is the manager

   b. Ms. Chang is the manager

4. **a.** the dress code is still very conservative

   b. the dress code that is still very conservative

5. **a.** Barker Bank has a strict dress code

   b. Barker Bank, which has a strict dress code

6. **a.** clothes were more formal

   b. clothes that were more formal

7. **a.** the men, who don't have to wear ties anymore

   b. the men don't have to wear ties anymore

8. **a.** my boss dresses very casually

   b. my boss, who dresses very casually

Work with a partner. Find the relative clauses in the conversation. Underline them and circle the noun phrases that they modify. Then practice the conversation.

Paul: What should I wear to my job interview?

Rita: How about your gray suit and (the shirt) that matches it?

Paul: Do you mean my new blue shirt, which is at the cleaners?

Rita: Oh. Well, what about the shirts that are hanging on the bedroom door?

Paul: Hmm . . . should I wear the white one or the one that has pinstripes?

Rita: Wear the one that feels more comfortable. What time is the interview?

Paul: The boss's secretary, who called to confirm yesterday, said 10:15, although the manager who originally contacted me said 10:30. I'd better be there at 10:15.

Rita: By the way, was the Department of Labor booklet helpful?

Paul: Yes, especially part 3, which had a lot of practical advice.

Rita: Is the position that's open a new one?

Paul: No. I know the person who has it now. She's leaving to work in the Boston branch, which opens after the first of the year.

Build as many meaningful sentences as possible. Use an item from each column. Punctuate your sentences correctly.

We like the man that works in the bakery.

we like	the man Gary, the new phone cards, cars	that who which	works in the bakery are affordable

B4 Working on Placement of Relative Clauses

A. Rewrite these sentences about dress codes, inserting the restrictive relative clause in parentheses after the appropriate noun.

1. Dress codes can make employees unhappy. (that are too strict)

   Dress codes that are too strict can make employees unhappy.

2. Some employers won't hire applicants. (who dress too casually)

3. Employees believe that clothing is a form of free expression. (who oppose dress codes)

4. Some companies restrict clothing. (that has sports logos on it)

5. A company dress code may not allow women to wear skirts. (that are very short)

B. Rewrite these sentences, inserting the nonrestrictive relative clause in parentheses after the appropriate noun. Remember to add commas.

1. This T-shirt is inappropriate for work. (which has slogans on it)

   This T-shirt, which has slogans on it, is inappropriate for work.

2. What do you think about rule number 3? (which restricts very tight clothing)

3. My nephew Dan often wears very unusual clothing. (who works for a high-tech company)

4. My boss is trying to enforce a new dress code. (who has been here only for a year)

5. Casual dress has become the new standard in many companies. (which is hard to define)

B5 Working on Verb Agreement in Relative Clauses

Work with a partner. Complete each sentence with an appropriate subject relative pronoun and the correct form of the verb in parentheses. (Some items will have two possible answers.) Then practice the conversations with a partner.

1. A: Who is the person _____who sits_____ (sit) next to you in English class?
                          1

   B: I don't know her name, but she's also in our chemistry class. She's the woman

   _____ (ask) a lot of questions.
           2

2. A: My notebook, _____ (be) on the table before, is missing.
                              1

   B: There's one over there _____ (look) like your notebook.
                                      2

3. A: Sami, _____ (live) across the street, plays with my son. Do you
    ₁

   know his family?

   B: No. I thought that the people _____ (own) that house didn't
       ₂

   have any children.

4. A: I need to see a doctor _____ (treat) skin problems. Do you
        ₁

   know any?

   B: Yes. Dr. Wu, _____ (have) an office near here, is a
       ₂

   dermatologist.

5. A: Koji and Susan, _____ (finish) the project yesterday, can leave
           ₁

   early today. Everyone else must stay in class until they finish.

   B: But what about the people _____ (be) not in class yesterday?
           ₂

6. A: AC Express, _____ (have) an office downtown, can probably
        ₁

   ship that package overseas. You should call them.

   B: OK. I will. But first I need to finish packing the items _____
               ₂

   (be) on this list.

B6 Combining Sentences with *Who, That,* or *Which*

Combine each pair of sentences to make a restrictive relative clause using *who, that,* or *which*. There are two possible answers for each item.

1. I picked up the package. It was lying on the front step.

   I picked up the package that/which was lying on the front step.

2. The professor called me. He teaches Russian.

3. My sister has a cat. It has three kittens.

4. Did you buy the socks? They were on sale.

5. The little girl was crying. She hurt her knee.

6. They gave us an exam. It lasted an hour.

7. I spoke to two women. They saw the accident.

8. The child went home. He was sick.

Identifying Nouns with Restrictive Relative Clauses

Examining Meaning and Use

Read the sentences and answer the questions below. Then discuss your observations and read the Meaning and Use Notes to check them.

1a. <u>A man</u> wore a tuxedo today.
1b. <u>A man</u> who works with me wore a tuxedo today.

2a. A dress code is a <u>set of rules</u>.
2b. A dress code is a <u>set of rules</u> that describes the appropriate kind of clothing for work.

1. Compare 1a and 1b. Which sentence gives information that identifies the underlined noun?

2. Which sentence is a more complete definition, 2a or 2b?

Meaning and Use Notes

> **Identifying Nouns**
>
> **1A** Restrictive relative clauses identify nouns. They distinguish one person or thing from other people or things. They answer the question *Which one(s)?* Restrictive relative clauses express necessary information. They cannot be omitted without affecting the meaning of the sentence.
>
> *With a Relative Clause*
> A: Are your children in that group over there?
> B: Yes, <u>the girl</u> **that's wearing the red sweater** and <u>the boy</u> **who's wearing the gray sweatshirt** are mine.
> (The relative clauses clearly identify B's children and distinguish them from the other children.)
>
> *Without a Relative Clause*
> A: Are your children in that group over there?
> B: Yes, <u>the girl</u> and <u>the boy</u> are mine.
> (B's children have not been clearly identified. The meaning is incomplete.)
>
> **1B** Restrictive relative clauses are used in definitions.
>
> A locksmith is <u>a person</u> **who makes and repairs locks and keys.**
> A penguin is <u>a black and white bird</u> **which lives in the Antarctic.**

1C Restrictive relative clauses are often used to provide information about a noun when it is first mentioned. If the information is new to the listener, the relative clause quickly identifies the noun. If the information is shared with the listener, it reminds the listener of the noun.

New Information
Guess what? <u>A guy</u> **who works with me** just won the lottery.
Shared Information
Look. There are <u>the dresses</u> **that are on sale**.

Reducing Restrictive Relative Clauses

2 Subject relative pronouns + *be* are often omitted from restrictive relative clauses.

Full Form	*Reduced Form*
Take the food **that/which is on the table**.	Take the food **on the table**.
Look at the man **who/that is wearing a tuxedo**.	Look at the man **wearing a tuxedo**.

C1 Listening for Meaning and Use

▶ Notes 1A, 1C

Listen to the questions. Choose the most appropriate answer.

1. **a.** The woman who is near the window.
   b. The one which is near the window.

2. **a.** The rules are too strict.
   b. The rules that are too strict.

3. **a.** The one that's over there.
   b. The one who's over there.

4. **a.** The man who called yesterday.
   b. The man called yesterday.

5. **a.** The man is working downstairs.
   b. The man who is working downstairs.

6. **a.** The guy who fixes up old cars.
   b. The guy fixes up old cars.

7. **a.** The ones that got wet.
   b. The ones who got wet.

8. **a.** A suit is worn on formal occasions.
   b. A suit that is worn on formal occasions.

Work with a partner. In each picture one object belongs to you. Describe it using a restrictive relative clause.

1. You're at the airport, and you're looking for your luggage. There are four suitcases that look like yours.

   My suitcase is the one that has a round luggage tag.

4. You hung up your raincoat on the coat rack at the restaurant. So did two other people.

2. It's dark, and you can't find your car in the parking lot. There are some cars in a row that look like yours.

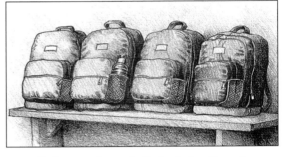

5. All the students left their backpacks outside the language lab. Several students have backpacks just like yours.

3. You took off your snow boots when you entered the doctor's office. As you're leaving, you notice that there are three other pairs of boots similar to yours.

6. You've lost your keys in a department store. When you go to the lost and found, the clerk shows you three sets of keys.

Work with a partner. Read each passage and use the information to answer each question with a sentence containing a relative clause.

1. Georgia O'Keeffe was a twentieth-century American artist. She painted well into her eighties. She is famous for painting flowers. The flowers were colorful.

   a. Who was Georgia O'Keeffe?

   Georgia O'Keeffe was a twentieth-century American artist who painted well into her eighties.

   b. What is she famous for?

2. Gene therapy is a new branch of genetic engineering. It may someday help prevent cancer. This serious medical condition causes tumors to grow in the body.

   a. What is gene therapy?

   b. What is cancer?

3. Martin Luther King, Jr., was an African American. He led the civil rights movement in the 1960s. He fought for equal rights through passive resistance. This nonviolent method of protest was previously used by Mahatma Gandhi in the 1940s.

   a. Who was Martin Luther King, Jr.?

   b. What is passive resistance?

4. Phobias are exaggerated fears. These fears can prevent a person from leading a normal life. Some people suffer from agoraphobia. They have a fear of being in open places. Others suffer from claustrophobia. They have a fear of being in closed places.

   a. What is a phobia?

   b. Which people suffer from agoraphobia? Which suffer from claustrophobia?

C4 **Defining Words with Relative Clauses** ► Note 1B

Work with a partner. Describe these different types of doctors by writing sentences with relative clauses. If necessary, use a dictionary.

1. A dermatologist *is a doctor who treats skin problems.*

2. A neurologist _____

3. A pediatrician _____

4. A dentist _____

5. A cardiologist _____

6. A podiatrist _____

Work with a partner. Look at each picture and answer the question using full and reduced relative clauses. Make up as many answers as possible for each item.

1. Which pair of shoes did you buy?

The shoes that were made in Italy.
The shoes made in Italy.

2. Which one is your son?

3. Which woman is the office manager?

4. Which man is your father?

5. Which hat are you going to wear?

6. Which iced tea mix do you prefer?

Beyond the Sentence

Combining Sentences with Relative Clauses

A paragraph with many short sentences may seem disconnected and hard to understand. You can use a relative clause to combine sentences that refer to the same noun or noun phrase. Relative clauses help avoid repetition and make the information flow more smoothly.

A Paragraph Without Relative Clauses

This story is about a young woman. She graduated from college with an engineering degree. After college, she worked for a small Internet company. The company sold books. Her friends, on the other hand, worked for well-known companies. These companies paid high salaries. She was frustrated and thought about quitting her job, but she didn't. That decision paid off. That small Internet company was one of the first "dot-coms." It became popular worldwide. Today, at the age of 33, she is worth millions of dollars.

A Paragraph with Relative Clauses

This story is about a young woman **who graduated from college with an engineering degree**. After college, she worked for a small Internet company **that sold books**. Her friends, on the other hand, worked for well-known companies **that paid high salaries**. She was frustrated and thought about quitting her job, but she didn't. That decision paid off. That small Internet company was one of the first "dot-coms" **that became popular worldwide**. Today, at the age of 33, she is worth millions of dollars.

C6 Connecting Ideas with Relative Clauses

A. Rewrite the following paragraph using relative clauses to make the information flow more smoothly. Make any changes that you think will improve the paragraph.

School dress codes are becoming popular again, although this doesn't necessarily mean that students have to wear uniforms. A school dress code is a set of rules. The rules restrict certain types of clothing. Some dress codes prohibit certain T-shirts. The T-shirts have offensive writing or pictures on them. Other dress codes prohibit certain types of pants or shirts. They prohibit very baggy pants, very tight pants, and very tight shirts. Many others prohibit certain types of skirts and dresses, too. The skirts and dresses are several inches above the knee. Some dress codes go even further. They don't allow sports clothing. This clothing has logos on it.

B. In small groups, compare your rewritten paragraphs. Discuss any differences between your paragraphs. Decide which changes you prefer and why. Combine your paragraphs into one version that you all agree on.

D Adding Extra Information with Nonrestrictive Relative Clauses

Examining Meaning and Use

Read the sentences and answer the questions below. Then discuss your observations and read the Meaning and Use Notes to check them.

a. <u>My brother who lives in Maine loves to fish.</u> My other brother loves to ski.
b. <u>My brother, who lives in Maine, loves to fish.</u> He takes us fishing when we visit.

1. Which relative clause gives necessary information that identifies *my brother*? Which relative clause adds information that is not essential?

2. Which underlined sentence implies that the speaker has only one brother?

Meaning and Use Notes

> **Adding Extra Information About Nouns**
>
> **1A** A nonrestrictive relative clause adds extra information about a noun, but it is not needed to identify the noun. This information is often new to the listener, but it isn't essential; it can be omitted without affecting the meaning of the sentence.
>
> *Without a Relative Clause*
> My son Scott always wears a baseball cap. My son Greg doesn't.
>
> *With a Relative Clause*
> <u>My son Scott</u>, **who is 11**, always wears a baseball cap. <u>My son Greg</u>, **who is 13**, doesn't. (The relative clauses give extra information about Scott and Greg but do not change the meaning of the sentences.)
>
> **1B** Nonrestrictive relative clauses can add extra information about proper nouns and other unique nouns. They can also add information about a definite noun that has already been identified.
>
> *Proper Noun*
> <u>Boston</u>, **which is in Massachusetts**, has many colleges and universities.
>
> *Unique Noun*
> <u>My sister</u>, **who is 17**, is in high school.
>
> *Noun Already Identified*
> <u>My antique desk</u> was damaged by the flood. <u>The desk</u>, **which is worth a lot of money**, can probably be repaired.

2 Restrictive relative clauses provide essential information in order to distinguish one noun from other similar nouns. Nonrestrictive relative clauses are used when there is only one particular noun or set of nouns. They do not distinguish nouns or provide essential information.

Restrictive Relative Clause

My brother **who lives in Baltimore** calls me every weekend.
   (The relative clause distinguishes *my brother* from a brother who lives elsewhere. It implies that the speaker has more than one brother.)

Nonrestrictive Relative Clause

My brother, **who lives in Baltimore,** calls me every weekend.
   (The relative clause is not used to distinguish *my brother* from anyone else. It implies that the speaker has only one brother.)

3 Subject relative pronouns + *be* are often omitted from nonrestrictive relative clauses.

Full Form	*Reduced Form*
I spoke to Pedro, **who is the boss.**	I spoke to Pedro, **the boss.**

D1 **Listening for Meaning and Use** ► Notes 1A, 1B, 2

🎧 **Listen to these situations. Choose the sentence that you hear.**

1. **(a.)** My sister, who lives in New York, has two children.
   b. My sister who lives in New York has two children.

2. **a.** Have you met her brother, who works at the bank?
   b. Have you met her brother who works at the bank?

3. **a.** Give me the sheet of paper, which has the list of names.
   b. Give me the sheet of paper which has the list of names.

4. **a.** The man, who is talking, is my boss.
   b. The man who is talking is my boss.

5. **a.** She showed me her necklace which had beautiful stones.
   b. She showed me her necklace, which had beautiful stones.

6. **a.** Her grandmother, who lived until 80, was a teacher.
   b. Her grandmother who lived until 80 was a teacher.

A. Complete each main clause with a proper noun or other unique noun. Then add more information with a nonrestrictive relative clause at the end of the sentence.

1. I come from _____Queens_____, which _is in New York City._____

2. I once visited _____, which _____

    _____

3. I've never met _____, who _____

    _____

4. I'd like to meet _____, who _____

    _____

B. Complete these sentences by first adding a nonrestrictive relative clause, and then completing the main clause.

1. My next vacation, _which will be in March, is for one week._____

2. My best friend, _____

3. My birthday, _____

4. My home, _____

Work with a partner. Read each situation and related statement. Decide whether the relative clause in each statement is restrictive or nonrestrictive. If the clause is nonrestrictive, add commas to the sentence.

1. **Situation:** My parents moved to Florida a few years ago. They used to live in New York City.

   Statement: My parents, who used to live in New York City, moved to Florida a few years ago. nonrestrictive

2. **Situation:** I have two aunts on my mother's side. One of them lives in Seattle. The other one lives in New York. One of them invited me for Christmas.

   Statement: My aunt who lives in Seattle invited me for Christmas.

3. **Situation:** We live in the South. It's very warm and humid here.

   Statement: We live in the South which is very warm and humid.

4. Situation: My father lives next to a golf course. He loves to play golf.

   Statement: My father who loves to play golf lives next to a golf course.

5. Situation: My dentist has several dental hygienists. The same one always cleans my teeth. A different one cleans my son's teeth.

   Statement: The dental hygienist who cleans my teeth doesn't clean my son's teeth.

6. Situation: One of my sons is in the second grade, one is in the fourth grade, and one is a sophomore in high school.

   Statement: My son who is in the second grade loves math.

7. Situation: You've invited your friends Jane and Tina to dinner. Jane and Tina work at the same company. You tell this to Tina.

   Statement: I've invited my friend Jane who works in the legal division at your company.

8. Situation: A newspaper article describes pollution.

   Statement: Pollution which is still a major problem was a political issue in the last presidential election.

D4 Describing People

Write two sentences about each person. In the first sentence, identify the person with a restrictive relative clause. In the second sentence, provide further information using a nonrestrictive relative clause. Be ready to tell the class about one of these people.

1. an aunt

   My aunt that lives in San Francisco loves cats.
   Her daughter, who was just married, has a lot of cats, too.

2. an uncle

3. a friend

4. a teacher

5. a neighbor

6. a classmate

E Combining Form, Meaning, and Use

E1 Thinking About Meaning and Use

Read each sentence and the statements that follow. Write *T* if the statement is true or *F* if it is false. Then discuss your answers in small groups.

1. The woman who works for my mother bought a new car.

   __T__ **a.** A woman works for my mother.

   _____ **b.** My mother bought a new car.

2. My brother, who just called my father, lives in Dallas.

   _____ **a.** My brother lives in Dallas.

   _____ **b.** My father called my brother.

3. The man who looked at my car was very old.

   _____ **a.** My car was very old.

   _____ **b.** A man looked at my car.

4. An explosion, which injured 20 people, occurred at about 11:00 last night.

   _____ **a.** An explosion injured 20 people.

   _____ **b.** An explosion occurred at about 11:00.

5. I spoke to my brother, who is very worried about something.

   _____ **a.** I have a brother.

   _____ **b.** I am very worried about something.

6. My son who talked to Mary looks like John.

   _____ **a.** I have more than one son.

   _____ **b.** Mary looks like John.

7. The milk, which is still on the first shelf, is spoiled.

    a. The milk is spoiled.

    b. There's probably milk on another shelf, too.

8. I took the umbrella, which was in the car.

    a. There was only one umbrella.

    b. The umbrella was in the car.

E2) Editing

Find the errors in these paragraphs and correct them. There may be more than one way to correct an error.

What kind of clothing should people ~~which~~ *who* visit a place of worship wear? Is it acceptable to wear jeans to mosques, churches, or synagogues? Should a worshiper wear something, that is sporty and comfortable or something what is more dressy? These are questions who concern many religious leaders these days.

Opinions are strongly divided about the type of clothing is appropriate for worship. According to some religious leaders, people which come to pray should wear clothing that show respect and admiration for their religion. They shouldn't be wearing clothes that is for jogging, shopping, or attending a ball game. On the other hand, there are many religious leaders don't care about such material issues. They believe that religion, which is a spiritual matter isn't concerned with clothing. They welcome everyone who attend religious services.

Most people think that the issue actually goes beyond clothing. More formal clothing usually accompanies an atmosphere which more traditional and serious. Informal clothing, on the other hand, is more acceptable in religious services that they are more contemporary and informal.

Beyond the Classroom

Searching for Authentic Examples

Find examples of English grammar in everyday life. Choose one of the tasks below. Be prepared to discuss your findings.

A. Look in a dictionary. Write down five definitions that have relative clauses with subject relative pronouns, and bring them to class. Look for definitions of nouns, particularly of various kinds of people, animals, and other living things. Why do you think the relative clauses are used?

B. Watch the news or another TV program. Listen for three examples of relative clauses with subject relative pronouns. Write down as much of the whole sentence as you can for each example. Are your examples restrictive or nonrestrictive? Are they full or reduced?

Speaking

In small groups, follow these steps to prepare a discussion about dress codes in your native country.

1. On your own, think about dress codes and clothing styles in your native country. Are there any rules for what to wear at different kinds of jobs? at school? Are the rules changing? Write down your ideas.

2. With your group, compare the dress codes in various countries using relative clauses when you can. Where are the dress codes more formal? Where are they more casual? Where are they changing? Do you think that dress codes and clothing styles suggest anything about a culture? How does clothing affect people's behavior and attitudes?

3. Prepare a short summary of your group's discussion and choose one person to present it to the class. Ask your classmates to share their opinions with you.

Relative Clauses with Object Relative Pronouns

The New Face of a Role Model

A1 Before You Read

Discuss these questions.

A role model is a person who is an example for other people to follow. What are some qualities of a role model?

A2 Read

Read this magazine article about soccer star Mia Hamm to find out what she thinks about being a role model.

THE NEW FACE OF A ROLE MODEL

In women's soccer, girls finally get the role model (they deserve): Mia Hamm

The Women's World Cup, <u>which the media called the biggest female sporting event in history</u>, arrived for the first time in the United States in 1999. Three television networks televised all 32 games, with an
5 estimated 1 billion viewers. One of the stars was Mia Hamm, <u>who many people call the Michael Jordan of women's soccer</u>.

Though her ballerina mom tried to interest her in dance, it was her father's soccer passion <u>that she</u>
10 <u>followed</u>. Hamm led the University of North Carolina to four championships in the early nineties, won Olympic gold in 1996, won the U.S. Soccer Player of the Year award many times, and broke the international goal-scoring record for males and females.

15 None of this would have been possible without a law called Title IX, <u>which the U.S. government passed in 1972</u>. This law requires equal funding for girls' school sports. Until 1972, the only role models <u>that female athletes had</u> were female skaters, female gymnasts,
20 and male athletes. Now, more than 7 million girls play soccer, and they all want to be like Mia.

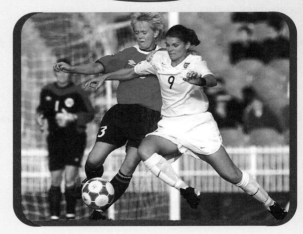

Mia Hamm

Mia Hamm is more than an amazing athlete. She is a very admirable role model. She has created the Mia Hamm Foundation, <u>which she has dedicated to</u>
25 <u>two causes</u> that are very important to her: encouraging young female athletes and research on bone marrow diseases. (Her brother Garrett died from aplastic anemia.)

Hamm juggles her personal relationships with her
30 busy career. Here are some things <u>that she says about life as sport's newest kind of role model</u>:

Q: Girls today have a wider variety of role models than ever before and you're one of them. What's it like to be a role model?

35 **A:** I take it very seriously. I didn't have the role models (these girls have.) Most of my athletic role models were men.

Q: Will playing team sports help girls as they grow up? How has it helped you?

40 **A:** Sports can do so much. It's given me a framework: meeting new people, confidence, self-esteem, time management, discipline, motivation. I learned all these things, whether I knew I was learning them or not, through sports.

45 **Q:** What's the most important thing (your mother taught you?)

A: Everyone has goodness. It's just a matter of how it's nurtured. Hopefully, I can do the same thing, nurture my son or daughter to grow up with love in his or her
50 heart for everyone. . . .

---

anemia: a disease of the blood
bone marrow: the soft tissue in the center of the bone
foundation: an organization that gives out money for special purposes (e.g., research)

juggle: to do many things at once
the media: television, radio, and newspapers
nurture: to encourage to develop

A3 **After You Read**

Choose the answer that best completes each sentence.

1. The Women's World Cup _____.
   a. began in the United States
   b. became well known through television
   c. started in 1999

2. Mia Hamm developed her love for soccer because of _____.
   a. her mother
   b. her father
   c. her brother

3. Mia Hamm has won _____ only once.
   a. an Olympic gold medal
   b. a college championship
   c. the Soccer Player of the Year award

4. Hamm broke the international goal-scoring record for _____.
   a. women
   b. men
   c. men and women

5. Title IX is a law that requires equal _____ for girls' and boys' sports.
   a. athletes
   b. stadiums
   c. money

6. Mia Hamm grew up without _____.
   a. an opportunity to dance
   b. a female role model
   c. a busy career

B Relative Clauses with Object Relative Pronouns

Examining Form

Look back at the article on page 302 and complete the tasks below. Then discuss your observations and read the Form charts to check them.

1. Look at the underlined relative clauses. Circle the object relative pronoun in each clause (*who, which,* or *that*) and the noun or noun phrase it modifies.

2. Look at the circled relative clauses. These clauses do not have object relative pronouns. Which object relative pronoun is omitted from each clause?

RESTRICTIVE RELATIVE CLAUSES

Relative Clauses After the Main Clause				
MAIN CLAUSE		RELATIVE CLAUSE		
	NOUN	OBJECT RELATIVE PRONOUN	SUBJECT	VERB (PHRASE)
Mia Hamm is	an athlete	who/whom that/Ø	I	admire.
Mia didn't have	the opportunities	which/that/Ø	girls	have now.

Relative Clauses Inside the Main Clause				
	MAIN CLAUSE			
	RELATIVE CLAUSE			
NOUN	OBJECT RELATIVE PRONOUN	SUBJECT	VERB (PHRASE)	
An athlete	who/whom that/Ø	I	admire a lot	is Mia Hamm.
The game	which/that/Ø	the girls	won	was on TV.

NONRESTRICTIVE RELATIVE CLAUSES

Relative Clauses After the Main Clause

MAIN CLAUSE		RELATIVE CLAUSE		
	NOUN	OBJECT RELATIVE PRONOUN	SUBJECT	VERB (PHRASE)
I met	Mia Hamm,	who/whom	I	admire a lot.
Mia was at	the World Cup,	which	we	saw on TV.

Relative Clauses Inside the Main Clause

MAIN CLAUSE				
	RELATIVE CLAUSE			
NOUN	OBJECT RELATIVE PRONOUN	SUBJECT	VERB (PHRASE)	
Mia Hamm,	who/whom	I	admire,	is a soccer player.
The World Cup,	which	we	saw on TV,	was a big media event.

Restrictive and Nonrestrictive Relative Clauses

- Relative clauses (restrictive and nonrestrictive) modify nouns (or noun phrases). They have a subject and a verb and cannot stand alone as complete sentences.
- Relative clauses can be thought of as a combination of two sentences.
  Mia Hamm is an athlete. I admire <u>her</u>. = Mia Hamm is an athlete **who** I admire.
- Restrictive clauses distinguish one noun from another. Nonrestrictive relative clauses add extra information about a noun and are separated by commas.

Object Relative Pronouns

- When *who, whom, which,* or *that* is the object of a relative clause, it is an object relative pronoun.
- In restrictive clauses, *who, whom,* and *that* are used for people. *Which* and *that* are used for things and animals. In nonrestrictive clauses, *who* or *whom* is used for people and *which* is used for things.
- Object relative pronouns are followed by a subject + verb (phrase). The verb agrees with the subject before it. It does not agree with the noun that the clause refers to.
  Mia Hamm is an athlete **who I admire a lot.**
- Object relative pronouns can be omitted from restrictive relative clauses.
  A swimmer **who I know** won a medal. = A swimmer **Ø I know** won a medal.
- Object relative pronouns are never omitted from nonrestrictive relative clauses.
  *I met Mia Hamm, I admire a lot. (INCORRECT)
- Do not repeat the object noun or pronoun in the relative clause.
  *I met Mia Hamm, who I admire her. (INCORRECT)

Listening for Form

🎧 **Listen to these sentences and choose the sentence you hear.**

1. **a.** The team that we played didn't do very well.
   b. The team that played didn't do very well.

2. **a.** The equipment we broke is expensive to repair.
   b. The equipment which broke is expensive to repair.

3. **a.** Did you hear about the team that we beat?
   b. Did you hear about the team that beat us?

4. **a.** We didn't know about the rules that changed.
   b. We didn't know about the rules they changed.

5. **a.** I didn't meet the player they called.
   b. I didn't meet the player that called.

6. **a.** The man he called wanted to join the team.
   b. The man who called wanted to join the team.

B2 **Examining Relative Clauses with Object Relative Pronouns**

Read the paragraphs and look at the underlined relative clauses. Circle the noun or noun phrase that each clause modifies and write *S* over the subject of each relative clause.

Kay Valera used to be a "soccer mom." She sat on the sidelines while she watched her children play soccer. But now the 40-year-old mom has become a soccer player in a women's league <u>which she joined last spring</u>. One of the things <u>that she has learned</u> is how challenging it is to play a sport that requires players to think, kick, and run at the same time. As she plays, she recalls all the advice <u>that she has given her kids</u>. Everything that looked so easy from the sidelines is now so challenging.

Many kids and dads come to the games to cheer on the moms. And what happens when mom makes a mistake or her team loses? The kids can be very encouraging, but they also love to discuss the mistakes <u>that mom made</u> and the moves <u>that she should have made</u>. They might say, "Don't feel bad, you did your best, but you know that kick <u>that you tried in midfield</u>, well . . ."

Vocabulary Notes

Object Relative Pronouns

Who and Whom In restrictive and nonrestrictive relative clauses, *whom* expresses a much more formal tone than *who*. It is less common than other relative pronouns.

Formal Speech: Let me introduce you to the person **whom I admire most**, my friend and colleague, Stanley Chen.

That and Ø In restrictive relative clauses, *that* is used more often than *who*, *whom*, and *which*. Omitting the object relative pronoun (Ø) is also very common in speech and writing.

News Broadcast: The judge **(that) the president will appoint next week** is a woman.

B3 Using Object Relative Pronouns

Complete the sentences by circling all the words (and Ø) that can form correct sentences.

1. A man { (that) / (who) / which / (Ø) } we { (know) / knows } sells cars.

2. Marcus, { that / who / which / Ø } we saw on Tuesday, { doesn't / don't } work with us.

3. The bike { that / who / which / Ø } they bought { is / are } missing.

4. Ellen, { that / who / which / Ø } works with me, { is / are } always late for work.

5. The people { that / who / which / Ø } she { visit / visits } live nearby.

6. The teacher { that / who / which / Ø } I like { is / are } not here today.

B4) Combining Sentences Using Relative Clauses

Work in small groups. Imagine that you are visiting your 45-year-old aunt, who is showing you family photos and souvenirs. Combine the sentences below to describe the underlined noun phrase. Use restrictive or nonrestrictive relative clauses with an object relative pronoun. Practice different alternatives.

1. Let's look at <u>some things</u>. I've been saving them for a long time.

   Let's look at some things that I've been saving for a long time. OR
   Let's look at some things which I've been saving for a long time. OR
   Let's look at some things I've been saving for a long time.

2. Here is a photo of <u>your grandfather</u>. I still miss him so much.

3. <u>Our dog Teddy</u> is in this picture. We loved him a lot.

4. <u>The dress</u> is in this box. I wore it to my wedding.

5. I'll never forget <u>the guests</u>. I invited them to my wedding.

6. I remember <u>my high school teacher Miss Pullman</u>. I liked her so much.

7. Here is <u>a poem</u>. I wrote it in her class.

8. This is <u>an award</u>. I received it for my poem.

B5) Asking and Answering Questions with Object Relative Pronouns

Work with a partner. Take turns asking and answering *what* or *who* questions with restrictive relative clauses, using the words given. Practice different alternatives in your questions and answers.

1. a person/you call every day

   A: *Who is a person (that/who) you call every day?*
   B: *My sister is a person (that/who) I call every day.*

2. a game/you liked to play as a child

3. the relative/you look like most

4. the person/you call when you're in trouble

5. a food/you have never tasted

6. a teacher/you will always remember

7. a book/you like to read over and over again

8. a thing/you can't live without

Identifying Nouns and Adding Extra Information

Examining Meaning and Use

Read the sentences and complete the tasks below. Then discuss your observations and read the Meaning and Use Notes to check them.

1a. The coat that costs $200 is on sale now.
1b. The coat you wanted is on sale now.

2a. Megan Quann, who was only 16, was on the Olympic swimming team.
2b. Megan Quann, who I know, was on the Olympic swimming team.

1. Underline the relative clause in each sentence. Circle the noun that each clause refers to.

2. In which pair of sentences do the relative clauses help identify the noun? In which pair do they add extra information about the noun?

Meaning and Use Notes

> **Identifying Nouns**
>
> **1A** Restrictive relative clauses with object relative pronouns distinguish one person or thing from other similar people or things. They cannot be omitted without affecting the meaning of the sentence.
>
> *With a Relative Clause*
> Three women tried out. <u>The woman</u> **that I met** made the team.
>   (The relative clause clearly identifies which woman made the team.)
>
> *Without a Relative Clause*
> Three women tried out. <u>The woman</u> made the team. (It is unclear which woman made the team. The meaning is incomplete.)
>
> ---
>
> **1B** Restrictive relative clauses are often used to provide information about a noun when it is first mentioned, or to remind the listener about previously mentioned information. The relative clause immediately identifies the noun to the listener.
>
> *First Mentioned (New Information)*
> <u>A man</u> **Ø I know** is a champion swimmer.
>
> *Previously Mentioned (Shared Information)*
> <u>The tennis racket</u> **that we saw yesterday** is now on sale.

(Continued on page 310)

Adding Extra Information

2A Nonrestrictive relative clauses with object relative pronouns add extra information about a noun but aren't needed to identify it. They can be omitted without affecting the meaning of the sentence.

With a Relative Clause

The decathlon world record, **which Dvorak set in 1999,** had previously been set in 1992.
　(The relative clause gives extra information about the decathlon world record.)

Without a Relative Clause

The decathlon world record had previously been set in 1992.
　(Without the relative clause, the meaning of the sentence is still complete.)

2B Especially at the end of a sentence, nonrestrictive relative clauses with object relative pronouns are a simple way to add extra information to a sentence without starting a new one.

Many young girls now play soccer, **which my high school didn't offer in the 1960s.**

C1 Listening for Meaning and Use ▶ Notes 1A, 1B, 2A, 2B

Listen to the situations carefully. Then choose the sentence that would most appropriately follow each one.

1. **a.** Really? Do you know her?
   b. Really? How did you meet her?

2. **a.** Why did she quit the girls' team?
   b. What was the name of the girls' team?

3. **a.** She was lucky.
   b. That's too bad.

4. **a.** What sports did they play?
   b. Too bad you didn't know them.

5. **a.** That's not good!
   b. That's surprising!

6. **a.** Was that before the laws were changed?
   b. Why didn't they offer sports in your high school?

A. Add a restrictive relative clause with an object relative pronoun to complete the meaning of each sentence.

1. I once had a teacher _who I admired a great deal._

2. My neighbor is a person _____

3. I know a man _____

4. I'd like a job _____

5. Someday I'm going to live in a house _____

6. I have a friend _____

7. I shop in stores _____

8. My father is someone _____

B. Choose one of your sentences as the first sentence of a paragraph describing that person, place, or thing. First make a list of five or six characteristics or details that you will include. Then use your list to write a descriptive paragraph with at least two more relative clauses with object relative pronouns.

I once had a teacher who I admired a great deal. He was my role model. He taught history classes that everyone enjoyed. . . .

A. Write five simple sentences about specific people, places, or objects related to sports.

1. Pedro Martinez pitches for the Boston Red Sox.
2. A popular women's sport is soccer.

B. Work with a partner. Exchange papers and add extra information to your partner's sentences. Use nonrestrictive relative clauses with object relative pronouns.

1. Pedro Martinez, who I saw on TV, pitches for the Boston Red Sox.
2. A popular women's sport is soccer, which most of the world calls football.

C4

Write two sentences that give your opinion about the nouns in parentheses. Begin one sentence with *I like* and the other sentence with *I don't like*. Use restrictive relative clauses with object or subject relative pronouns.

1. (cars) <u>I like cars that go fast.</u>

   <u>I don't like cars (that) you have to fix all the time.</u>

2. (teachers) _____

   _____

3. (clothes) _____

   _____

4. (newspapers) _____

   _____

5. (friends) _____

   _____

6. (TV shows) _____

   _____

7. (foods) _____

   _____

8. (music) _____

   _____

9. (books) _____

   _____

10. (pets) _____

   _____

D Object Relative Pronouns with Prepositions

Examining Form

Read the sentences and complete the tasks below. Then discuss your observations and read the Form charts to check them.

> **a.** We saw the movie that everyone is talking about.
> **b.** We saw the movie about which everyone is talking.

1. The relative pronoun in each relative clause is the object of a preposition. Underline each object relative pronoun and circle each preposition.

2. Compare a and b. Where does the preposition occur in each relative clause? What other difference do you see?

RELATIVE CLAUSES ENDING IN PREPOSITIONS

Restrictive Relative Clauses					
MAIN CLAUSE		RELATIVE CLAUSE			
	NOUN	OBJECT RELATIVE PRONOUN	SUBJECT	VERB	PREPOSITION
There's	the coach	who/whom that/Ø	I	spoke	to.
He coaches	the team	which/that/Ø	she	plays	on.

Nonrestrictive Relative Clauses					
MAIN CLAUSE		RELATIVE CLAUSE			
	NOUN	OBJECT RELATIVE PRONOUN	SUBJECT	VERB	PREPOSITION
There's	Coach Smith,	who/whom	I	spoke	to.
He coaches	the Liberty team,	which	she	plays	on.

(Continued on page 314)

Relative Clauses Ending in Prepositions

- An object relative pronoun (*who, whom, that,* or *which*) can be the object of a preposition.
  There's the coach. I spoke <u>to him</u>. = There's the coach **who** I spoke **to**.
- Relative clauses ending in prepositions are usually used in spoken English and less formal written English.
- In restrictive relative clauses that end in prepositions, the object relative pronoun can be omitted.

RELATIVE CLAUSES BEGINNING WITH PREPOSITIONS

Restrictive Relative Clauses

	MAIN CLAUSE	RELATIVE CLAUSE			
	NOUN	PREPOSITION	OBJECT RELATIVE PRONOUN	SUBJECT	VERB
There's	<u>the coach</u>	to	whom	I	spoke.
He coaches	<u>the team</u>	on	which	she	plays.

Nonrestrictive Relative Clauses

	MAIN CLAUSE	RELATIVE CLAUSE			
	NOUN	PREPOSITION	OBJECT RELATIVE PRONOUN	SUBJECT	VERB
There's	<u>Coach Smith,</u>	to	whom	I	spoke.
He coaches	<u>the Liberty team,</u>	on	which	she	plays.

Relative Clauses Beginning with Prepositions

- In very formal English, a preposition can begin a relative clause. The preposition is followed by either *whom* for people or *which* for things. It cannot be followed by *who* or *that*.
- *Whom* and *which* are never omitted after prepositions.

🎧 Listen and choose the sentences you hear.

1. **a.** Do you know the woman he's married to?
   b. Do you know the woman to whom he's married?

2. **a.** The man he spoke to helped quite a bit.
   b. The man who he spoke to helped quite a bit.

3. **a.** Let's look at the book I brought in.
   b. Let's look at the book. I brought it in.

4. **a.** Did you meet the people he works with?
   b. Did you meet the people who we work with?

5. **a.** Did you see the doctor I was waiting for?
   b. Did you see the doctor? I was waiting for her.

D2 **Building Relative Clauses Ending in Prepositions**

Work in small groups. Add the information that follows each sentence, using a relative clause ending in a preposition.

1. <u>A man</u> called me last night. (My sister works with him.)

   A man who my sister works with called me last night. OR
   A man that my sister works with called me last night. OR
   A man my sister works with called me last night.

   (I always talk to him at the supermarket.)
   (I went to high school with him.)
   (I used to live next door to him.)

2. <u>The movie</u> was great.
   (We went to the movie last night.)
   (You told us about the movie.)
   (I didn't want to go to it.)
   (You reported on it in class.)

3. Do you know <u>the doctor</u>?
   (Young-soo lives across from him.)
   (Eva fell in love with him.)
   (Luisa works for him.)
   (I was waiting for him.)

4. Have you read <u>the book</u>?
   (The whole class is interested in it.)
   (The teacher looked for it last week.)
   (Julie wrote about it.)
   (I brought in the book.)

5. Today we're going to read <u>the story</u>.
   (You've heard a lot about it.)
   (You listened to it on tape.)
   (I was working on it.)
   (The lecturer talked about it.)

A. Work in small groups. Read these situations. Use restrictive relative clauses ending in prepositions to distinguish between the people or things.

1. Bill needs to ask one of his neighbors to water his plants while he's away. He works with one of them, but he doesn't work with the other one.

   He decides to ask the person _(who/that) he works with._

2. You know that your friend was born in one small town, but that she grew up in a different small town.

   You ask her the name of the town _____

3. Martha and Stefan are in a store looking for a new desk chair. Martha is sitting on one of them, and Stefan is sitting on another one.

   A salesman recommends the one _____

4. Anna has called her doctor's office twice this week. She spoke to one nurse on Tuesday and another nurse on Wednesday.

   Today she asked for the nurse _____

5. Two movies are playing nearby. Martin has heard about one of them, but he hasn't heard about the other one.

   He decides to see the movie _____

6. Your friend borrowed two cassettes from the library. She listened to one of them last night, and she will listen to the other one tomorrow.

   She decided to return the one _____

7. Two players on the soccer team were carded for bad language. The coach talked to one right after the game, but didn't get a chance to talk to the other.

   Today he will talk to the player _____

8. I saw two new ads for teachers in the paper yesterday. I'm more interested in one, but I'm more qualified for the other.

   I think I'll apply for the one _____

B. Now rewrite items 1–4 from part A in very formal English. Use restrictive relative clauses beginning with prepositions.

1. He decides to ask the person with whom he works.

E   Reducing Relative Clauses

Examining Meaning and Use

Read the sentences and answer the question below. Then discuss your observations and read the Meaning and Use Notes to check them.

   a. Give the names of two professors who you have taken courses with.
   b. Give the names of two professors with whom you have taken courses.
   c. Give the names of two professors you have taken courses with.

Which sentence sounds the most formal?

Meaning and Use Notes

> **Reducing Relative Clauses**
>
> **1A** In both conversation and writing, object relative pronouns are often omitted from restrictive relative clauses. Remember, prepositions must go at the end of reduced relative clauses.
>
> *Conversation*
> The meal **Ø we ate yesterday evening** was delicious. I'm going to write down the name of the restaurant **Ø we went to**. You should try it.
>
> *Newspaper Article*
> The suspect **Ø the police caught this morning** remains in custody.
>
> ---
>
> **1B** When relative clauses with prepositions are <u>not</u> reduced, they sometimes sound very formal if the preposition precedes the relative pronoun.
>
> *Sounds Formal*
> Write the name and address of the hotel **in which you are staying**.
>
> *Doesn't Sound Formal*
> Write the name and address of the hotel **which you are staying in**.

(Continued on page 318)

> **Avoiding Repetition**

2 Object relative pronouns are often omitted when many restrictive relative clauses are used in one context. When two restrictive relative clauses occur next to each other, the first object relative pronoun is often omitted. The second is not.

Interview Question

What is the most important thing Ø her mother taught her ① **that she can teach her** ② **children**?

Textbook

One issue Ø the study mentioned ① **that researchers need to consider further** ② is the effect of changing climate.

E1) **Listening for Meaning and Use**   ► Notes 1A, 1B

🎧 Listen to each situation and check (✓) whether you think it has a formal or informal tone. Then listen again and think of an appropriate context for each situation.

	FORMAL	INFORMAL	CONTEXT
1.		✓	a conversation between 2 students
2.			
3.			
4.			
5.			
6.			

E2) **Rephrasing Formal Relative Clauses**   ► Notes 1A, 1B

Work with a partner. Take turns changing the formal tone of each sentence to a conversational tone. Use relative clauses ending in prepositions.

Application for Travel Insurance

1. List the names of the family members with whom you will be traveling.

   List the names of the family members who/that/Ø you'll be traveling with.

2. List the city from which you will depart and the city to which you will return.

3. List the name of the tour operator with whom you will be traveling.

_____

4. List the hotel in which you will be staying.

_____

5. List the code numbers of any extra tours for which you have registered.

_____

Job Application

1. Name two colleagues with whom you have worked closely.

_____

2. Name one supervisor for whom you have worked.

_____

3. List two different projects on which you have worked.

_____

4. Name two decisions in which you have played an important role.

_____

5. Name the job for which you would like to apply.

_____

E3 **Reducing Relative Clauses Ending in Prepositions** ▶ Notes 1A, 1B

Work with a partner. Take turns finding out information about each other. Match a noun from the left box with a verb + preposition from the right box to form reduced relative clauses. Use appropriate tenses.

A: *Name a restaurant you've eaten at recently.*
B: *The Noodle House. It's really good. Now it's your turn. Name a sport. . . .*

NOUN		VERB + PREPOSITION	
a restaurant	a friend	vote for	disagree with
a sport	a CD	eat at	rely on
a politician	a relative	listen to	work on
an assignment	a magazine	participate in	subscribe to

Your company has sent you to another country for a long training program. You have been there for a week. Write an e-mail message to your family asking them to send five different items that you left at home. Describe the items carefully using relative clauses. Tell your family why you need them.

It's warm here during the day, but it gets cool at night. The jacket I brought is not warm enough. Please send the one that you gave me for my birthday. It's hanging in my closet next to ...

Vocabulary Notes

When and Where in Relative Clauses

Where and *when* can replace object relative pronouns to introduce relative clauses.

Where is used to express location. It can modify a noun that refers to a place. It can replace *which, that,* or Ø and the prepositions *in* or *at*.

That's <u>the building</u> **where** my father lives. = That's <u>the building</u> **in which** my father lives.
= That's <u>the building</u> **that/Ø** my father lives **in**.

When is used to express time. It can replace *that,* Ø, or *during which* to refer to a period of time.

<u>The year</u> **when** I lived in Vancouver was = <u>The year</u> **that/Ø/during which** I lived in
very special.   Vancouver was very special.

E5 **Using *Where, When,* and Object Relative Pronouns**

A. Complete the sentences below. Use *where, when, that, which, in which,* or Ø to introduce the relative clauses. More than one answer is possible. Discuss which alternatives you prefer in small groups.

Baseball, _____*which*_____ is the "national pastime" of the United States,
                    1
is also popular in the Dominican Republic. This small country is a place

_____ a large number of famous major-league baseball players
              2
have been born. In fact, one of its small cities, San Pedro de Macoris, is described

as the city _____ more players have been born than anywhere else
                        3
in the world. For example, 1998 was the year _____ eight of the
                                                          4
62 major-league Dominicans were from the area _____ is referred
                                                                      5
to simply as San Pedro.

Baseball star Sammy Sosa is one of the most-loved native sons of San Pedro. Every time he hits a home run, he touches two fingers to his mouth to blow a kiss to the city _____ _____ his family still lives. The kisses, _____ are for his mother, are also felt by all
$\underset{6}{}$
$\underset{7}{}$

125,000 citizens of his beloved city. Sosa has never forgotten the period of his life _____ he lived in San Pedro.
$\underset{8}{}$

B. Write three sentences each about a place and a time from your past. Use *where* and *when* to introduce a relative clause in each sentence.

The house where I grew up was very small for my big family.
Dinnertime, when all of us tried to eat together, was chaotic.

C. Exchange papers with a partner. Pick two of your partner's sentences to rewrite using object relative pronouns (*who, that, which, Ø*). Make any necessary changes.

The house (that) I grew up in was very small for my big family.
Dinnertime, during which all of us tried to eat together, was chaotic.

Combining Form, Meaning, and Use

F1 Thinking About Meaning and Use

Read each sentence and the statements that follow. Write *T* if the statement is true or *F* if it is false. Then discuss your answers in small groups.

1. My brother, who I resemble, lives in Jordan.

   __F__ **a.** I live in Jordan.

   _____ **b.** I resemble my brother.

2. The man my sister works with has a sailboat.

   _____ **a.** My sister has a sailboat.

   _____ **b.** My sister works on a sailboat.

3. The team I wanted to win lost in the semifinals.

   _____ **a.** The team lost.

   _____ **b.** I wanted to win.

4. Andrei still loves playing hockey, which he learned when he was five.

   _____ **a.** Andrei is five years old.

   _____ **b.** Andrei plays hockey.

5. I looked at some equipment that my neighbors were selling at a garage sale.

   _____ **a.** I sold some equipment at a garage sale.

   _____ **b.** My neighbors looked at some equipment at a garage sale.

6. Ms. Wang wrote the book I heard about on a radio show.

   _____ **a.** I listened to a radio show.

   _____ **b.** Ms. Wang heard about a book.

7. The professor assigned a book in which the history of baseball is discussed.

   _____ **a.** The professor gave an assignment.

   _____ **b.** The professor discussed the history of baseball.

8. Charlotte, who I once worked for, took over the company.

   _____ **a.** I once worked for Charlotte.

   _____ **b.** Charlotte took over the company.

F2 Editing

Find the errors in these paragraphs and correct them.

Sisleide Lima do Amor, ~~which~~ *who* soccer fans know as Sissi, was not discouraged as a child by the boys who wouldn't let her play the game with which she loved most. Eventually, she got her way on the streets of Salvador, Brazil, because the soccer ball that the boys wanted to play with it was hers. Still, she often ran home with her ball after she grew frustrated with the negative attitudes that the boys displayed. Sissi had learned to play soccer by practicing with all kinds of objects what she found around the house. These included rolled-up socks, oranges, bottle caps, and the heads of dolls that her parents had given her them. It was her father who finally decided that she needed a soccer ball to keep her from destroying her dolls.

Sissi showed her admiration for Brazil's male soccer heroes by choosing the jersey number who Romario wears and by shaving her head to resemble the style in which Ronaldo has made famous. During the Women's World Cup, Sissi displayed the type of skill fans will long remember. Left-footed Sissi scored seven goals for her team, including a goal that she kicked in with her weaker right foot. According to Sissi, her seventh goal is the one about which she keeps thinking about. During a 3-3 tie, she kicked the ball into a spot the goalkeeper couldn't reach it, and her team's 4-3 victory put them into the semifinals. Most fans would agree that it is Sissi's style of playing that has given her the kind of world recognition who she deserves.

Beyond the Classroom

Searching for Authentic Examples

Find examples of English grammar in everyday life. Choose one of the tasks below. Be prepared to discuss your findings.

A. Look in newspaper or magazine ads. Write down five examples of relative clauses with object relative pronouns and bring them to class. Look for some examples with prepositions, too. Why do you think the relative pronouns were kept or omitted?

B. Look in a textbook. Write down three examples of restrictive relative clauses and three examples of nonrestrictive relative clauses, and bring them to class. Look for examples with object relative pronouns. Why do you think the relative clauses were used? Why were the relative pronouns kept or omitted?

C. Watch the news or another TV program. Listen for three examples of relative clauses with object relative pronouns and write them down. Are your examples restrictive or nonrestrictive? Are they full or reduced? Did you hear any with prepositions?

Speaking

In small groups, follow these steps to discuss athletic opportunities for women in your native country.

1. On your own, think about the athletic opportunities for women in your country. What sports do women play? How popular are these sports among women? among men? among children? Are there any female role models in athletics? Write down your ideas.

2. With your group, discuss the differences in athletic opportunities for women in different countries. What sports are the most popular for women? What changes have there been in recent years? Are there any problems for women athletes? How does women's athletics compare with men's athletics?

3. Prepare a small summary of your group's discussion and choose one person to present it to the class. Ask your classmates to share their opinions with you.

Conditionals

Real Conditionals, Unreal Conditionals, and Wishes

A Reflections on Life

A1 Before You Read

Discuss these questions.

Do you ever make wishes? What do you wish for? Discuss your wishes and decide whether it is possible to achieve them.

A2 Read

Read these different perspectives on life. Which selection best reflects your outlook on life?

CHINESE PROVERB

If there is light in the soul,
there will be beauty in the person.

If there is beauty in the person,
there will be harmony in the house.

If there is harmony in the house,
there will be order in the nation.

If there is order in the nation,
there will be peace in the world.

—Anonymous

1.

If I Had My Life to Live Over

I'd dare to make more mistakes next time.
I'd relax, I would limber up. I would be
sillier than I have been this trip. I would
take fewer things seriously. I would take
5 more chances. I would climb more
mountains and swim more rivers. I would
eat more ice cream and fewer beans. I
would perhaps have more actual troubles,
but I'd have fewer imaginary ones.

10 You see, I'm one of those people who lives
sensibly and sanely hour after hour, day
after day. Oh, I've had my moments, and
if I had it to do over again, I'd have more of
them. In fact, I'd try to have nothing else.

15 If I had my life to live over, I would start
barefoot earlier in the spring and stay that
way later in the fall. I would go to more
dances. I would ride more merry-go-
rounds. I would pick more daisies.

—Nadine Stair (85-year-old woman)

2.

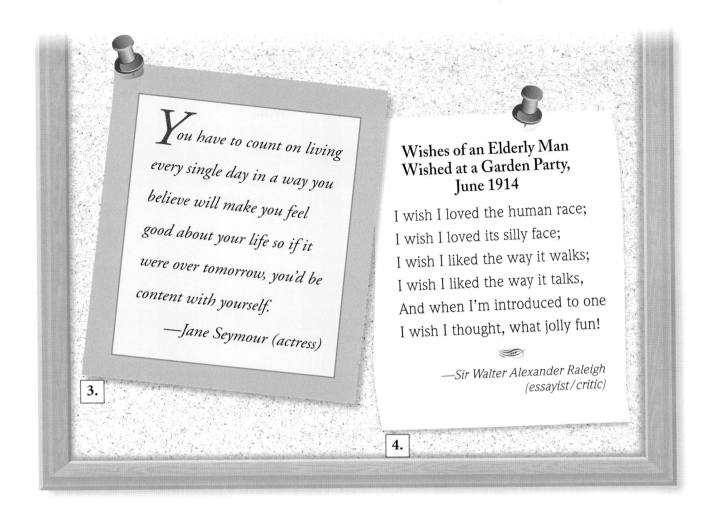

*Y*ou have to count on living every single day in a way you believe will make you feel good about your life so if it were over tomorrow, you'd be content with yourself.

—*Jane Seymour (actress)*

3.

Wishes of an Elderly Man Wished at a Garden Party, June 1914

I wish I loved the human race;
I wish I loved its silly face;
I wish I liked the way it walks;
I wish I liked the way it talks,
And when I'm introduced to one
I wish I thought, what jolly fun!

—*Sir Walter Alexander Raleigh (essayist/critic)*

4.

---

harmony: agreement, peaceful cooperation
jolly: cheerful, happy

limber up: to make the body more flexible, to stretch the muscles so that they move easily

A3 After You Read

Match each reading selection on the left with its main idea on the right.

_d_ **1.** Chinese proverb

a. The writer regrets not taking advantage of more of the joys in life.

_____ **2.** *If I Had My Life to Live Over*

b. The writer doesn't like people very much.

_____ **3.** Quotation by Jane Seymour

c. It is important to be satisfied with the kind of life you lead.

_____ **4.** *Wishes of an Elderly Man*

d. There is a logical connection between the individual and the rest of the world.

B Real Conditionals, Unreal Conditionals, and Wishes

Examining Form

Look back at the selections on pages 328–329 and complete the tasks below. Then discuss your observations and read the Form charts to check them.

1. An example of the simple present in an *if* clause is underlined in selection 1. Find three more examples.

2. Find two sentences that show the simple past in an *if* clause in selections 2 and 3. What verb form do you find in each main clause?

3. Look at the sentences that contain *wish* in selection 4. What is the tense of *wish*? What verb form is used in each clause that follows *wish*?

Present and Future Real Conditionals

┌── IF CLAUSE ──┐		┌── MAIN CLAUSE ──┐
IF + SIMPLE PRESENT	*(THEN)*	SIMPLE PRESENT
If I'm on time,	(then)	**I walk** to work.
IF + SIMPLE PRESENT	*(THEN)*	FUTURE
If it's not too late,	(then)	**I'll walk** to work. **I'm going to walk** to work.
IF + SIMPLE PRESENT	*(THEN)*	MODAL
If I leave on time,	(then)	**I may walk** to work.
IF + SIMPLE PRESENT	*(THEN)*	IMPERATIVE
If you have time,	(then)	**walk** with me.

Present and Future Unreal Conditionals

┌── IF CLAUSE ──┐		┌── MAIN CLAUSE ──┐
IF + SIMPLE PAST	*(THEN)*	*WOULD* + VERB
If I had the time,	(then)	**I would walk** to work. **I'd walk** to work.
IF + SIMPLE PAST	*(THEN)*	*COULD* + VERB
If I left on time,	(then)	**I could walk** to work.
IF + SIMPLE PAST	*(THEN)*	*MIGHT* + VERB
If I left on time,	(then)	**I might walk** to work.

Real and Unreal Conditionals

- Conditional sentences have a dependent *if* clause and a main clause.
- When the *if* clause comes first, it is followed by a comma. *Then* is usually omitted before the main clause, but it is always implied.

    If I'm on time, (then) **I walk** to work.   **If I had** the time, (then) **I'd walk** to work.

- When the main clause is first, there is no comma and *then* is not used. The meaning is the same.

   I walk to work **if I'm** on time.   **I'd walk** to work **if I had** the time.

- In conditional sentences, either clause or both clauses can be negative.

   If I'm not on time, **I take** the bus.   **If I'm not** on time, **I won't walk** to work.

- Questions with conditionals are formed by putting the main clause in question word order.

   If it's not too late, **are you going to walk** to work?

   If you had the time, **would you walk** to work?

Real Conditionals

- In real conditionals, the verb in the *if* clause is in the present, even if it has future meaning.

   If you go tomorrow, **call** me.

- Real conditionals can also be formed with the present continuous in the *if* clause.

   If you're going tomorrow, **call me**.   **If it's raining, I might take** the bus.

Unreal Conditionals

- When an unreal conditional *if* clause contains the verb *be,* use *were* for all subjects.

   If I were on time, **I'd walk** to work.

- Unreal conditionals can also be formed with the past continuous in the *if* clause.

   If I were leaving now, **I might walk** to work.

- See Appendix 14 for contractions with *would.*

Wishes About the Present and Future	
⌐ *WISH* CLAUSE ⌐	⌐——————— *THAT* CLAUSE ———————
SIMPLE PRESENT	(*THAT* +) PAST FORM
I **wish**	(that) I **were** older. (that) I **didn't have** a cold. (that) you **were going** to the wedding. (that) you**'d help** me. (that) you **could come** with me.

- In sentences with *wish,* the *wish* clause is the main clause. The *that* clause is the dependent clause.
- In *that* clauses with the verb *be, were* is used for all subjects.
- *Could* and *would* (the simple past of *can* and *will*) are often used in the *that* clause.
- *That* is often omitted after *wish,* but it is always implied.
- Short answers with *wish* consist of a subject + *wish* clause + subject + *were/did.*

   A: Are you ready yet?   A: Does he have any money?

   B: No, **I wish I were**.   B: No, but **I wish he did**.

Vera and Jose are engaged, but they attend universities 3,000 miles apart. Listen to some sentences from their phone conversation. Choose the verb forms that you hear.

1. **a.** could spend
   b. spent

2. **a.** are married
   b. were married

3. **a.** will finish
   b. finish

4. **a.** 'll move
   b. 'd move

5. **a.** attended
   b. would attend

6. **a.** wouldn't matter
   b. doesn't matter

7. **a.** didn't want
   b. don't want

8. **a.** do you want
   b. would you want

B2 Working on Real and Unreal Conditionals

A. Work in small groups. Start a real conditional sentence chain with *If the teacher cancels class,* and finish it with a result clause. Use the end of the last person's sentence to begin your own sentence.

A: If the teacher cancels class, there will be more time to study.
B: If there's more time to study, we'll do better on the exam.
C: If we do better on the exam, . . .

B. Now start an unreal conditional chain with *If I had the day off, I'd. . . .* As before, use the end of the last person's sentence to begin your own sentence.

A: If I had the day off, I'd go shopping.
B: If I went shopping, I'd spend a lot of money.
C: If I spent a lot of money, I'd feel bad the next day.

B3 Building Conditional and *Wish* Sentences

Build as many meaningful sentences as possible. Use an item from each column or from two columns only. Punctuate your sentences correctly.

If I were ready, I'd leave.

if I wish	I were ready she is sick they were driving	I'd leave call for help he'll take over you could come later

A. Work with a partner. Complete these conversations using the appropriate form of the verbs. Add *would* when necessary. Then practice the conversations.

1. **A:** I wish I ____had____ (have) more money to spend.
      ₁

   B: If you _____ (do), you _____ (buy) things you don't need.
            ₂   ₃

2. **A:** I wish this place _____ (be/not) so crowded. If there
                              ₁

   _____ (be) fewer people, we _____ (get) better service.
   ₂   ₃

   B: I know. I wish we _____ (can leave), but it's too late to go anywhere else.
                          ₄

3. **A:** Do you ever wish you _____ (have) a different job?
                              ₁

   B: Yes, quite often. If I _____ (have) a different job, I _____
                              ₂   ₃

   (have) more free time.

4. **A:** Can you help me fix my car?

   B: I wish I _____ (can), but I'm late. If I _____ (have/not)
                  ₁   ₂

   an appointment at three, I _____ (stay) to help.
                              ₃

B. Write four wishes. Then write a second sentence explaining each one with a related unreal conditional.

I wish it weren't so hot. If it weren't so hot, we could go for a walk.

A. Complete these sentences with your own ideas. Use an appropriate verb form in the *if* clause or the main clause.

1. If I missed the bus, I'd have to walk to work. _____

2. If I'm late for an appointment, _____

3. If I were sick, _____

4. I'm embarrassed if _____

5. I'd quit my job if _____

6. I'll buy a new computer if _____

B. Now write two real and two unreal *if* clauses or main clauses on a separate sheet of paper. Give them to a classmate to complete.

Informally Speaking

Using *Was*

 Look at the cartoon and listen to the conversation. How is each underlined form in the cartoon different from what you hear?

Speech bubble (woman trying on coat): I need a jacket, but nothing fits me. I wish I <u>were</u> taller.

Speech bubble (woman in striped dress): If it <u>were</u> earlier, we could go to another store. Let's do that tomorrow.

In informal speech, *was* is often used instead of *were* for unreal conditionals and wishes with *I, he, she,* and *it.*

STANDARD FORM	WHAT YOU MIGHT HEAR
If I **weren't** so busy, I'd go out tonight.	"If I wasn't so busy, I'd go out tonight."
I wish I **weren't** so busy.	"I wish I wasn't so busy."

B6 Understanding Informal Speech

Listen and write the standard form of the words you hear.

1. If _____ I weren't so tired _____, I'd go out for a cup of coffee with you.

2. What would you do if it _____ to take the bus?

3. I wish my boss _____.

4. If he _____, we could leave now.

5. She'd tell you if she _____ at you.

6. Don't you wish he _____ with us?

Real Conditionals

Examining Meaning and Use

Read the sentences and answer the questions below. Then discuss your observations and read the Meaning and Use Notes to check them.

a. If two hydrogen atoms combine with one oxygen atom, they form a water molecule.
b. If you help me, I'll help you.
c. If you finish the test early, turn over your paper.
d. If you don't hurry, you'll miss the train.

Which real conditional sentence do you think is a promise? a statement of fact? a warning? an instruction to do something?

Meaning and Use Notes

Overview of Real Conditionals

1 In real conditional sentences, the *if* clause and main clause have a cause-and-effect relationship. The *if* clause introduces a possible condition or event (it may or may not happen). The main clause expresses a possible result (what happens or may happen after the *if* clause).

—— POSSIBLE CONDITION ——⌐ ⌐ POSSIBLE RESULT ⌐

If she finds another apartment, she'll move.
  (She may find an apartment. Under those circumstances, she'll move. Otherwise, she won't.)

Expressing Certainty

2A Some conditionals are used to express results that the speaker is certain of. These sentences are sometimes called factual conditionals; the speaker thinks the results will occur whenever the condition in the *if* clause is true.

If you lose your credit card, the bank replaces it in a day.
  (This is a fact you are certain of.)

(Continued on page 336)

2B When the result clause is in the simple present, real conditionals can express the kinds of routines and habits, facts, or general truths usually found in simple present sentences.

Routines and Habits

If I **take** the 8:05 train, I **get** to work at 8:50.

If I **drive**, I **get** to work earlier.

Facts or General Truths

If air **is heated**, it **rises**.

If you **overcook** fish, it **dries out**.

2C Facts or general truths can also be expressed with the *will* future.

Facts or General Truths

If air **is heated**, it **will rise**.

If you **overcook** fish, it **will dry out**.

Expressing Predictions and Promises

3 When the result clause is in a future form, real conditionals can express predictions with varying degrees of certainty. In the first person, they can also express promises.

Predictions

If it **rains** tonight, the game **may be canceled**.

If it **rains** tonight, the game **will be canceled**.

Promises

If you **come over** tomorrow, **I'll help** you.

Expressing Advice, Warnings, and Instructions

4 Real conditionals are often used to give advice, warnings, and instructions. The result clause may use the imperative, a modal, or the future.

Advice

If your **throat** hurts, **try** salt water.

If your **throat** hurts, you **should try** salt water.

If you **gargle** with salt water, you**'ll get** immediate relief.

Warnings

If you **don't get** enough sleep, you**'ll get** sick.

Instructions

If the printer **runs out** of paper, **refill** it immediately.

C1 Listening for Meaning and Use

🎧 Listen to these sentences. How is each conditional sentence used? Check (✓) the correct column.

	FACTS OR GENERAL TRUTHS	ADVICE, WARNINGS, INSTRUCTIONS	PROMISES
1.		✓	
2.			
3.			
4.			
5.			
6.			
7.			
8.			

C2 Describing Factual Conditions

► Notes 2A–2C

Work with a partner and read this chart about fees at a ski resort. Use factual conditional sentences to describe the different conditions for membership and discounts.

If you're between 7 and 15, it costs $50 to buy a full-season pass.
If you're a member, you get a 15 percent discount on equipment rentals.

WINTER SEASON
Membership Prices (per person)

Age	Full-Season Pass	Half-Season Pass
7–15*	$50	$30
16 & up	$75	$45

*Children 6 and under ski free when accompanied by an adult ticket holder.

Members receive the following year-round:
- 15% discount on equipment rentals
- Two free days of skiing: once before December 23, once after March 6 (One guest allowed each time)

On Membership Appreciation Days (dates to be announced):
- 50% discount on lift tickets for members
- Free lift ticket for one guest per member

C3 Making Promises ► Note 3

Work with a partner. Imagine you are a candidate running for mayor.
Make promises using the words and phrases in real conditional sentences.

1. create jobs

   If I am elected mayor, I will create jobs. OR
   If you vote for me, I will create jobs. OR
   If I become mayor, I will create jobs.

2. improve education

3. build new schools

4. reduce crime

5. hire more police

6. expand health care

7. open more hospitals

8. cut taxes

9. employ more women

10. employ more minorities

C4 Rephrasing Advice with Conditional Sentences ► Note 4

Work in small groups. Read these statements of advice and think of different ways
to rephrase them using real conditional sentences. Try to use the future, modals, or
the imperative in your different result clauses.

1. Turn down your thermostat at night. You won't use so much fuel.

   If you turn down your thermostat at night, you won't use so much fuel.
   *If you don't want to use so much fuel, (you should) turn down your thermostat
       at night.*

2. Study hard, and you won't fail the test.

3. Make calls at night, and your telephone bill won't be so high.

4. Don't eat so much. You won't get indigestion.

5. Read a book for a while. You'll fall asleep easily.

6. Call the doctor, and you'll get some good advice.

Vocabulary Notes

If and Unless

Sentences with *unless* in the dependent clause often have the same meaning as sentences with negative *if* clauses.

UNLESS	IF
Unless the cab **comes** at three, you won't make it to the airport.	**If** the cab **doesn't come** at three, you won't make it to the airport.
Unless you **finish** your work, we'll lose the account.	**If** you **don't finish** your work, we'll lose the account.

C5 Giving Warnings with *If* and *Unless* Clauses

A. Complete these health warnings. Use *will* or *won't* in the result clause.

1. If you don't eat more vegetables, _you won't have a balanced diet._

2. _____ if you eat too much fat.

3. If you go to bed too late, _____

4. If you don't get enough calcium, _____

5. If you don't exercise, _____

B. Complete these safety warnings by writing negative conditions in the *if* clauses that could lead to the harmful results.

1. You'll get into an accident if _you don't drive more carefully._

2. If _____, you'll slip.

3. You'll damage your eyes if _____

4. If _____, you'll get sick.

5. You'll start a fire if _____

C. Look at the warnings your partner wrote in part B. Rewrite the warnings that can be rephrased using *unless* instead of *if*.

You'll get into an accident unless you drive more carefully.

Unreal Conditionals

Examining Meaning and Use

Read the sentences and answer the questions below. Then discuss your observations and read the Meaning and Use Notes to check them.

1a. If my plane is late, I'll miss the meeting.
1b. If my plane were late, I'd miss the meeting.

2a. If I were you, I'd leave now.
2b. You should leave now.

1. Compare 1a and 1b. Which one expresses something that is more likely to happen? Which one expresses something that is probably imaginary?

2. Compare 2a and 2b. Which sentence sounds more direct? Which one seems more indirect?

Meaning and Use Notes

> ### Unreal Conditionals
>
> **1A** Unreal conditional sentences express imaginary situations. The *if* clause introduces the imaginary condition or event (it is not true at the present time). The main clause expresses the imaginary result (what would or could happen after the *if* clause).
>
>   ——— IMAGINARY CONDITION ———   ——— IMAGINARY RESULT ———
>
> **If** she **found** another apartment, she **would move**.
> (She hasn't found an apartment, so she isn't moving.)
>
> ---
>
> **1B** In the *if* clause, the simple past or past continuous does not indicate past time; it indicates that the situation is unreal. In the result clause, *would, could/would be able to,* or *might* also indicate that the result is unreal.
>
> **If I had** a problem, **I'd ask** for your help. (I don't have a problem right now, so I don't need help.)
>
> **If I had** the money, **I could buy** a new car. (Right now I don't have the money, so I can't buy a new car.)
>
> **If we were staying in Moscow, we'd be able to visit** them. (We're not staying in Moscow, so we can't visit them.)

1C *Would* in the result clause expresses more certainty than *could* or *might* about the imaginary results. *Could* or *might* indicates one of several possible outcomes.

If I **had** the money, I **would buy** a new car. (*Would* expresses more certainty about the imaginary outcome.)

If I **had** the money, I **might buy** a new car. (*Might* expresses one imaginary outcome. There are other possible outcomes.)

Giving Advice and Opinions

2 Unreal conditionals beginning with *If I were you* can be used as an indirect way of giving advice. Unreal conditionals sound softer than modals like *should* or *ought to*.

Advice with Unreal Conditionals
If I **were** you, I**'d** speak to the instructor.

Advice with Modals
You **should** speak to the instructor.

Asking Permission

3 Unreal conditionals with *would you mind, would it bother you,* or *would it be OK* can be used to ask for permission. Notice that a negative response to the first two questions means you are giving permission.

Permission with Unreal Conditionals
A: **Would you mind if I opened** the window?
B: **No,** go right ahead.

A: **Would it bother you if I opened** the window?
B: **No,** not at all.

A: **Would it be OK if I opened** the window?
B: **Yes,** go ahead.

Permission with Modals
A: **May I open** the window?
B: **Yes,** go right ahead.

D1 **Listening for Meaning and Use**   ▶ Notes 1A–1C, 2, 3

Listen and choose the best response.

1. **a.** Sure, it would be a pleasure.
   b. No, not at all.

2. **a.** I took a taxi.
   b. I'll call you.

3. **a.** I might.
   b. I did.

4. **a.** I'll have dinner with Cleopatra.
   b. I'd choose John F. Kennedy.

5. **a.** I would.
   b. Maybe.

6. **a.** No, go right ahead.
   b. Yes, if no one is using it.

A. Complete these unreal conditionals. Try to think of unusual or interesting situations that people might like to talk about. Then take turns asking and answering the questions with a partner.

1. What would you do if _you found a million dollars?_____

   I'd probably report it to the police and hope to get a reward.

2. What would you say if _____

3. How would you feel if _____

4. Where would you go if _____

5. Who would you invite if _____

6. Who would you ask for help if _____

B. Ask the class one of your questions.

D3 **Giving Advice with** *If I Were You* ► Notes 1A–1C

Work in small groups. Give advice with *If I were you, I'd* . . . or *If I were you, I wouldn't.* . . . Brainstorm different solutions for each problem.

1. There's a big mistake on my electric bill.

   If I were you, I wouldn't ignore it.
   If I were you, I'd call the electric company and explain the situation.

2. My landlord doesn't repair things when I ask him to.

3. I accepted two invitations to go out, and now I don't know what to do.

4. I get a lot of phone calls, but most of them are wrong numbers.

5. My boss isn't very nice to me.

6. I tried to put a quarter into a parking meter, but the quarter got stuck. When I returned to my car, there was a parking ticket on my windshield.

7. I want to buy a computer, but I don't know much about them.

8. I'm not doing very well in my English class.

D4) Asking Permission

Work with a partner. Read each situation and take turns asking for permission in at least two different ways. Use *Would you mind if . . .* , *Would it bother you if . . .* , or *Would it be OK if . . .* , and respond with appropriate positive or negative answers.

1. You're supposed to pick your friend up at eight o'clock, but you'd prefer to pick her up earlier.

   A: *Would you mind if I picked you up earlier?*
   B: *No, not at all.*

2. You want to listen to the news while your roommate is studying. You don't want to disturb him.

3. You think it's too hot in the classroom. You want to open the window.

4. Your friend has an interesting book. You want to borrow it.

Beyond the Sentence

Omitting *If* Clauses

When a single condition has many results, the *if* clause is usually stated only once. The imaginary results are expressed in new sentences with *would*.

> **If I were the boss,** I <u>would</u> try to be considerate of my employees' needs to balance work and family. I <u>would</u> give them more time off for family responsibilities. I <u>would</u> even encourage my employees to volunteer in their children's schools during work hours. I <u>would</u> . . .

D5) Using Conditionals with Many Results

A. If you could be anyone in the world for one day, who would you like to be? Make a list of things you would do if you were that person.

B. Write a paragraph describing what you would do if you were the person you chose in part A. Start your paragraph with *If I were . . . , I'd . . . .* Continue expressing imaginary results using sentences with *would*. Do not use any more *if* clauses in your paragraph.

> If I were Bill Gates for one day, I'd fly on one of my private jets to a beautiful tropical paradise. I'd spend the day swimming, relaxing, and having fun with my family. I'd have the finest chefs prepare all of my favorite foods, and . . .

Wishes

Examining Meaning and Use

Read the sentences and answer the questions below. Then discuss your observations and read the Meaning and Use Notes to check them.

1a. I wish you'd leave work early tomorrow and come to the picnic.

1b. I wish I were wearing a sweater. It's cold.

2a. I wish you would clean up your room more often.

2b. I wish I could help you, but I don't know the answer.

1. Look at sentences 1a and 1b. Which sentence is a wish about the present? Which is a wish about the future?

2. Look at sentences 2a and 2b. Which expresses a complaint? Which expresses a regret?

Meaning and Use Notes

> **Making Wishes**
>
> **1** Use *wish* to express a desire for something that does not exist now. It is a desire to change a real situation into an unreal or impossible one. As in unreal conditional sentences, the past form does not indicate past time; it indicates that the situation is unreal. The past form can be simple past, past continuous, *could,* or *would.*
>
> *Wishes About the Present*
> I live in an apartment, but I **wish** I **lived** in a house.
> I **wish** I **were living** in Chicago.
> I **wish** I **could swim,** but I can't.
>
> *Wishes About the Future*
> I **wish** you **would come** with me tonight.
> I **wish** you **were coming** with me tonight.
> I **wish you could come** with me tonight.

2A Sometimes *wish* sentences with *would* express complaints, especially when you want something to change but think it probably won't.

I **wish** it **would stop** raining. We can't go anywhere in this weather.
I **wish** you **wouldn't leave** the car windows open.

2B *Wish* sentences often express regret about a current situation.

A: Can you help me this afternoon?
B: No, I'm sorry. I **wish** I **could**, but I have a doctor's appointment.

Using *If Only*

3 Sentences with *if only* often have a similar meaning to sentences with *wish*, but they are more emphatic. *If only* sentences focus on the desire to change a negative situation. Unlike other *if* conditionals, an *if only* clause is often used alone without a result clause.

If Only	*Wish*
If only I **had** a car!	I **wish** I **had** a car.
If only I **felt** better, then I'd go out.	I **wish** I **felt** better. Perhaps I'd go out.
If only it **would stop** raining.	I **wish** it **would stop** raining.

E1 **Listening for Meaning and Use** ► Note 1

Listen to each situation and check (✓) whether the item exists or doesn't exist.

		EXISTS	DOESN'T EXIST
1.	a cold	✓	
2.	pictures		
3.	free time		
4.	a car		
5.	a safety lock		
6.	a limit		
7.	a credit card		
8.	your guitar		

E2 **Making Wishes About the Present** ► Note 1

Work in small groups. Take turns making up as many wishes as possible for each situation. Explain your wishes with unreal conditional sentences.

1. Your apartment is too small.

    I wish I had more space. If I had more space, I'd get a pet.
    I wish I could move. If I moved, I'd get a much bigger apartment.

2. You're broke. You have no money.

3. Your new teacher is boring.

4. You're very busy.

5. You live in a big city.

6. You drive to work during rush hour.

7. You need more exercise.

8. You're lost in the woods.

E3 **Making Wishes About the Future** ► Notes 1, 3

Work with a partner. Take turns expressing your wishes for the future by using *wish* and *if only* sentences with *would*.

1. You are waiting to receive your grades in the mail. The mail is late.

    I wish the mail would come!
    If only the mail would come!

2. You want your sister to take better care of herself, but you're afraid that she won't.

3. You're afraid to go out alone at night, but your best friend is always busy. You want her to go out with you.

4. You think that your father is working too hard. You want him to take a vacation.

5. The weather is very bad. Your friend dropped by for a few minutes. You want him to stay until the weather improves, but he seems to be in a hurry.

6. Your brother has just announced that he wants to quit school and go back home. You want him to stay in college.

E4 **Complaining with *Wish* and *If Only* Sentences** ► Notes 2A, 3

Work with a partner. Imagine you are very unhappy with your college roommate for the reasons listed below. Complain about your roommate's bad habits using *wish* and *if only* sentences with *would* or *wouldn't*.

1. makes a lot of noise in the morning

   I wish he wouldn't make so much noise in the morning. OR
   I wish he would be quieter in the morning. OR
   If only he wouldn't make so much noise!

2. uses up all the hot water in the shower

3. stays in the bathroom a long time

4. doesn't write down phone messages

5. doesn't clean up the kitchen

6. talks on the phone for hours

E5 **Expressing Regret with *Wish* Sentences** ► Note 2B

Work with a partner. Complete these conversations with expressions of regret. Use the simple past and then give a reason with *but*, explaining the real situation. Then practice the conversations, switching roles.

1. **Roommate A:** Could you please help me with this?
   Roommate B: I'm sorry, I can't. I wish <u>I could, but I have to leave right now.</u>

2. **Customer:** Do you have any more wallets?
   Salesclerk: No, I'm sorry. I wish _____

3. **Student A:** Can you lend me yesterday's notes?
   Student B: Well, I wish _____

4. **Friend A:** Do you have any free time later this afternoon?
   Friend B: No, I wish _____

5. **Child:** Are there any more cookies left?
   Parent: No, I wish _____

6. **Friend A:** Is it warm outside this morning?
   Friend B: No, I wish _____

Combining Form, Meaning, and Use

F1 Thinking About Meaning and Use

Read each situation and the statements that follow. Write *T* if the statement is true or *F* if it is false. Then discuss your answers in small groups.

1. We'd leave if it stopped raining.

   __F__ **a.** We left.

   _____ **b.** It's raining.

2. I'd go to the meeting if I weren't so busy.

   _____ **a.** I'm not very busy.

   _____ **b.** I'm going to the meeting.

3. Unless I call, I'll be home at six.

   _____ **a.** I might call.

   _____ **b.** I plan to be home at six.

4. If it weren't on sale, I couldn't afford it.

   _____ **a.** It's on sale.

   _____ **b.** I can't afford it.

5. If the light flashes, the bell rings five seconds later.

   _____ **a.** The bell won't ring until the light flashes.

   _____ **b.** The light flashes before the bell rings.

6. I wish I didn't have to take the exam.

   _____ **a.** I've taken the exam.

   _____ **b.** I don't have a choice.

7. If you lived in that neighborhood, you'd know Joseph Taylor.

   _____ **a.** You know Joseph Taylor.

   _____ **b.** You don't live in that neighborhood.

8. If only you spoke more slowly, then I'd understand you better.

_____ **a.** You speak slowly.

_____ **b.** I understand you very well.

Find the errors in this text and correct them.

                would you
What you would do if there were an earthquake in your area? Would you know

what to do? Some people are too frightened to find out about safety precautions. They

wish they live somewhere else. If you could, won't you rather find out what to do in

advance? Here is some advice about what to do before, during, and after an

earthquake.

1. If you don't have a box of emergency equipment and supplies, you will need to prepare one in advance.

2. If you would be indoors during an earthquake, you should stay away from windows, bookcases, and shelves.

3. If it were possible, you should turn off the gas, water, and electricity.

4. If you will be able, stand in a doorway or get under a sturdy desk or table.

5. After the earthquake, don't walk around unless you are not wearing shoes to protect your feet from broken glass.

Don't wait. Don't wish you are prepared. Be prepared!

Beyond the Classroom

Searching for Authentic Examples

Find examples of English grammar in everyday life. Choose one of the tasks below. Be prepared to discuss your findings.

A. Find three or four advertisements in a newspaper or magazine that use real conditionals, unreal conditionals, or wishes. Bring the ads to class. Why do you think each of these forms is used in your ads? How do you think they help to make the ads effective?

B. Look in a science textbook. Write down five examples of factual conditionals and bring them to class. Why do you think each one is used?

C. Listen to native-speaker conversations or watch a television show or movie. Listen for and write down examples of wishes, regrets, complaints, and promises expressed by real and unreal conditionals and *wish* sentences, and bring them to class. Why do you think these forms were used? Did you hear any uses of conversational *was* instead of *were*?

Writing

In small groups, follow these steps to write a one-page public service ad titled "Ten Home Safety Tips." Your ad will appear in newspapers and magazines, and it will also be used as a poster.

1. Brainstorm different things that people can do to be safe at home, such as installing smoke alarms or child-proof electrical outlets. Write down the ten most useful and important ideas.

2. Use your notes to write a first draft of your ad. Think of interesting ways to use unreal conditionals and wishes to attract attention and make people think. Use factual conditionals to express some of your safety tips.

3. Read over your work carefully and circle grammar, spelling, and punctuation errors. Pay particular attention to the verb forms that you used in your real and unreal conditional sentences. Work with your group to decide how to fix your errors. Then rewrite your draft with the changes that you and your group discussed.

Past Unreal Conditionals and Past Wishes

A   The Ifs of History

Discuss these questions.

Think of a decision that you regret. What should you have done differently? Think of a decision that you have never regretted. Why not?

Read this magazine article to find out about some possible alternatives to actual historical events. Do you agree with this writer's ideas?

The Ifs of History

by Hans Koning

Franklin Delano Roosevelt

The ifs of history are numberless. For everything that has happened we can, of course, line up infinite alternatives. But
5 not much is gained from this, except for the obvious observation that human history is very iffy.

The ifs I am talking about
10 here are last-minute ifs—that is, I am not going to lose myself and my readers by guessing what would have happened if there had been no Bering Strait or
15 English Channel or no Franklin Delano Roosevelt. A last-minute if is: What would have happened if, in February 1933, Giuseppe Zangara's hand had not been
20 pushed aside in Miami, and his bullet had killed Franklin Roosevelt rather than the mayor of Chicago?

This example gets right to
25 the point. Most of my ifs are life-or-death ifs. And that raises the well-known dilemma: Are certain individuals of greater importance to the flow of
30 history? I find it hard to accept that the chance life or death of one person could decide the lives and deaths of millions. But I suspect that the truth lies
35 somewhere in between. A few individuals have influenced destiny, but in the long run, history exhibits its own logic.

If that German officer in
40 Hitler's headquarters who moved a briefcase had minded his own business, then the bomb in the briefcase would have killed Hitler. A different government would
45 have taken over in Berlin and World War II would have ended. The Allies would have occupied Germany ten months sooner. As many as a million prisoners'
50 lives would have been saved.

If Cleopatra had been less attractive, Marc Antony would have kept his mind on the affairs of state and not been eliminated
55 from the race for Roman emperor. He would have continued sharing power with his brother-in-law Octavian, whom he hated, and he would
60 have worked to oppose Octavian's unjust use of force. If Marc Antony had done that, it would have hastened the rise of Christianity and the fall of
65 the Roman Empire by a hundred years. Everything thereafter would have happened one hundred years sooner.

If Joseph Ginoux, a café
70 owner in Arles, had allowed Vincent van Gogh to pay for his lodging in paintings instead of evicting him, then Vincent would have had some peace
75 and security. His nervous breakdown might have happened later and been less severe. He would have painted for five, perhaps ten years more.
80 The people of Arles wouldn't have drawn up their petition to have him put in an asylum. In a less hostile and threatening

Vincent van Gogh,
Self-Portrait

world, his later work would have
85 reached an unimaginable perfection. Gauguin and Picasso would have been influenced differently; twentieth-century painting would have been
90 different. (And Ginoux's heirs would have been the richest people in France.)

Sculpture of Cleopatra

Adapted from *Harper's Magazine*

---

asylum: a psychiatric hospital
destiny: fate, the influence of uncontrollable forces
dilemma: a difficult choice between alternatives
evict: to force a renter out of his or her apartment

hasten: to cause to happen sooner
iffy: full of uncertainty, doubtful
last-minute: at the final moment before an important event

A3 **After You Read**

Check (✓) the events that actually happened or are true, according to the article.

1. __✓__ A man tried to kill Franklin Delano Roosevelt in Miami.

2. _____ Hitler was killed by a bomb in a briefcase.

3. _____ Marc Antony was attracted to Cleopatra.

4. _____ Van Gogh was evicted from where he was living.

5. _____ Joseph Ginoux received paintings from van Gogh.

B Past Unreal Conditionals and Past Wishes

Examining Form

Look back at the article on page 352 and complete the tasks below. Then discuss your observations and read the Form charts to check them.

1. A past unreal conditional sentence is underlined. Find three more examples.

2. What form is used in each *if* clause? What form is used in each main clause?

PAST UNREAL CONDITIONALS

Past Unreal Conditionals		
IF CLAUSE	(THEN)	MAIN CLAUSE
IF + PAST PERFECT	*(THEN)*	*WOULD HAVE* + PAST PARTICIPLE
If I **had known** the answer,	(then)	I **would have passed** the test.
If I**'d known** the answer,	(then)	I**'d have passed** the test.
IF + PAST PERFECT	*(THEN)*	*COULD HAVE* + PAST PARTICIPLE
If I **had known** the answer,	(then)	I **could have passed** the test.
IF + PAST PERFECT	*(THEN)*	*MIGHT HAVE* + PAST PARTICIPLE
If I **had known** the answer,	(then)	I **might have passed** the test.

- The contraction of both *had* and *would* with pronouns is *'d*.
- When the *if* clause comes first, it is followed by a comma. When the main clause is first, there is no comma and *then* is not used.
  If I had known the answer, (then) **I would have passed** the test.
  I would have passed the test **if I had known** the answer.
- Either clause or both clauses can be negative.
  If I hadn't known the answer, **I would have asked** for help.
  If I hadn't known the answer, **I wouldn't have passed** the test.
- Questions are formed by putting the main clause in question word order.
  If you had known the answer, **would you have passed** the test?
- See Appendix 14 for contractions with *had* and *would*.

Past Wishes

⎧ WISH CLAUSE ⎫	⎧ THAT CLAUSE ⎫
SIMPLE PRESENT	(THAT +) PAST PERFECT
I **wish**	(that) I **had taken** a vacation last year.

SIMPLE PRESENT	(THAT +) COULD HAVE + PAST PARTICIPLE
I **wish**	(that) you **could have come** to the show.

- *That* is often omitted after *wish,* but it is always implied.
- Notice the use of past perfect or past modal short forms when a *wish* clause follows *but.*
    I didn't take a vacation last year, but **I wish I had.**
    I invited Joe to the party, but **I wish I hadn't.**
    I didn't go to the show, but **I wish I could have.**

B1 Listening for Form

Listen to each conversation and choose the response that you hear.

1. **a.** Not really. If it had been me, I would have interrupted him.
   (b.) Not really. If it had been me, I wouldn't have interrupted him.

2. **a.** If I had another chance, I'd prepare more for the interview.
   b. If I'd had another chance, I'd have prepared more for the interview.

3. **a.** No, I wouldn't.
   b. No, I wouldn't have.

4. **a.** If I had listened to my roommate, I would have taken it.
   b. If I had listened to my roommate, I wouldn't have taken it.

5. **a.** Yes, if I'd had my way, we would have moved to Seattle.
   b. Yes, if I had my way, we would move to Seattle.

6. **a.** I know. I would have called if it had been so late.
   b. I know. I would have called if it hadn't been so late.

B2 Completing Past Conditional Sentences

A. Complete these sentences with *would have, could have,* or *might have* in a past result clause.

1. If I had studied medicine, <u>I would have become a doctor.</u>

2. If I had known ten years ago what I know now, _____

3. If I had listened to my parents, _____

4. If I hadn't ever learned to read, _____

5. If I had been born in Australia, _____

6. If I had lived in another century, _____

7. If I hadn't studied English, _____

8. If I hadn't come to school today, _____

B. On a separate sheet of paper, write three more past *if* clauses. Then trade papers with your partner and complete the sentences.

B3 Working on Past Conditionals

Work in small groups. Start a past unreal conditional sentence chain with *If I hadn't slept well last night,* and finish it with a result clause. Use the end of the last person's sentence to begin your own sentence.

A: *If I hadn't slept well last night, I'd have been exhausted this morning.*
B: *If I'd been exhausted this morning, I would have stayed home from work.*
C: *If I'd stayed home from work, . . .*

Informally Speaking

Reduced Forms of Past Conditionals

 Look at the cartoon and listen to the conversation. How is each underlined form in the cartoon different from what you hear?

The waiter overcharged me for lunch today, but I didn't say anything.

Well, I <u>would have</u> shown him the mistake. I sure <u>wouldn't have</u> paid the extra money.

In informal speech, *would have, could have,* and *might have* are often reduced like other past modals (see Chapter 8, page 175). *Have* may sound like /əv/. If it is reduced even more, it sounds like /ə/. Notice the reduction of the past perfect in the *if* clauses as well.

STANDARD FORM	WHAT YOU MIGHT HEAR
If **Tim had** driven, he **would have** arrived earlier.	"If /'tɪməd/ driven, he /'wʊdəv/ arrived earlier." OR "If /'tɪməd/ driven, he /'wʊdə/ arrived earlier."
If **Tim had** driven, he **could have** arrived earlier.	"If /'tɪməd/ driven, he /'kʊdəv/ arrived earlier." OR "If /'tɪməd/ driven, he /'kʊdə/ arrived earlier."
If **Joe had** been there, I **would not have** gone.	"If /'dʒoʊəd/ been there, I /'wʊdntəv/ gone." OR "If /'dʒoʊəd/ been there, I /'wʊdntə/ gone."
If **Joe had** been there, I **might not have** gone.	"If /'dʒoʊəd/ been there, I /'maɪtnɑdəv/ gone." OR "If /'dʒoʊəd/ been there, I /'maɪtnɑdə/ gone."

B4 Understanding Informal Speech

Listen and write the standard form of the words you hear.

1. <u>Would you have chosen</u> a different career if you hadn't married so young?

2. If I had studied, I _____ much better on the quiz.

3. We _____ so late if the car had been working.

4. If I hadn't been careful, I _____ an accident.

5. I _____ late if I'd missed the bus.

6. If I hadn't scored, we _____ the game.

A. Work with a partner. Complete these conversations with the appropriate forms
of the verbs in parentheses to form past wishes. Then practice the
conversations.

1. **A:** <u>Does he ever wish</u> (he/ever/wish) that he <u>had chosen</u> (choose)
   _____
   1   2
   a different career when he graduated?

   B: Yes. Sometimes he _____ (wish) he _____ (go)
                                    3   4
   to graduate school right after college.

2. **A:** My sister _____ (wish) she _____ (see)
                          1   2
   the apartment upstairs when she was looking for one.

   B: I didn't know she was interested in a two-bedroom apartment.

   I _____ (wish) I _____ (show) it to
          3   4
   her. Then we could have been neighbors.

3. **A:** _____ (you/ever/wish) you _____
              1   2
   (learn) to ski when you were younger?

   B: Yes, I _____ (wish) I _____ (be)
                      3   4
   braver when my school offered lessons.

B. Complete these sentences with the short form.

1. I never learned to swim, but I wish <u>I had.</u>

2. He didn't graduate this year, but he wishes _____

3. We didn't see that movie, but we wish _____

4. They took the train, but they wish _____

5. She couldn't attend the meeting yesterday, but she wishes _____

C Past Unreal Conditionals

Examining Meaning and Use

Read the sentences and answer the questions below. Then discuss your observations and read the Meaning and Use Notes to check them.

    a. If she had been a better student, she would have graduated on time.
    b. If she were a better student, she would graduate on time.

1. Which sentence refers to a situation that was not true in the past?

2. Which sentence refers to a situation that is not true in the present?

Meaning and Use Notes

> **Past Unreal Conditionals**
>
> **1A** Past unreal conditional sentences express imaginary situations that were actually not true in the past. In the *if* clause, the past perfect indicates the situation was unreal in the past. In the result clause, *would have, could have,* or *might have* also indicate the result was unreal in the past.
>
> **If I had been** the boss, I **would have fired** her. (I wasn't the boss, so I didn't fire her.)
>
> **1B** *Could have* or *might have* in the result clause indicates one of several possible imaginary outcomes. *Would have* indicates that the speaker is more certain about the imaginary results.
>
> **If** you**'d had** your car, you **could have left** earlier.
> **If** you**'d had** your car, you **might not have left** so late. (*Could have* and *might have* both express one of several possible imaginary outcomes.)
> **If** you**'d had** your car, you **wouldn't have left** so late. (*Would have* expresses more certainty about the imaginary outcome.)

(Continued on page 360)

2 Unreal conditionals beginning with *If I had been you* can be used as an indirect way of giving advice. The *if* clause is often omitted. Unreal conditionals sound softer than modals like *should have*.

Advice with Past Unreal Conditionals	*Advice with Modals*
(If I**'d been** you,) I **would have left** early.	You **should have left** early.

Restating Past Unreal Conditionals with *But*

3 Often, a sentence with *would have* is used without an *if* condition. Instead, the main clause is joined to a true (not imaginary) sentence with *but*. The true sentence with *but* implies the unreal past condition.

True Sentence with But	*Past Unreal Conditional*
I would have come to the party, **but I had to study.**	I would have come to the party **if I hadn't had to study.**
I would have left earlier, **but my car didn't start.**	I would have left earlier **if my car had started.**

C1 **Listening for Meaning and Use**   ► Notes 1A, 1B

Listen and choose the best answer to each question.

1. (**a.**) I don't know.
   b. I didn't know.

2. **a.** Yes, he did.
   b. He could have.

3. **a.** Maybe, but he'd be quite old.
   b. Maybe he hadn't.

4. **a.** It's hard to say.
   b. They certainly were.

5. **a.** Maybe not.
   b. Yes, they did.

6. **a.** It might be.
   b. It might have.

7. **a.** No, it won't.
   b. No, I doubt it.

8. **a.** No one knows.
   b. No one knew.

C2 Giving Indirect Advice

Work with a partner. Take turns giving indirect advice to your partner by telling what you would have done. The *if* clauses may be omitted.

1. **A:** I didn't understand last week's homework, but I didn't do anything about it.

   B: _(If I'd been you,) I would have gone to see the instructor._

2. **A:** My best friend asked to borrow a lot of money. I gave it to him without asking any questions.

   B: _____

3. **A:** A salesperson was rude to me yesterday when I was buying a gift.

   B: _____

4. **A:** My doctor didn't answer all my questions.

   B: _____

5. **A:** My boss didn't offer me the raise that I wanted. I was disappointed.

   B: _____

6. **A:** The airline refused to change my ticket, even though it was an emergency.

   B: _____

C3 Distinguishing Fact and Fiction

Work with a partner. List the two facts that each conditional sentence implies. Then paraphrase the conditional sentence using *would have* followed by a true sentence with *but*.

1. If Robert Kennedy had become president of the United States, he would have ended the Vietnam War in 1969.

   Facts: 1. _Robert Kennedy didn't become president of the United States._

   2. _The Vietnam War didn't end in 1969._

   Paraphrase: _Robert Kennedy would have ended the Vietnam War in 1969, but he didn't become president._

(Continued on page 362)

2. If Napoleon's armies had had proper nails for horseshoes, they would have conquered Russia.

Facts: 1. _____

2. _____

Paraphrase: _____

_____

3. If *Apollo 13* hadn't had an explosion during its flight, it would have landed on the moon as planned.

Facts: 1. _____

2. _____

Paraphrase: _____

_____

4. If Mozart hadn't died young, he would have finished his famous piece *Requiem*.

Facts: 1. _____

2. _____

Paraphrase: _____

_____

5. If I hadn't been worried about the "Y2K" problem, I would have enjoyed my friend's party on December 31, 1999.

Facts: 1. _____

2. _____

Paraphrase: _____

_____

C4 **Describing the Ifs of History**   ▶ Notes 1A, 1B

Work in small groups. Think of five historical events that you know something about. Make up two past unreal conditional sentences about each event.

Apollo 13: If an oxygen tank hadn't exploded during the flight into space, the astronauts' lives wouldn't have been in danger. If the explosion hadn't happened, the astronauts would have landed on the moon.

D Past Wishes

Examining Meaning and Use

Read the sentences and answer the questions below. Then discuss your observations and read the Meaning and Use Notes to check them.

> **1a.** I wish the temperature were warmer. I am freezing.
> **1b.** I wish the temperature had been warmer. I was freezing.
>
> **2a.** If only he didn't have a cold. He really wants to go out.
> **2b.** If only he hadn't had a cold. He really wanted to go out.

1. Which sentences are about present situations? Which are about past situations?

2. Which pair of sentences seems to express stronger feelings?

Meaning and Use Notes

Making Wishes About the Past

1 Past *wish* sentences refer to past situations that did not occur. They express a desire to change something that happened in the past.

I **wish** the weather **had been** nice yesterday. (It rained yesterday.)
I **wish** you **could have seen** the movie. (You didn't see the movie.)

Expressing Regret or Dissatisfaction

2 When you use a past *wish* sentence, you express regret or dissatisfaction about a past situation.

I **wish** I **had gone** to the meeting. I completely forgot about it. I **wish** someone **had called** to remind me.

Using *If Only*

3 *If only* is often used in place of a past wish to express strong regret. *If only* sentences focus on the wish to change a negative outcome.

If only I **hadn't lost** my wallet!
If only the war **had ended** sooner!

Listen to each situation and choose the sentence that is true.

1. **a.** I read about World War II.
   (b.) I saw a movie.

2. **a.** I wasn't home.
   b. I answered the phone.

3. **a.** She wasn't elected.
   b. She represents us now.

4. **a.** You called.
   b. The exam ended.

5. **a.** They got reservations.
   b. They didn't fly home.

6. **a.** There was a tree on the driveway.
   b. I wasn't leaving.

7. **a.** You took a day off last week.
   b. You took today off.

8. **a.** I didn't have a headache.
   b. I didn't stay.

D2 **Expressing Regret**   ▶ Notes 2, 3

Work with a partner. Take turns making up past *wish* and *if only* sentences that express regret. Think of as many sentences as possible for each situation.

1. You refused to lend your brother money. He had to drop out of school for a semester because he couldn't pay his tuition.
   I wish I'd lent him the money.
   If only I'd helped him.

2. You lost your temper today when you were baby-sitting your nephew. He began to cry.

3. You didn't tell your boss how overworked you've been feeling. Now he has changed your schedule, and you can't take a day off.

4. You didn't call the doctor last week when you got sick. Now you've missed a week of classes.

5. You forgot your best friend's birthday. There was a big party for your friend and you didn't go.

6. You accepted a job offer on Monday. On Tuesday you got a better offer from another company.

D3 **Expressing Regret or Dissatisfaction** ▶ Notes 2, 3

A. Work with a partner. Take turns reacting to the statements by using a past *wish* sentence or *if only* sentence with short forms.

1. **A:** The library was closed yesterday.
   B: _I wish it hadn't been._

2. **A:** Our team didn't win first prize.
   B: _If only we had._

3. **A:** The president raised taxes again.
   B: _____

4. **A:** My TV stopped working.
   B: _____

5. **A:** The train was late.
   B: _____

6. **A:** I didn't invite Peter.
   B: _____

7. **A:** It snowed a lot.
   B: _____

8. **A:** They didn't call back.
   B: _____

B. With your partner, expand one of the examples above into a longer conversation between two people. (Try to have each person speak three or four times.) Give more details about the situation and try to use at least one more *wish* sentence, *if only* sentence, or past unreal conditional sentence.

A: *The library was closed last night.*
B: *I know. I wish it hadn't been.*
A: *I needed to work on my paper. If only I had checked the schedule a few days ago, I would have been able to finish on time.*

D4 **Explaining Wishes** ▶ Note 1

A. Think of two past events in your life that you wish you could have changed. Write a past *wish* sentence about each one. Then write a past *if* sentence to explain your wish.

I wish my family hadn't moved when I was young.
If they hadn't moved, I wouldn't have been so lonely.

B. Now expand one of the events from part A into a paragraph. First, make a list of details that would have been different if your wish had come true. Then use your list to write your paragraph. Use *would have, could have,* and *might have.*

I wish my family hadn't moved when I was young. If we hadn't moved, I wouldn't have been so lonely. I wouldn't have had to leave my best friend. Who knows? We might have remained friends forever. We could have . . .

Combining Form, Meaning, and Use

E1 Thinking About Meaning and Use

Read each sentence and the statements that follow. Write *T* if the statement is true or *F* if it is false. Then discuss your answers in small groups.

1. I would have reached you if the phone had been working.

   __F__ **a.** The phone was working.

   _____ **b.** I didn't reach you.

2. I wish I had taken a vacation.

   _____ **a.** I should have taken a vacation.

   _____ **b.** I took a vacation.

3. She wouldn't have taken the medication if she had known about the risks.

   _____ **a.** She knew about the risks.

   _____ **b.** She took the medication.

4. If only I hadn't followed his advice.

   _____ **a.** I didn't follow his advice.

   _____ **b.** I shouldn't have followed his advice.

5. I would have come over, but my car broke down.

   _____ **a.** I couldn't come over because my car broke down.

   _____ **b.** If my car hadn't broken down, I would have come over.

6. If I had been there, I'd have complained to the manager.

   _____ **a.** I complained to the manager.

   _____ **b.** I'd have complained to the manager, but I wasn't there.

7. If we hadn't bought our tickets already, we wouldn't have gone to the show.

_____ **a.** We had already bought our tickets.

_____ **b.** We went to the show.

8. If only we'd been told about the delay.

_____ **a.** No one told us about the delay.

_____ **b.** I regret that we weren't told about the delay.

E2 Editing

Find the errors in these paragraphs and correct them.

Historians love to think about the dramatic "what-ifs" of history. They have even given the name "counterfactual history" to this pursuit. How would history *have* ~~had~~ changed if some key event had been different? What would the consequences been if the weather has been different in a certain battle? What would had happened if a famous person had lived instead of died? These are the sorts of questions that are asked in two recent books that imagine how history might been under different circumstances: *What If?*, edited by R. Cowley and S. Ambrose; and *Virtual History,* edited by N. Ferguson.

Don't just wish you've been alive in a different era. Go back and explore what could have, should have, or might have happened at various times in history. You won't be sorry. You'll wish you'll gone back sooner!

Beyond the Classroom

Searching for Authentic Examples

Find examples of English grammar in everyday life. Choose one of the tasks below. Be prepared to discuss your findings.

A. Look in a newspaper or news magazine. Write down three examples of past unreal conditionals and bring them to class. Look for events with controversial, questionable, or surprising results. Why do you think the past unreal conditionals were used?

B. Watch a news program or documentary on TV and listen for one example each of past wishes and past unreal conditionals. Write down as much of each sentence as you can and bring them to class. How were the sentences used in context? What meanings do they express?

Writing

Follow these steps to write a letter of apology.

1. Think about a mistake that you have made that affected someone you know. Write down your ideas. What was the mistake? How did it affect this person? What regrets do you have? What could/should you have done differently?

2. Use your notes to write a first draft of your letter. Express your regret and explain why you are sorry. Be specific in explaining what you did wrong, how much you regret what you did, and what you should have or could have done instead. Try to use at least one past *wish* or *if only* sentence and one past unreal conditional sentence with *if*.

3. Read over your draft and correct any errors that you find.

4. Exchange papers with a partner. Underline errors in punctuation, spelling, and grammar. Pay particular attention to the form, meaning, and use of past unreal sentences and past wishes. Discuss the errors with the writer. Then rewrite your own paper, making the appropriate corrections.

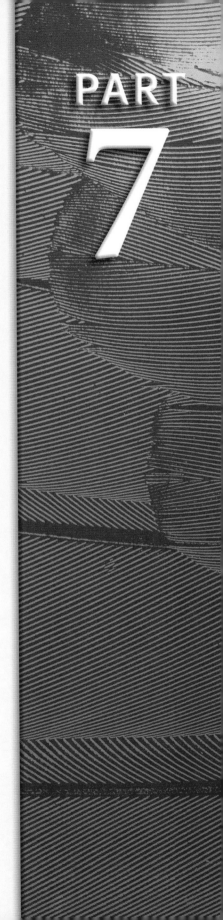

Noun Clauses and Reported Speech

Noun Clauses

A   Career Currents

A1   Before You Read

Discuss these questions.

What is the best way to find a new job? Would you quit your job before you found a better one? Why or why not?

A2   Read

Read this article from a website to find out some of the benefits of looking for a new job.

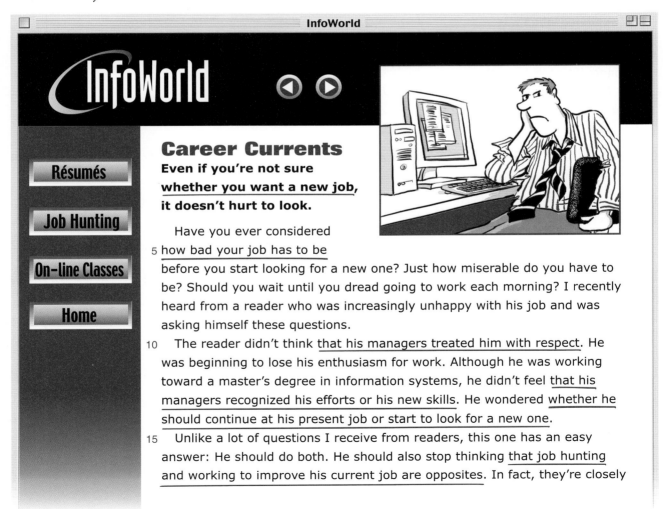

InfoWorld

Career Currents
Even if you're not sure whether you want a new job, it doesn't hurt to look.

Have you ever considered
5 how bad your job has to be
before you start looking for a new one? Just how miserable do you have to be? Should you wait until you dread going to work each morning? I recently heard from a reader who was increasingly unhappy with his job and was asking himself these questions.

10   The reader didn't think that his managers treated him with respect. He was beginning to lose his enthusiasm for work. Although he was working toward a master's degree in information systems, he didn't feel that his managers recognized his efforts or his new skills. He wondered whether he should continue at his present job or start to look for a new one.

15   Unlike a lot of questions I receive from readers, this one has an easy answer: He should do both. He should also stop thinking that job hunting and working to improve his current job are opposites. In fact, they're closely

Résumés

Job Hunting

On-line Classes

Home

related. A traditional job hunt can lead to a new job with a new company. But the steps that you go through to look for a new job can also help you
20 improve your current job.

The first step in a job hunt is to find out <u>what opportunities are out there</u>. You learn <u>what kinds of skills and experience are required to get those jobs</u>. You also learn <u>how much these positions pay</u>. Then you update your résumé and begin selling yourself to potential employers in cover letters and
25 interviews.

You may not know <u>if you would actually end up switching jobs</u>. Nevertheless, having an updated résumé is still a good idea because you now have one if you need it, and creating a résumé forces you to think of all that you have accomplished in your current job. When you try to match
30 your résumé to the jobs that are available, you will discover <u>which areas you need more experience in</u> and <u>which skills you need to improve</u>. You will also learn <u>what opportunities are available</u> and <u>what the salaries are</u>. This information could put you in a good position to get a better deal from your current employer if you realize <u>that you are not making enough money</u>.
35 Try to use <u>what you learn during your job hunt to improve your current position</u>. This may mean <u>that you should present your boss with the results of your salary research and a list of your accomplishments, and then ask for a raise</u>. Or perhaps you should take some classes or find out <u>if you can work on different types of projects to expand your opportunities</u>.

Adapted from *InfoWorld.com*

dread: to have feelings of anxiety about something
miserable: extremely unhappy

potential: possible, though not yet actual or real
update: to make something current

 After You Read

Check (✓) the advice that is true according to the article.

✓ 1. It's a good idea to find out about other available jobs even if you're not really thinking about quitting.

_____ 2. Don't update your résumé.

_____ 3. Quit your job before you look for a new one.

_____ 4. Find out the salaries of jobs that are similar to yours before you ask for a raise.

_____ 5. You can sometimes improve your current job by looking for a new job.

B Noun Clauses

Examining Form

Look back at the article on page 372 and complete the tasks below. Then discuss your observations and read the Form charts to check them.

1. There are many noun clauses underlined in the article. Find at least three examples of each of these types:

   a. noun clauses beginning with *wh-* words (e.g., *what, how, which*)

   b. noun clauses beginning with *if/whether*

   c. noun clauses beginning with *that*

2. Circle the subject and verb in one noun clause of each type. Are they in statement word order or question word order?

NOUN CLAUSES

Wh- Clauses	
MAIN CLAUSE	*WH-* CLAUSE
He wondered	**who I was.** **what she was wearing.** **why I called.**
Can you tell me	**where he is?** **when the train arrives?** **how they do it?**

If/Whether Clauses	
MAIN CLAUSE	*IF/WHETHER* CLAUSE
I wonder	**if he left (or not).**
I don't know	**if he's still here (or not).**
Can you tell me	**whether he arrived (or not)?** **whether (or not) he arrived?** **if he arrived (or not)?**

That Clauses	
MAIN CLAUSE	*THAT* CLAUSE
I think	**(that) he called.**
Did they doubt	**(that) he would call?**

Noun Clauses

- There are three different types of noun clauses: *wh-* clauses, *if/whether* clauses, and *that* clauses.
- Noun clauses are dependent clauses that can occur in the same place as a noun or noun phrase in a sentence. All noun clauses have a subject and a verb.

Wh- Clauses

- *Wh-* clauses are sometimes called indirect questions or embedded questions. Although *wh-* clauses begin with *wh-* words, they use statement word order.

  I wonder **where he is.** *I wonder where is he. (INCORRECT)

- Use a question mark only if the main clause is a question.

  <u>Can you tell me</u> **what happened**?

If/Whether Clauses

- *If/whether* clauses are also sometimes called indirect questions or embedded questions. They also use statement word order.

  Do you know **if you're coming with us**?

  *Do you know if are you coming with us? (INCORRECT)

- *Or not* can be added to the end of *if/whether* clauses if the clauses are not very long.

  I wonder **whether she left <u>or not</u>.**   I wonder **if she left <u>or not</u>.**

- *Or not* can also immediately follow *whether*, but it can't follow *if*.

  I wonder **whether <u>or not</u> she left.**   *I wonder if or not she left. (INCORRECT)

That Clauses

- *That* can usually be omitted.

B1 **Listening for Form**

Listen to the sentences. Do you hear a *wh-* clause, an *if/whether* clause, or a *that* clause? Check (✓) the correct column.

	WH- CLAUSE	*IF/WHETHER* CLAUSE	*THAT* CLAUSE
1.	✓		
2.			
3.			
4.			
5.			
6.			
7.			
8.			

Read this information about résumés. Find the *wh-*, *if/whether,* and *that* noun clauses and underline them. Then circle the verb in the main clause related to each noun clause.

Many employment counselors (believe) <u>that your résumé is a kind of personal advertisement</u>. It summarizes what you have accomplished and describes what kind of work you want. Hopefully, it tells why *you* should be hired. A good résumé doesn't always determine whether you will get an interview, but a bad one will certainly eliminate your chances.

Résumés are only one tool that you need to use in your employment search. Many employers don't even use them; employers often decide whether they should hire you based on other information. Nevertheless, most employment counselors believe that it is worthwhile to write a good résumé. It helps you get organized. Most importantly, it helps you figure out what kind of job you really want and whether or not you have the qualifications.

Work with a partner. Complete the noun clauses with the subjects and verbs in parentheses and the correct tense. Then practice the conversations.

1. Person A is looking for Yuki.

   A: Do you know where _____<u>Yuki went</u>_____ (Yuki/go) after lunch?
   ₁

   B: No, and I don't know what time _____<u>she came back</u>_____ (she/come back).
   ₂

2. Person A didn't receive any mail.

   A: I wonder why _____ (the mail/not/come) today.
   ₁

   B: Maybe I'll call the post office and ask what _____ (happen).
   ₂

   Do you know what time _____ (the post office/close)?
   ₃

3. Person A needs information about the chemistry exam.

   A: Do you know when _____ (the chemistry exam/be)?
   ₁

   B: Yes, it's on Thursday, but I'm not sure when _____
   ₂

   (it/start) or how long _____ (it/last).
   ₃

4. Person A is in a department store.

A: I'd like to find out how much _____ (this/cost).

           1

B: I'm not sure, but I'll ask the manager as soon as I find out where

_____ (he/be).

     2

Work with a partner. Use your own words to complete the *if/whether* clauses. Use appropriate tenses depending on the context. Then practice the conversations.

1. Two friends are on the way home from work.

A: Do you know if the bank _is open today?_

                             1

B: I'm not sure if _it is or not._ They've recently changed their hours.

                    2

2. Person A is getting ready to leave for work.

A: I wonder whether _____

                         1

B: Take your umbrella if you're not sure.

3. Person A is buying groceries.

A: Can you tell me if _____

                         1

B: I'm not sure if _____ or not. I'll ask the manager.

                  2

4. Person A is buying tickets for a concert.

A: I was wondering if you could tell me whether _____

                         1

B: There aren't any seats left on that date. Should I check whether

_____

     2

5. Person A needs to make a telephone call.

A: Do you know if _____ near here?

                        1

B: I'm not certain if _____. Maybe you should ask

                    2

someone else.

6. Person A is planning a weekend trip.

A: I wonder if _____ this weekend.

                    1

B: I didn't see the weather forecast, so I don't know whether

_____ or not.

     2

B5) Unscrambling Sentences with *That* Clauses

Work with a partner. Unscramble the words to make a statement or a question with a *that* clause. Use every word. The first word of each sentence is underlined for you. *That* has been omitted from some of the sentences.

1. was/that/you/he/angry/notice/<u>did</u>

   Did you notice that he was angry?

2. predict/it/soon/happen/<u>they</u>/will

   _____

3. help/<u>I</u>/some/need/I/that/guess

   _____

4. that/due/remembered/my/is/rent/<u>I</u>/tomorrow

   _____

5. proved/could/<u>he</u>/do/it/he

   _____

B6) Completing Noun Clauses

A. Use the questions in parentheses to complete each main clause. You may have to add *if* or *whether* at the beginning of some noun clauses.

1. I was wondering <u>what experience you have.</u>
   (What experience do you have?)

2. Could you tell me _____
   (How long did you work there?)

3. I was wondering _____
   (Did you like your job?)

4. Can you tell me _____
   (What is your greatest strength?)

5. Could you explain _____
   (Why are you changing jobs?)

B. Work with a partner. Pretend you are at a job interview. Take turns asking and answering the questions in part A.

Wh- and *If/Whether* Clauses

Examining Meaning and Use

Read the sentences and complete the tasks below. Then discuss your observations and read the Meaning and Use Notes to check them.

1a. Sara: I can't decide what I need for the trip. Did you get everything on your list?
1b. Pam: I don't know whether I did or not. I lost my list. I wonder if it's in the car.

2a. Excuse me. Is the bus late?
2b. Excuse me. Can you tell me if the bus is late?

1. Underline the noun clauses in sentences 1a and 1b. Circle the verb that comes before each clause. Which verbs express mental activities?

2. Which question sounds more polite, 2a or 2b?

Meaning and Use Notes

> ### Noun Clauses After Mental Activity Verbs
>
> **1A** *Wh-* clauses and *if/whether* clauses often follow mental activity verbs. These sentences frequently express uncertainty, curiosity, decisions, and other mental activities.
>
> A: I don't <u>know</u> **how to start my job search**. I can't <u>decide</u> **what kind of job to look for**.
> B: I <u>wonder</u> **whether the Career Center is open**. They'll be able to get you started.
>
> ---
>
> **1B** Below are some common mental activity verbs. See Appendix 11 for more verbs commonly followed by noun clauses.
>
> | | | | | | |
> |---|---|---|---|---|---|
> | consider | figure out | guess | learn | realize | understand |
> | decide | forget | know | notice | remember | wonder |
>
> ---
>
> **1C** *Wh-* and *if/whether* clauses often follow these expressions of uncertainty.
>
> I'm not <u>sure</u> **how to start**.
> I'm not <u>certain</u> **if he's coming tonight**.
> I have no <u>idea</u> **where he is**.

(Continued on page 380)

Wh- and *If/Whether* Clauses After Other Verbs

2 Many other verbs and phrases are commonly followed by *wh-* and *if/whether* clauses.

ask	depend on	hear	rely on	see	tell (someone)
demonstrate	explain	notice	say	show	write

Indirect Questions

3A *Wh-* or *if/whether* clauses often follow certain phrases to express indirect questions. Indirect questions sound more polite than *Wh-* questions or *Yes/No* questions.

Direct Questions	*Indirect Questions*
When does the train arrive?	Can you (please) tell me **when the train arrives**?
	I was wondering **when the train arrives**.
Has the train arrived yet?	Do you know **if the train has arrived yet**?
	I'd like to find out **if the train has arrived yet**.

3B Below are some common expressions used to introduce indirect questions.

Do you know . . . ?	Do you remember . . . ?
Can/Could you tell me . . . ?	Do you have any idea . . . ?
Can you remember . . . ?	I'd like to know/find out. . . .
Could you explain . . . ?	I wonder/was wondering. . . .

C1 Listening for Meaning and Use

▶ Notes 1A, 3A, 3B

Listen to these situations. Choose the sentence that most appropriately follows what you hear.

1. **a.** Yes, it is.
   b. Yes, around eight.

2. **a.** So was I. Let's ask him.
   b. No, I don't.

3. **a.** Yes, she works.
   b. No, I don't.

4. **a.** I wonder who.
   b. I wonder why.

5. **a.** It did.
   b. I did.

6. **a.** Yes. It's over there.
   b. Yes. I know it.

7. **a.** In room 2.
   b. Sure. Let me look it up.

8. **a.** Yes. Be patient.
   b. It certainly is.

Work with a partner. Imagine you are witnesses at the scene of a traffic accident. Take turns asking and answering the police officer's questions. Use a *wh-* clause and a statement of uncertainty: *I can't remember, I'm not sure, I don't know, I'm not certain, I have no idea.*

1. Who was driving the truck?

   I'm not sure who was driving it.

2. What time did the accident occur?

3. What did the truck look like?

4. How many people were in the truck?

5. What was the license plate number on the truck?

6. How fast was the truck going?

7. What color was the truck?

8. What did the driver look like?

Vocabulary Notes

If and *Whether*

If and *whether* have the same meaning when they begin noun clauses. They are both found in informal situations, but *whether* is probably more common in formal situations.

I don't know **if she's at home.**   I don't know **whether she's at home.**

We often add *or not* to *if/whether* clauses if the clauses are not very long. In *if* clauses, *or not* goes at the end of the clause. In *whether* clauses, *or not* can appear in two positions.

I don't know **if she's at home <u>or not</u>.**   I don't know **whether <u>or not</u> she's at home.**

I don't know **whether she's at home <u>or not</u>.**

C3) **Adding *If/Whether* Clauses to Expressions of Uncertainty**

A. Work with a partner. Read each situation and complete the sentences with an *if/whether* clause in the correct tense. Add *or not* to some of your noun clauses.

1. This is the first day of Sheila's new job. She's nervous on her way to work.

   a. She wonders <u>if she'll like her new job.</u>

   b. She's not sure _____

   c. She has no idea _____

2. Min-woo has met the woman of his dreams. He's going to meet her parents tonight. He's been worrying about it all day.

   a. He wonders _____

   b. He doesn't know _____

   c. He's not sure _____

B. Work on your own. Think of a situation in which you did something for the first time and you were uncertain about it. Make a list of some of the problems you had. Then write a paragraph explaining your uncertainty in detail. Use some statements of uncertainty followed by *if/whether* clauses.

   Before I moved to France, I had a lot of decisions to make. I wasn't sure whether I should sell my furniture or not. I wondered if it would be cheaper to buy new furniture after I arrived in France. However, I was surprised when I found out how much new furniture costs.

C4 Asking Indirect Questions with *If/Whether* Clauses

▶ Notes 3A, 3B

Work with a partner. Make each question less direct by using *I was wondering, Can/Could you (please) tell me, Do you know,* or *Do you have any idea* + an *if/whether* clause.

1. Did you have any trouble with the last assignment?

   I was wondering if you had any trouble with the last assignment.

2. Is the library closed during vacation?

3. Is the teacher going to show a film today?

4. Is the assignment due tomorrow?

5. Is the new language lab open yet?

6. Did I miss anything important yesterday?

C5 Asking Indirect Questions with *Wh-* Clauses

▶ Notes 3A, 3B

Work with a partner. Make up a polite question for each situation, using a *wh-* clause. Take turns asking and answering each question.

1. *At the airport*
   a. You're looking for a restroom.

      A: Excuse me. Can you please tell me where the restroom is?
      B: It's downstairs on the left.

   b. You're looking for the baggage claim.

2. *At a bus stop*
   a. You're asking someone for the time.
   b. You're looking for the bus schedule.

3. *In a department store*
   a. You're asking a salesperson the price of a shirt.
   b. You're asking a salesperson the size of a pair of pants.

4. *In the supermarket*
   a. You're looking for the manager.
   b. You're asking the clerk for the price of broccoli.

5. *On campus*
   a. You're looking for the history department.
   b. You want to pay your tuition bill.

That Clauses

Examining Meaning and Use

Read the sentences and answer the questions below. Then discuss your observations and read the Meaning and Use Notes to check them.

1a. I know that he left.
1b. I know that he's leaving.

2a. I remembered that the answer to the question was *ten*.
2b. I remembered that the answer to the question is *ten*.

1. Which pair of sentences has the same meaning?

2. Which pair does not? Why?

Meaning and Use Notes

That Clauses After Mental Activity Verbs

1A Noun clauses beginning with *that* often follow mental activity verbs to express thoughts and opinions.

> I <u>remembered</u> **(that) she called yesterday.**
> I <u>believe</u> **(that) employers should read résumés carefully.**

1B Below are some common mental activity verbs that are followed by *that* clauses. See Appendix 11 for more verbs commonly followed by noun clauses.

agree	believe	doubt	feel	hope	recognize	suppose
assume	bet	expect	find	imagine	regret	think

1C *That* clauses often follow these expressions:

> I'm <u>not sure</u> **(that) he can come.**　　I'm <u>afraid</u> **(that) I can't come.**
> I'm <u>not certain</u> **(that) he's coming.**　It <u>appears</u> **(that) he didn't come.**
> I <u>had no idea</u> **(that) he was coming.**　It <u>seems</u> **(that) he couldn't come.**

2A When the mental activity verb is in the present tense, the verb in the noun clause can be in the present, past, or future. The tense depends on the meaning of the sentence.

Present + Present   *Present + Past*   *Present + Future*

I <u>think</u> **it's OK.**   I <u>believe</u> **she sent the letter.**   I <u>assume</u> **they'll come** later.

2B When the mental activity verb is in the past, the verb in the noun clause usually takes a past form to express the speaker's past perspective.

Past + Past

I <u>thought</u> **that she was sleeping.**   *I <u>thought</u> that she is sleeping. (INCORRECT)

I <u>assumed</u> **he was happy when he called.**   *I <u>assumed</u> he is happy when I called. (INCORRECT)

2C When the mental activity verb is in the past, and you want to refer to an earlier past time, use the past perfect in the noun clause.

Earlier Time (Past + Past Perfect)

I <u>knew</u> **that she had left.**

2D When the mental activity verb is in the past, and you want to refer to a time that follows the past time, use *was/were going to* or *would* in the noun clause.

Later Time (Past + Past Continuous)   *Later Time (Past +* Would*)*

I <u>thought</u> **she was going to come** later.   I <u>thought</u> **she would come** later.

 If a noun clause is a generalization that is true at the present, the present tense can be used in the noun clause instead of the past tense.

Columbus <u>believed</u> **that the world is round.**

 If a past mental activity took place quickly, the present, past, or future tense can be used in the noun clause. Spontaneous mental activity verbs include *decide, discover, figure out, forget, find out, learn, notice, prove, realize, recall,* and *remember.*

Last night, I <u>realized</u>
Last night, I <u>decided</u>
{
(that) my report is too long.
(that) my report was too long.
(that) my report will be too long.

D1 Listening for Meaning and Use

🎧 Listen to these situations. Choose the sentence that most appropriately follows.

1. **a.** I hope she's on time.
   b. I hope she was on time.

2. **a.** I think it's Joan. I'll go find out.
   b. I thought it was Joan. I'll go find out.

3. **a.** Why did he leave?
   b. Why doesn't he leave?

4. **a.** How much did you buy?
   b. How much will you buy?

5. **a.** Yes, he was right.
   b. Good for him.

6. **a.** She was.
   b. She is.

D2 Thinking About Tense Agreement with *That* Clauses

A. Complete the sentences by circling all of the phrases that can form grammatical sentences.

1. I thought it (is snowing/was going to snow/snowed) in the mountains last night.

2. He doubts that (they'll accept / they accept / they accepted) credit cards.

3. I hoped my plane (won't be / wouldn't be / isn't) late.

4. I left the game early because I assumed our team (will win / had won / wins) the championship.

5. She decided that she (needs / needed / will need) help.

6. He's certain that the show (will start / starts / started) at 8:00.

B. Choose two of the grammatical sentences from part A and write two short dialogues using the sentences in appropriate contexts.

A: We can't ski today.
B: You're kidding. I thought it was going to snow in the mountains last night.
I'm so disappointed.

D3 Giving Opinions Using *That* Clauses

A. Work in small groups. Take turns expressing your own opinions about each statement. Use as many mental activity verbs as you can with *that* clauses.

1. Smokers are often treated unfairly.

   I agree that smokers are often treated unfairly. I think . . .

2. Most people are basically honest.

3. Marriage contracts are a good idea.

4. You can't really change someone.

5. All children should leave home at 18.

6. We learn from our mistakes.

B. On your own, make up two more statements. Read them aloud and ask your group to give opinions using mental activity verbs.

D4 **Expressing Opinions About Work** ▶ Notes 1A–1C

A. Read these survey results on job satisfaction in the United States. Do people in your country have the same concerns? Discuss your ideas with a partner.

U.S. Workers find some major problems in the workplace. *In a survey of 1,000 adults it was found that:*
95% are concerned about spending more time with their family.
92% don't have enough flexibility in their schedules to take care of family needs.
88% are concerned about work-related stress.
87% say they don't get enough sleep.
60% would take training courses if they were paid for by the employer.
49% believe on-site child care is important, but only 12% of employers offer this benefit.
46% work more than 40 hours per week: 18% work more than 50 hours per week.
45% had to work overtime with little or no advance notice.
44% think the opportunity to telecommute is important, but only 17% of employers offer telecommuting opportunities.

from U.S. Newswire

B. How do you feel about the workers' concerns in part A? Use the mental activity verbs below and *that* clauses to organize your ideas. Then discuss with a partner.

I think/believe/agree that . . .   I don't believe/think that . . .
I feel/imagine/suppose that . . .   I doubt that . . .
It appears/seems that . . .   I hope/expect that . . .

I agree that most workers want to spend more time with their families.

Combining Form, Meaning, and Use

E1) Thinking About Meaning and Use

Read each sentence and the statement that follows. Write *T* if the statement is true, *F* if it is false, and *?* if you do not have enough information to decide. Then discuss your answers in small groups.

1. I regret that Mary left.

   __F__ Mary is going to leave.

2. I think she passed the test.

   _____ She passed the test.

3. I'm not sure who rang the bell.

   _____ Someone rang the bell.

4. She realized how late it was.

   _____ She didn't know if it was late.

5. I wonder whether they left or not.

   _____ They didn't leave.

6. She doubts that she will come tonight.

   _____ She doesn't think she'll come.

7. He regretted that he left early.

   _____ He wasn't sorry that he left early.

8. We assumed they had won.

   _____ They won.

Find the errors in these sentences and correct them.

1. I wonder where ~~is he~~. *he is*

2. I asked her if could borrow her pen.

3. I thought that she is sleeping when I called.

4. I can't remember who called?

5. Do you know if are you coming with us?

6. I didn't realize, that she was absent.

7. She thought he will come later.

8. Do you know if or not he's staying?

9. I need John's phone number, but I don't know where the phone book.

10. Frederica didn't understand what was saying the teacher.

 # Beyond the Classroom

Searching for Authentic Examples

Find examples of English grammar in everyday life. Choose one of the tasks below. Be prepared to discuss your findings.

A. Look at editorials in newspapers or letters to the editor for mental activity verbs followed by *that* clauses. Write down three examples with *that* clauses and three examples where *that* was omitted, and bring them to class. Which examples were easier to find?

B. Look at advertisements or advice columns. Write down four examples each of noun clauses beginning with *wh-* words and *if/whether*, and bring them to class. What kinds of verbs introduce these noun clauses? Why do you think the noun clauses are used?

C. Watch a television movie or situation comedy in which there is a lot of dialogue. Listen for and write down four examples of direct questions and four examples of indirect questions with noun clauses. Why do you think the speaker uses each type of question in each context? Did you find any contexts where the different types of questions would be interchangeable?

(Continued on page 390)

Writing

Follow these steps to create a poster.

1. You work for a travel agent. Your boss has asked you to design a poster with tips for traveling to a foreign country. In small groups, make a list of what travelers need to do in advance, what they need to find out, and so on. Use mental activity verbs and noun clauses of different types.

2. On your own, decide which of the ideas are the most important and then choose ten of them. Write a rough draft of your poster, using a noun clause in each tip.

   Tips for Traveling to a Foreign Country
   1. Find out whether you need a visa.
   2. Decide where you're going to stay.
   3. Don't assume that . . .

3. Exchange posters with a partner. Underline errors in punctuation, spelling, and grammar. Pay particular attention to the form, meaning, and use of noun clauses. Discuss any errors with the writer. Then rewrite your own poster and make the appropriate changes.

Reported Speech

A Doctor-Patient Relationship in Critical Condition

A1 Before You Read

Discuss these questions.

What are some qualities of a good doctor? Have you ever been to a doctor that you didn't like? What were the problems?

A2 Read

Read this magazine article to find out what happens when doctors and patients don't communicate well.

Doctor-Patient Relationship
in Critical Condition

Have you ever walked out of the doctor's office feeling frustrated? Did you understand what the doctor said? Did your doctor understand what you said?

Concerns about doctor-patient communication are
5 as important as health problems themselves. Like most other interpersonal relationships, success greatly depends on effective communication between doctors and patients. But what if communication fails?

In a study at the Mayo Clinic, patients were asked
10 to fill out a detailed questionnaire right after they had completed a comprehensive medical examination. The survey asked patients to list their most serious health problems, according to their recent examination. At the same time, their physicians were
15 asked what health problems they had discussed with each patient. More than half of the patients did not know what their doctors considered to be their most important health problems. For example, when physicians reported that cholesterol was a major
20 concern, only 45 percent of those patients reported that they had such problems. Similarly, although doctors said their patients were suffering from obesity, high blood pressure, or certain heart problems, 73 percent of the patients didn't report that they had an

obesity problem, 62 percent didn't say they had high blood pressure, and 48 percent never said that there was concern about their heart. The survey concludes that patients often misunderstand their doctors. It also proposes that doctors may be missing the most important concerns of their patients.

The results suggest very clearly that doctors and patients both need to make improvements. First of all, during a discussion, doctors need to make sure to establish eye contact with their patients and frequently ask them <u>if they understand</u>. Doctors should also stop and periodically ask whether there are any questions, and at the end of the visit, they should summarize the discussion in simple terms. Experts suggest that doctors limit their use of medical jargon as much as possible.

Patients also have a lot of work to do. Experts tell patients to plan their visits to the doctor very carefully. They urge making a list of questions, symptoms, and any other concerns, in order of importance, if possible. For example, if there are several issues to discuss, they recommend that patients concentrate on the questions that are most important first. Many doctors complain that too often patients wait until the end of the visit before bringing up important information. In other words, don't mention the wart on your finger before you tell your doctor that you have been experiencing chest pains. And don't be embarrassed about certain issues. Research shows that no matter how embarrassing your problem may be, your doctor has probably dealt with it before.

Perhaps the research confirms something that you have already noticed: The authoritarian doctor and passive patient relationship no longer seems to work. It needs to be replaced by a partnership based more on careful planning, good communication, and shared decision making. In fact, your life may depend on it.

---

authoritarian: demanding that people do exactly what you tell them to do
cholesterol: a substance found in the cells of the body that helps to carry fats
concern: a worry or a matter of importance

critical: very serious or dangerous
jargon: the special language of a profession or trade
obesity: the condition of being very fat
passive: accepting what happens without questioning it
wart: a small, hard, dry growth on the skin caused by a virus

---

 After You Read

Check (✓) the suggestions that would be appropriate for either doctors or patients to follow.

✓ **1.** Make sure the discussion is summarized at the end of the visit.

____ **2.** Learn more medical jargon.

____ **3.** Plan visits carefully.

____ **4.** Don't discuss embarrassing issues.

____ **5.** Don't ask a lot of questions.

____ **6.** Try to improve your communication skills.

B ## Reported Speech

Examining Form

Look back at the article on page 392 and complete the tasks below. Then discuss your observations and read the Form charts to check them.

1. Examine the underlined examples of reported speech clauses. Each one follows a reporting verb in a main clause. Circle the reporting verb related to each example.

2. Which underlined reported speech clause is a *wh-* clause? a *that* clause? an *if/whether* clause? an infinitive?

3. Find other examples of reported speech in the third paragraph (lines 9–30). What reporting verbs are used?

OVERVIEW

Statements
QUOTED SPEECH
"The report is on my desk."

⟶

REPORTED SPEECH WITH *THAT* CLAUSE
She says (that) the report is on her desk.

***Yes/No* Questions**
QUOTED SPEECH
"Are you staying?"

⟶

REPORTED SPEECH WITH *IF/WHETHER* CLAUSE
He asked if I was staying.

Information Questions
QUOTED SPEECH
"Where did you go?"

⟶

REPORTED SPEECH WITH *WH-* CLAUSE
I asked where she had gone.

Imperatives
QUOTED SPEECH
"Press the green button."
"Don't press the red button."

⟶

REPORTED SPEECH WITH INFINITIVE
He told me to press the green button.
He said not to press the red button.

PRESENT TENSE REPORTING

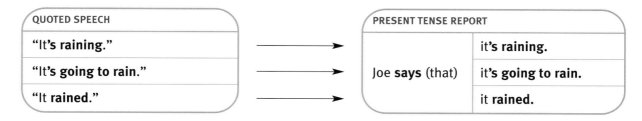

QUOTED SPEECH		PRESENT TENSE REPORT	
"It's raining."	→	Joe **says** (that)	it's raining.
"It's going to rain."	→		it's going to rain.
"It rained."	→		it rained.

PAST TENSE REPORTING

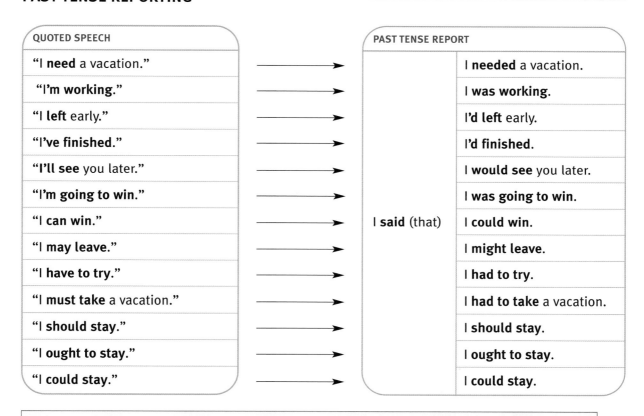

QUOTED SPEECH		PAST TENSE REPORT	
"I **need** a vacation."	→	I **said** (that)	I **needed** a vacation.
"I'm working."	→		I **was working**.
"I **left** early."	→		I'd **left** early.
"I've finished."	→		I'd **finished**.
"I'll see you later."	→		I **would see** you later.
"I'm going to win."	→		I **was going to win**.
"I can win."	→		I **could win**.
"I may leave."	→		I **might leave**.
"I have to try."	→		I **had to try**.
"I must take a vacation."	→		I **had to take** a vacation.
"I should stay."	→		I **should stay**.
"I ought to stay."	→		I **ought to stay**.
"I could stay."	→		I **could stay**.

Reported Speech

- Reported speech (also called indirect speech) has a reporting verb in the main clause (for example, *say* or *ask*) followed by a noun clause or an infinitive.
- See the Vocabulary Notes on page 402 and Appendix 12 for a list of more reporting verbs.
- Reported speech often differs from quoted speech (also called direct speech) in tense, pronouns, and adverbs.
- Reported speech has no quotation marks or question marks.
- See Appendix 13 for punctuation rules for quoted speech.

(Continued on page 396)

> **Present Tense Reporting**
> - If the reporting verb (for example, *say*) is in the present tense, the tense in the *that* clause does not change from the tense of the original quotation.
>
> **Past Tense Reporting**
> - If the reporting verb is in the past tense (for example, *said*), the tense in the *that* clause often changes to a past form.
> - The modals *should, ought to,* and *could* do not change forms in reported speech.

B1 Listening for Form

🎧 **Listen to these sentences and choose the clause that you hear.**

1. **a.** that he didn't know
   b. if he didn't know

2. **a.** if he wanted some books
   b. if he wants some books

3. **a.** that we'd call him back on Monday
   b. we'd call him back on Monday

4. **a.** could we call on Tuesday instead
   b. if we could call on Tuesday instead

5. **a.** he had a special date on Monday night
   b. he has a special date on Monday night

6. **a.** who was he going out with
   b. who he was going out with

7. **a.** that it was none of our business
   b. that we were none of his business

8. **a.** did he have any secrets
   b. if he had any secrets

B2 Identifying Reported Speech

Underline all the examples of reported speech in these conversations. Circle the reporting verb in each sentence. What other reporting verbs besides *tell, ask,* and *say* did you find?

1. **A:** I don't think that the new manager is doing a good job.

   B: Me neither. He told me to come in early yesterday, and he forgot to show up.

   A: You're kidding. Julia said the same thing happened to her on Tuesday. I wonder whether we should complain to Allison. She hired him.

   B: I'm not sure if we should say anything yet. I asked Tom what he thought. He said that we should wait one more week.

2. **A:** Did you hear the news? Channel 7 reported that the superintendent just resigned.

   B: I know. I wonder if something happened. Everyone says he was pleased with the way things were going.

   A: Yesterday's news mentioned that he hadn't been feeling well lately. Maybe it's something serious and his doctor told him to resign.

3. A: Did you speak to the travel agent?

B: Yes. I asked whether I needed to change the flight. He admitted that he'd made a mistake, but he said that he would take care of it. He assured me that everything would work out.

A: Let's hope so. I told you to be careful during the holiday season. They're so busy that they often make mistakes.

Vocabulary Notes

Tell, Say, and Ask

Tell is used to report statements. It is followed by a noun or pronoun and a *that* clause. This noun or pronoun refers to the original listener.

He **told me** that he was late.   I **told Julia** I'd be there soon.

Say is also used to report statements. Unlike *tell*, it is not followed by a noun or pronoun.

He **said** that he was late.   *He said me that he was late. (INCORRECT)

Ask is used to report questions. It can be followed by a noun or pronoun. *Say* and *tell* are not used to report questions.

She **asked** if it was time to leave.

She **asked him** if it was time to leave.

*She said if it was time to leave. (INCORRECT)

Tell, say, and **ask** are used to report imperatives.

He **told me** to go.   He **said** to go.   He **asked me** to go.

B3) Building Sentences with *Tell, Say,* and *Ask*

Build as many meaningful sentences as possible. You may omit the second or third column in some of your sentences. Punctuate your sentences correctly.

He asked them if it was raining.

he asked		if	leave early
I said	them	that	it was raining
she told		to	I had called earlier

B4) Restating Questions with Reported Speech

A. List questions people might ask when they first meet you.

1. <u>What's your name?</u>

2. _____

3. _____

4. _____

5. _____

6. _____

B. Use your questions to complete these sentences.

1. People often ask me <u>what my name is.</u>

2. They also ask me _____

3. They usually want to know _____

4. They sometimes want to know _____

5. Someone typically asks _____

6. Some people even ask _____

B5) Reporting Statements, Questions, and Imperatives

Work with a partner. Read this conversation between a doctor and his patient.
Report what each person said, using the verbs *asked, said,* and *told.* Change tenses
and pronouns where appropriate.

1. **Patient:** How long do I have to stay home from work?
   Doctor: Stay home for a couple of days.

   The patient asked how long she had to stay home from work.
   The doctor said to stay home for a couple of days. OR
   The doctor told her to stay home for a couple of days.

2. **Patient:** Can I have a copy of the test results?
   Doctor: The lab is sending one.

3. **Patient:** How often should I take the medicine?
   Doctor: Don't take it more than three times a day.

4. **Patient:** Do I need to come back?
   Doctor: That won't be necessary unless there's a problem.

5. **Patient:** I need to be better by the weekend.
   Doctor: Why?

6. **Patient:** I'm going out of town for a few days.
   Doctor: You'll be fine. Get lots of sleep.

Reported Speech

Examining Meaning and Use

Read the sentences and answer the questions below. Then discuss your observations and read the Meaning and Use Notes to check them.

    a. Emily said she has a headache. She needs to rest.
    b. Emily said she'd had a headache. It was very painful.
    c. Emily said she had a headache. Don't disturb her.

1. In which two sentences does Emily still have a headache?

2. In which sentence is Emily's headache gone?

Meaning and Use Notes

The Reporter's Point of View

1   Reported speech is used to tell what someone has said or written. It expresses the same meaning as quoted speech, but it expresses the speech from the reporter's point of view rather than from the original speaker's point of view.

Quoted Speech	*Reported Speech*
(Speaker's Point of View)	*(Reporter's Point of View)*
"I'm having a great time." ⟶	**He said he was having** a great time.

Tense Changes

2   The tense in the noun clause may change to a past form if the reporting verb is in the past tense. This tense change usually depends on whether the reporter thinks of the quoted sentences as part of the past.

Quoted Speech	*Past Tense Report*
Alice: How **are** you? ⟶	Alice asked Barbara how she **was.**
Barbara: I'm fine. ⟶	Barbara said she **was** fine.

(Continued on page 400)

3A There are several reasons why the reporter may *not* change the reported speech to a past tense. If the quoted speech just happened, the reporter often keeps the same tense because the time has not changed very much.

Quoted Speech   *Immediate Reports (with Tense Unchanged)*

"I'm going out for a while."

A: What did she say? ⟶ She said she**'s going out** for a while.
(This sentence was spoken only a few seconds after the first speaker's sentence.)

"Flight 403 **has arrived** at gate 9."

A: What did the announcement say? ⟶ It said that flight 403 **has arrived** at gate 9.
(This sentence was spoken only a few seconds after the announcement.)

3B If the reporter wants to show that the quoted speech is a generalization that is always true, the present tense is used.

Quoted Speech   *Generalizations (with Tense Unchanged)*

"We don't accept checks." ⟶ The manager told me that the store **doesn't accept** checks.
(The statement is true all the time, not just when the manager spoke.)

3C If the event in the quoted speech hasn't happened yet, the future is often used.

Quoted Speech   *Future Events (with Tense Unchanged)*

"I am going to appoint a new ⟶ The president announced that she **is going to** judge next week." **appoint** a new judge next week.
(The event hasn't happened yet.)

4A Personal pronouns and possessive adjectives often change to represent the reporter's point of view, instead of the original speaker's point of view.

Quoted Speech   *Reported Speech*

"I need a vacation." ⟶ He said **he** needed a vacation.

"Please take **your** book." ⟶ She told me to take **my** book.

"I like **your** hat." ⟶ I said I liked **his** hat.

4B The words can stay the same when the reporter is repeating his or her own words.

Quoted Speech   *Reported Speech*

"**I** can't find **my** keys." ⟶ <u>I said</u> **I** can't find **my** keys.

Adverb Changes

5 Adverbs of time (e.g., *today, yesterday*) and place (e.g., *here, there*) may change depending on the time of the reported speech and the location of the reporter. They change when the reporter's point of view is different from the speaker's.

Quoted Speech   *Reported Speech*

"I'll call you **tomorrow**." ⟶ He said he would call me **the next day**.

⟶ He said he'd call me **on Monday**.

⟶ He said he'll call me **tomorrow**.

"I'll be **here** until 6:00 P.M." ⟶ He said he'd be **there** until 6:00 P.M.

⟶ He said he'll be **here** until 6:00 P.M.

C1 **Listening for Meaning and Use**   ► Notes 1–5

Listen to the reported speech. Then choose the quoted speech that most closely expresses the meaning of the reported speech.

1. **a.** "Do you need a prescription?"
    (b.) "Do I need a prescription?

2. **a.** "She has a headache."
    b. "She had a headache."

3. **a.** "I called when I got the results."
    b. "I'll call when I get the results."

4. **a.** "When did the results come?"
    b. "When will the results come?"

5. **a.** "They had come the next day."
    b. "They'll come tomorrow."

6. **a.** "You missed your last appointment."
    b. "You'd miss your last appointment."

7. **a.** "Your ankle is sprained."
    b. "My ankle is sprained."

8. **a.** "We'd call back that day."
    b. "We'll call back today."

Vocabulary Notes

More Reporting Verbs

Although *say, tell,* and *ask* are the most common reporting verbs, there are many others.

Verbs Like *Tell* These verbs are followed by a noun or pronoun and a *that* clause. The noun or pronoun refers to the original listener.

assure   convince   inform   notify   persuade   remind

He **assured me** (that) he had an appointment at three o'clock.

The president **informed the Congress** (that) he was going to form a special committee.

Verbs Like *Say* The following verbs may be used without mentioning the original listener.

admit   complain   indicate   remark   shout
announce   confess   mention   reply   state
comment   explain   point out   report   swear

He **complained** it was too late.   I **explained** that I'd be there soon.
I **admitted** that I'd made a mistake.   She **replied** that she was pleased.

Note that if the original listener is mentioned, *to* is needed.

He **admitted to me** that he was sorry.

See Appendix 12 for a list of more reporting verbs.

C2 Understanding Reporting Verbs

Circle the word that best completes the meaning of each sentence.

Kenji left school yesterday. He ((said)/ told) that he couldn't complete the semester.
1

He (informed / explained) me that he had fallen behind in all of his courses. He
2

(assured / confessed) that he hadn't attended two of his courses for over a month. I
3

was shocked. He (reminded / explained) that he'd been looking for a job instead of
4

going to classes. I (told / asked) him if he could go to school part-time instead of
5

quitting. He (replied / persuaded) that it was too late. I (said / advised) him to speak
6   7

to his advisor. He (convinced / promised) that he would, but then he just left town.
8

When I spoke to one of his friends the next day, she (told / asked) me that Kenji
9

had (admitted / told) to her that he had found the work very difficult.
10

Today is Thursday, March 23. Your friend in the hospital has asked you to listen to and report back the messages on his answering machine at home. The messages are from March 20 to 23. Change each message to reported speech using appropriate verb tenses, pronouns, and adverbs.

1. *Monday, March 20*

    a. "This is Nora Green. Please call me back."

    Nora Green called on Monday. She said to call her back. OR
    She asked you to call her back.

    b. "This is Joe's Repair Shop. Call us back. We will be here until 6:00 P.M."

2. *Tuesday, March 21*

    a. "This is Bob. I'll call back later."

    b. "My name is Richard Smith. I'd like to speak to you about an insurance policy. My number is 555-1221."

3. *Wednesday, March 22*

    a. "This is Rosa. I'm just calling to say hello."

    b. "This is Stuart Lee. I've been calling for several days. Is anything wrong? Please call me back soon."

4. *Thursday, March 23*

    a. "This is Eric Martin. Where are you? I have some questions."

    b. "This is Gibson's. We'll be able to deliver the desk you ordered on Monday, March 27."

    c. "This is Tanya. I'm sorry I haven't called. I should have called sooner."

A. Read this recent news item. Write three or four sentences explaining it, using reported speech. Think about the meaning of the article. Is the situation part of the present or past? How does that affect the tenses used in your report?

A recent news article reported that schools have begun . . .

Medical Schools Stress Communication

Medical schools have begun to put communication skills into the curriculum. "The time has come," says a spokesman for the Medical Association, "to focus more on doctor-patient communication."

The public seems to agree. According to the latest Smith Public Opinion Poll, "the best doctors talk with their patients. They encourage questions, they explain procedures, and they discuss alternatives. They also know how to listen. Sometimes they even use humor."

As a result, first-year medical students are spending more time speaking and listening in retirement homes, homeless shelters, soup kitchens, and other community agencies. Back in the classroom, they're discussing what kinds of communication skills they need to treat these patients. They're learning how to interact with patients in a variety of situations, instead of just studying diseases.

B. Compare your sentences with a partner's and discuss any differences you find.

Vocabulary Notes

Reporting Verbs Used for Advising

Base Form in *That* Clauses When the verbs below are followed by a *that* clause, they are often used to tell someone to do something. To express this meaning, the verb in the *that* clause is always in the base form, even if the main clause is in the past.

advise   ask   demand   insist   propose   recommend   suggest

> I **recommend** (that) he stay.   They **suggest** (that) she take a vacation.
> I **recommended** (that) he stay.   They **suggested** (that) she take a vacation.

Should* in *That* Clauses with *Say/Tell With the verbs *say* and *tell*, *should* is often used in a *that* clause to tell someone to do something. Remember that *say* and *tell* can also occur with an infinitive to express the same meaning. However, *say* and *tell* do *not* occur in the base form pattern of the verbs like *advise* above.

> Doctor: Don't eat any spicy foods for a few days.
> Patient: The doctor **said/told me that I shouldn't eat** any spicy foods for a few days.
>   The doctor **said/told me not to eat** any spicy foods for a few days.

A. Maria is a 30-year-old elementary school teacher. She is thinking about finding a new career. Her family and friends have given her a lot of different advice. Complete each sentence by reporting each person's advice with an infinitive, a clause with *should,* or a clause with the base form of the verb.

1. Maria's friend told her <u>not to quit</u> <u>her job until she knows what she</u> <u>wants to do.</u>

   She also recommended that _____

   _____

   _____

2. Her husband suggested _____

   _____

   _____

   He also advised _____

   _____

   _____

3. Her grandmother proposed _____

   _____

   _____

   She also said _____

   _____

   _____

(Continued on page 406)

Meaning and Use • Reported Speech   405

4. Her father insisted _____

_____

_____

He also advised _____

_____

_____

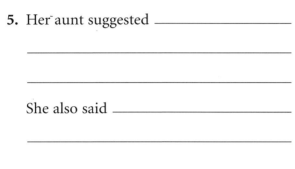

5. Her aunt suggested _____

_____

_____

She also said _____

_____

_____

B. Work in small groups. First, discuss what parents and other family members used to tell you to do when you were growing up. Use reported speech and try to include different types of reporting verbs such as *suggest, insist, demand, advise,* and so on.

My father always insisted that I be on time.
He said that I shouldn't keep people waiting.

C. Write a paragraph describing one of your examples in more detail.

Punctuality was important to my father. He always insisted that I be on time. He said that I shouldn't keep people waiting. He even suggested that I wake up 15 minutes earlier than necessary in the morning in order to be prepared for anything that might cause delay. Unfortunately, I didn't listen to my father at all. One day . . .

Combining Form, Meaning, and Use

Read each sentence and the statements that follow. Write *T* if the statement is true, *F* if it is false, or *?* if you do not have enough information to decide. Then discuss your answers in small groups.

1. Charles told me that I got a raise.

   _F_   **a.** Charles got a raise.

   _____   **b.** I got a raise.

2. Sandra told me that Amy had been sick.

   _____   **a.** Amy is sick.

   _____   **b.** Sandra spoke to Amy.

3. Hector asked his sister to pick up his CD player.

   _____   **a.** The CD player belongs to Hector.

   _____   **b.** Hector spoke to his sister.

4. I said I'd see Marie.

   _____   **a.** I saw Marie.

   _____   **b.** When I said that, I hadn't seen Marie yet.

5. She suggested that I go home.

   _____   **a.** I went home.

   _____   **b.** She wanted me to go home.

6. Amelia asked if I was sick.

   _____   **a.** I was sick.

   _____   **b.** Amelia inquired whether I was sick.

(Continued on page 408)

7. We told him not to drive.

_____ **a.** He didn't drive.

_____ **b.** We said he shouldn't drive.

8. It is recommended that we make a reservation.

_____ **a.** Reservations are suggested.

_____ **b.** Reservations are required.

D2 **Editing**

Find the errors in these paragraphs and correct them.

Linguist Deborah Tannen claims men and women have different conversational styles. She argues that the differences can cause miscommunication between the sexes. Here's a typical example of what Professor Tannen means.

A married couple met at the end of the day. They greeted each other, and he asked her how had her day been. She replied that she has a very busy day. She explained him that she had attended several different meetings, and she had seen four clients. She described how she had felt and what had she been thinking. After that, she eagerly turned to her husband and asked how your day had been. He replied that it had been the same as usual. She looked disappointed, but quickly forgot about it until later that evening when they met friends for dinner. During the meal, her husband told the group that something extraordinary had happened to him today. He went on to explain the amusing details. Everyone laughed except his wife. She felt quite frustrated and confused. She didn't understand why he hadn't told _her_ the story earlier in the evening.

According to Tannen, the answer relates to the difference in conversational styles between men and women. She tells that women use conversation to establish closeness in a relationship, but men consider conversation to be more of a public activity. Men use it to establish their status in a group. Do you agree with this distinction? Do you know men or women like this?

Beyond the Classroom

Searching for Authentic Examples

Find examples of English grammar in everyday life. Choose one of the tasks below. Be prepared to discuss your findings.

A. Listen to a news report. Write down five examples of reported speech and bring them to class. What tenses were used? Why? Can you think of other ways to express the same meaning?

B. Look in a newspaper, in a magazine, or on the Internet. Write down five examples of reported speech and bring them to class. Why do you think reported speech was used instead of quoted speech in each context? What other ways can you paraphrase your examples?

Speaking

In groups of four, follow these steps to role-play customers complaining to a manager in a store.

1. Decide on a context for your role-play—for example, a supermarket, a department store, or a sporting goods store. Then brainstorm different problems that customers might have. For example, the salesperson doesn't know how to refund your money, no one knows where a certain product is, the cashier overcharged you, and so on. Make notes.

2. Choose a manager and three customers. Customers decide which problems they have and the manager decides how he or she will respond. Use reported speech if possible.

   Customer: I told the cashier that she overcharged me, but she said . . .
   Manager: I'll tell her to cancel the transaction. But first, let's ask . . .

3. Present your role-play to the class.

Appendices

❶ Spelling of Verbs and Nouns Ending in -*s* and -*es*

1. For most third-person singular verbs and plural nouns, add -*s* to the base form.

Verbs	**Nouns**
swim — swims	lake — lakes

2. If the base form ends with the letters *s, z, sh, ch,* or *x,* add -*es.*

Verbs	**Nouns**
miss — misses	box — boxes

3. If the base form ends with a consonant + *y,* change *y* to *i* and add -*es.*
    (Compare vowel + *y:* obey — obeys; toy — toys.)

Verbs	**Nouns**
try — tries	baby — babies

4. If the base form ends with a consonant + *o,* add -*s* or -*es.* Some words take -*s, -es,*
    or both -*s* and -*es.* (Compare vowel + *o:* radio — radios; zoo — zoos.)

    -s
    auto — autos
    photo — photos
    piano — pianos
    solo — solos

    -es
    do — does
    echo — echoes
    go — goes
    hero — heroes
    potato — potatoes
    tomato — tomatoes

    Both -s and -es
    tornado — tornados/tornadoes
    volcano — volcanos/volcanoes
    zero — zeros/zeroes

5. If the base form of certain nouns ends in a single *f* or in *fe,* change the *f* or *fe* to *v*
    and add -*es.*

    calf — calves
    shelf — shelves
    knife — knives

    Exceptions
    belief — beliefs
    chief — chiefs
    roof — roofs
    scarf — scarfs/scarves

② Pronunciation of Verbs and Nouns Ending in -s and -es

1. If the base form of the verb or noun ends with the sounds /s/, /z/, /ʃ/, /ʒ/, /tʃ/, /dʒ/, or /ks/, then pronounce -es as an extra syllable /ɪz/.

Verbs

slice — slices   watch — watches

lose — loses   judge — judges

wash — washes   relax — relaxes

Nouns

price — prices   inch — inches

size — sizes   language — languages

dish — dishes   tax — taxes

garage — garages

2. If the base form ends with the voiceless sounds /p/, /t/, /k/, /f/, or /θ/, then pronounce -s and -es as /s/.

Verbs

sleep — sleeps   work — works

hit — hits   laugh — laughs

Nouns

grape — grapes   cuff — cuffs

cat — cats   fifth — fifths

book — books

3. If the base form ends with any other consonant or with a vowel sound, then pronounce -s and -es as /z/.

Verbs

learn — learns

go — goes

Nouns

name — names

boy — boys

③ Spelling of Verbs Ending in -ing

1. For most verbs, add -ing to the base form of the verb.

sleep — sleeping   talk — talking

2. If the base form ends in a single e, drop the e and add -ing (exception: be – being).

live — living   write — writing

3. If the base form ends in ie, change ie to y and add -ing.

die — dying   lie — lying

4. If the base form of a one-syllable verb ends with a single vowel + consonant, double the final consonant and add -ing. (Compare two vowels + consonant: eat — eating.)

hit — hitting   stop — stopping

5. If the base form of a verb with two or more syllables ends in a single vowel + consonant, double the final consonant only if the stress is on the final syllable. Do not double the final consonant if the stress is not on the final syllable.

admít — admitting   begín — beginning   devélop — developing   lísten — listening

6. Do not double the final consonants x, w, and y.

fix — fixing   plow — plowing   obey — obeying

4 Spelling of Verbs Ending in *-ed*

1. To form the simple past and past participle of most regular verbs, add *-ed* to the base form.

   brush — brushed   play — played

2. If the base form ends with *e*, just add *-d*.

   close — closed   live — lived

3. If the base form ends with a consonant + *y*, change the *y* to *i* and add *-ed*. (Compare vowel +*y*: play — played; enjoy — enjoyed.)

   study — studied   dry — dried

4. If the base form of a one-syllable verb ends with a single vowel + consonant, double the final consonant and add *-ed*.

   plan — planned   shop — shopped

5. If the base form of a verb with two or more syllables ends in a single vowel + consonant, double the final consonant and add *-ed* only when the stress is on the final syllable. Do not double the final consonant if the stress is not on the final syllable.

   preférr — preferred   énter — entered

6. Do not double the final consonants *x, w,* and *y*.

   coax — coaxed   snow — snowed   stay — stayed

5 Pronunciation of Verbs Ending in *-ed*

1. If the base form of the verb ends with the sounds /t/ or /d/, then pronounce *-ed* as an extra syllable /ɪd/.

/t/	**/d/**
start — started	need — needed
wait — waited	decide — decided

2. If the base form ends with the voiceless sounds /f/, /k/, /p/, /s/, /ʃ/, /tʃ/, or /ks/, then pronounce *-ed* as /t/.

laugh — laughed	jump — jumped	wish — wished	fax — faxed
look — looked	slice — sliced	watch — watched	

3. If the base form ends with the voiced sounds /b/, /g/, /dʒ/, /m/, /n/, /ŋ/, /l/, /r/, /ð/, /v/, /z/, or with a vowel, then pronounce *-ed* as /d/.

rob — robbed	hum — hummed	call — called	wave — waved
brag — bragged	rain — rained	order — ordered	close — closed
judge — judged	bang — banged	bathe — bathed	play — played

6 Irregular Verbs

Base Form	Simple Past	Past Participle
arise	arose	arisen
be	was/were	been
beat	beat	beaten
become	became	become
begin	began	begun
bend	bent	bent
bet	bet	bet
bind	bound	bound
bite	bit	bitten
bleed	bled	bled
blow	blew	blown
break	broke	broken
bring	brought	brought
build	built	built
burst	burst	burst
buy	bought	bought
catch	caught	caught
choose	chose	chosen
cling	clung	clung
come	came	come
cost	cost	cost
creep	crept	crept
cut	cut	cut
deal	dealt	dealt
dig	dug	dug
dive	dove (or dived)	dived
do	did	done
draw	drew	drawn
drink	drank	drunk
drive	drove	driven
eat	ate	eaten
fall	fell	fallen
feed	fed	fed
feel	felt	felt
fight	fought	fought
find	found	found
fit	fit	fit
flee	fled	fled
fly	flew	flown
forbid	forbade	forbidden
forget	forgot	forgotten
forgive	forgave	forgiven

Base Form	Simple Past	Past Participle
freeze	froze	frozen
get	got	gotten
give	gave	given
go	went	gone
grind	ground	ground
grow	grew	grown
hang	hung	hung
have	had	had
hear	heard	heard
hide	hid	hidden
hit	hit	hit
hold	held	held
hurt	hurt	hurt
keep	kept	kept
know	knew	known
lay (= put)	laid	laid
lead	led	led
leave	left	left
lend	lent	lent
let	let	let
lie (= recline)	lay	lain
light	lit	lit
lose	lost	lost
make	made	made
mean	meant	meant
meet	met	met
pay	paid	paid
prove	proved	proven (or proved)
put	put	put
quit	quit	quit
read	read	read
ride	rode	ridden
ring	rang	rung
rise	rose	risen
run	ran	run
say	said	said
see	saw	seen
seek	sought	sought
sell	sold	sold
send	sent	sent
set	set	set
sew	sewed	sewn

Base Form	Simple Past	Past Participle	Base Form	Simple Past	Past Participle
shake	shook	shaken	strike	struck	struck
shine	shone	shone	string	strung	strung
shoot	shot	shot	swear	swore	sworn
show	showed	shown	sweep	swept	swept
shrink	shrank	shrunk	swim	swam	swum
shut	shut	shut	swing	swung	swung
sing	sang	sung	take	took	taken
sink	sank	sunk	teach	taught	taught
sit	sat	sat	tear	tore	torn
sleep	slept	slept	tell	told	told
slide	slid	slid	think	thought	thought
speak	spoke	spoken	throw	threw	thrown
speed	sped	sped	understand	understood	understood
spend	spent	spent	undertake	undertook	undertaken
spin	spun	spun	upset	upset	upset
split	split	split	wake	woke	woken
spread	spread	spread	wear	wore	worn
spring	sprang	sprung	weave	wove	woven
stand	stood	stood	weep	wept	wept
steal	stole	stolen	wet	wet	wet
stick	stuck	stuck	win	won	won
sting	stung	stung	wind	wound	wound
stink	stank	stunk	write	wrote	written

7 Common Intransitive Verbs

These verbs can only be used intransitively. (They cannot be followed by an object.)

ache	emerge	itch	sit
appear	erupt	laugh	sleep
arrive	faint	live	smile
be	fall	look	snow
come	frown	matter	stand
cry	go	occur	stay
depart	grin	rain	talk
die	happen	remain	weep
disappear	hesitate	seem	

8 Gerunds

Verb + Gerund

These verbs may be followed by gerunds, but not by infinitives:

acknowledge	detest	keep (= continue)	recall
admit	discuss	loathe	recollect
anticipate	dislike	mean (= involve)	recommend
appreciate	endure	mention	regret
avoid	enjoy	mind (= object to)	report
can't help	escape	miss	resent
celebrate	excuse	omit	resist
consider	feel like	postpone	resume
defend	finish	practice	risk
defer	go	prevent	suggest
delay	imagine	prohibit	tolerate
deny	involve	quit	understand

Verb with Preposition + Gerund

These verbs or verb phrases with prepositions may be followed by gerunds, but not by infinitives:

adapt to	believe in	depend on
adjust to	blame for	disapprove of
agree (with someone) on	care about	discourage (someone) from
apologize (to someone) for	complain (to someone) about	engage in
approve of	concentrate on	forgive (someone) for
argue (with someone) about	consist of	help (someone) with
ask about	decide on	

Be + Adjective + Preposition + Gerund

Adjectives with prepositions typically occur in *be* + adjective phrases. These phrases may be followed by gerunds, but not by infinitives:

be accustomed to	be famous for	be proud of
be afraid of	be fond of	be responsible for
be angry (at someone) about	be glad about	be sad about
be ashamed of	be good at	be successful in
be capable of	be happy about	be suitable for
be certain of/about	be incapable of	be tired of
be concerned with	be interested in	be tolerant of
be critical of	be jealous of	be upset about
be discouraged from	be known for	be used to
be enthusiastic about	be nervous about	be useful for
be familiar with	be perfect for	be worried about

9 Infinitives

These verbs may be followed by infinitives, but not by gerunds:

Verb + Infinitive

agree	decide	manage	struggle
aim	decline	plan	swear
appear	demand	pledge	tend
arrange	fail	pretend	volunteer
care	guarantee	refuse	wait
claim	hope	resolve	
consent	intend	seem	

Verb + Object + Infinitive

advise	get	persuade	tell
command	hire	remind	trust
convince	invite	require	urge
force	order	teach	warn

Verb + (Object) + Infinitive

ask	desire	need	promise
beg	expect	offer	want
choose	help	pay	wish
dare	know	prepare	would like

Adjective + Infinitive

afraid	distressed	hesitant	reluctant
alarmed	disturbed	impossible	right
amazed	eager	interested	sad
anxious	easy	likely	scared
astonished	embarrassed	lucky	shocked
careful	excited	necessary	sorry
curious	fascinated	pleased	surprised
delighted	fortunate	possible	unlikely
depressed	frightened	prepared	unnecessary
determined	glad	proud	willing
difficult	happy	ready	wrong
disappointed	hard	relieved	

⑩ Verb + Infinitive or Gerund

These verbs may be followed by infinitives or gerunds:

attempt	continue	neglect	start
begin	forget	prefer	stop
can't bear	hate	propose	try
can't stand	like	regret	
cease	love	remember	

⑪ Mental Activity Verbs

These mental activity verbs are followed by noun clauses:

agree	doubt	hope	recall
assume	dream	imagine	recognize
believe	expect	know	regret
bet	feel	learn	remember
calculate	figure out	mean	suppose
conclude	find (out)	notice	think
consider	forget	pretend	understand
decide	guess	prove	wonder
discover	hear	realize	

⑫ Reporting Verbs

Verb + Noun Clause

These reporting verbs are followed by noun clauses:

acknowledge	complain	inform (someone)	remind (someone)
add	conclude	insist	repeat
admit	confess	instruct (someone)	reply
advise (someone)	confirm	maintain	report
affirm	convince (someone)	mention	respond
agree	cry	murmur	roar
announce	declare	mutter	say
answer	demand	note	scream
argue	deny	notify (someone)	shout
ask	emphasize	observe	shriek
assert	estimate	persuade (someone)	sneer
assure (someone)	exclaim	point out	stammer
boast	explain	promise	state
brag	grumble	propose	suggest
caution	guess	protest	swear
claim	imply	recommend	tell (someone)
comment	indicate	remark	threaten

Verb + Infinitive

These reporting verbs are used with infinitives:

advise (someone) to
ask (someone) to
beg (someone) to
command (someone) to
direct (someone) to

forbid (someone) to
instruct (someone) to
oblige (someone) to
order (someone) to
request (someone) to

tell (someone) to
urge (someone) to
want (someone) to

13 Punctuation Rules for Quoted Speech

1. If quoted speech comes after the reporting verb:
   - Place a comma after the reporting verb.
   - Place quotation marks at the beginning and end of reported speech. Put them near the top of the letter.
   - Begin quoted speech with a capital letter.
   - Use the correct punctuation (a period, an exclamation mark, or a question mark) and place the punctuation inside the quotation marks.

   Examples
   He said, "We are staying."
   He shouted, "We are staying!"
   He asked me, "Are we staying?"

2. If quoted speech comes before the reporting verb:
   - Place quotation marks at the beginning and end of reported speech. Put them near the top of the letter.
   - Begin quoted speech with a capital letter.
   - Use a comma if the quoted speech is a statement. Use an exclamation mark if the quoted speech is an exclamation. Use a question mark if the quoted speech is a question. Place the punctuation inside the quotation marks.
   - Begin the phrase that follows the quoted speech with a lowercase letter.
   - Use a period at the end of the main sentence.

   Examples
   "We are staying," he said.
   "We are staying!" he shouted.
   "Are we staying?" he asked me.

⑭ Contractions with Verb and Modal Forms

Contractions with *Be*

I am	=	I'm
you are	=	you're
he is	=	he's
she is	=	she's
it is	=	it's
we are	=	we're
you are	=	you're
they are	=	they're

I am not	=	I'm not
you are not	=	you're not / you aren't
he is not	=	he's not / he isn't
she is not	=	she's not / she isn't
it is not	=	it's not / it isn't
we are not	=	we're not / we aren't
you are not	=	you're not / you aren't
they are not	=	they're not / they aren't

Contractions with *Be Going To*

I am going to	=	I'm going to
you are going to	=	you're going to
he is going to	=	he's going to
she is going to	=	she's going to
it is going to	=	it's going to
we are going to	=	we're going to
you are going to	=	you're going to
they are going to	=	they're going to
you are not going to	=	you're not going to / you aren't going to

Contractions with *Will*

I will	=	I'll
you will	=	you'll
he will	=	he'll
she will	=	she'll
it will	=	it'll
we will	=	we'll
you will	=	you'll
they will	=	they'll
will not	=	won't

Contractions with *Would*

I would	=	I'd
you would	=	you'd
he would	=	he'd
she would	=	she'd
we would	=	we'd
you would	=	you'd
they would	=	they'd
would not	=	wouldn't

Contractions with *Was* and *Were*

was not	=	wasn't
were not	=	weren't

Contractions with *Have*

I have	=	I've
you have	=	you've
he has	=	he's
she has	=	she's
it has	=	it's
we have	=	we've
you have	=	you've
they have	=	they've
have not	=	haven't
has not	=	hasn't

Contractions with *Had*

I had	=	I'd
you had	=	you'd
he had	=	he'd
she had	=	she'd
it had	=	it'd
we had	=	we'd
you had	=	you'd
they had	=	they'd
had not	=	hadn't

Contractions with *Do* and *Did*

do not	=	don't
does not	=	doesn't
did not	=	didn't

Contractions with Modals and Phrasal Modals

cannot / can not	=	can't
could not	=	couldn't
should not	=	shouldn't
have got to	=	've got to
has got to	=	's got to

⑮ Phrasal Verbs

Separable Phrasal Verbs

Many two-word phrasal verbs are separable. This means that a noun object can separate the two words of the phrasal verb or follow the phrasal verb. If the object is a pronoun *(me, you, him, her, it, us, them)*, the pronoun must separate the two words.

Noun Object	Pronoun Object
She **turned** the offer **down**.	She **turned** it **down**.
She **turned down** the offer.	*She turned down it. (INCORRECT)

These are some common separable phrasal verbs and their meanings:

Phrasal Verb	Meaning
ask (someone) out	invite someone to go out
ask (someone) over	invite someone to come to your house
blow (something) up	inflate, cause something to explode
boot (something) up	start or get a computer ready for use
bring (someone) up	raise a child
bring (something) up	introduce or call attention to a topic
burn (something) down	destroy by fire
call (someone) back	return a phone call to someone
call (something) off	cancel something
call (someone) up	telephone
call (something) up	retrieve from the memory of a computer
check (something) out	borrow a book, tape, video from the library; verify
clean (something) out	clean the inside of something thoroughly
clean (something) up	clean thoroughly and remove anything unwanted
clear (something) up	explain a problem
cross (something) out	draw a line through
cut (something) up	cut into little pieces
do (something) over	do something again
figure (something) out	solve a problem
fill (something) in	write in a blank or a space
fill (something) out	write information on a form
fill (something) up	fill completely with something
find (something) out	discover information
give (something) back	return something
give (something) up	quit something; get rid of something
hand (something) in	submit homework, a test, an application
hand (something) out	distribute something
hang (something) up	put on a clothes hanger; end a telephone call
keep (someone) up	prevent someone from going to sleep
kick (someone) out	force someone to leave
leave (something) out	omit

Phrasal Verb	Meaning
look (something) over	examine carefully
look (something) up	look for information in a book
make (something) up	create or invent something; do work that was missed
make (something) up to (someone)	return a favor to someone
pay (someone) back	return money owned to someone
pick (something) out	choose
pick (something/someone) up	lift something or someone; stop to get something or someone
point (something) out	mention, draw attention to something
put (something) away	put something in its usual place
put (something) back	return something to its original place
put (something) down	stop holding something
put (something) in	install
put (something) off	postpone
put (something) on	get dressed
put (something) out	extinguish a fire, cigarette, or cigar
put (something) over on (someone)	deceive someone
set (something) up	make something ready for use
shut (something) off	turn off a machine
start (something) over	start again
take (something) away	remove
take (a time period) off	have a break from work or school
take (something) off	remove
take (someone) out	accompany to the theater, a restaurant, a movie
take (something) out	remove something from something else
tear (something) down	destroy completely
tear (something) off	detach something
tear (something) up	tear into pieces
think (something) over	reflect upon something before making a decision
think (something) up	invent
throw (something) away	put something in the trash
throw (something) out	put something in the trash
try (something) on	put on clothing to see how it looks
turn (something) down	lower the volume; refuse an offer or invitation
turn (something) in	return; submit homework, a test, an application
turn (something) off	stop a machine or light
turn (something) on	start a machine or light
turn (something) up	increase the volume
use (something) up	use something until no more is left
wake (someone) up	cause someone to stop sleeping
wear (someone) out	cause someone to become exhausted
work (something) out	solve something
write (something) down	write something on a piece of paper

Nonseparable Phrasal Verbs

Some two-word verbs and most three-word verbs are nonseparable. This means that a noun or pronoun object cannot separate the two parts of the phrasal verb.

Noun Object

The teacher **went over** the lesson.

*The teacher went the lesson over. (INCORRECT)

Pronoun Object

The teacher **went over** it.

*The teacher went it over. (INCORRECT)

These are some common nonseparable phrasal verbs and their meanings:

Phrasal Verb	Meaning
blow up	explode
break down	stop functioning properly
break up with (someone)	end a relationship with someone
burn down	be destroyed by fire
call on (someone)	ask someone to answer or speak in class
catch up with (someone/something)	travel fast enough to overtake someone who is ahead
check out of (a hotel)	leave a hotel after paying the bill
clear up	become fair weather
come back	return
come over	visit
come up with (something)	think of a plan or reply
cut down on (something)	reduce
eat out	have a meal in a restaurant
face up to (something)	be brave enough to accept or deal with
fall down	leave a standing position; perform in a disappointing way
get away with (doing something)	not be punished for doing something wrong
get down to (something)	begin to give serious attention to
get off (something)	leave a plane, bus, train
get on (something)	enter a plane, bus, train
get over (something)	recover from an illness or serious life event
get up	arise from a bed or chair
give up	stop trying, lose hope
go back	return
go down	(of computers) stop functioning; (of prices or temperature) become lower; (of ships) sink; (of the sun or moon) set
go off	stop functioning; (of alarms) start functioning; explode or make a loud noise
go on	take place, happen
go out	leave one's house to go to a social event
go out with (someone)	spend time regularly with someone
go over (something)	review
grow up	become an adult
hold on	wait on the telephone
keep on (doing something)	continue doing something
keep up with	stay at the same level or position
look out for (something/someone)	be careful of something or someone

Phrasal Verb	Meaning
move out	stop occupying a residence, especially by removing one's possessions
pack up	prepare all of one's belongings for moving
put up with (something/someone)	tolerate
run out	come to an end, be completely used up
run out of (something)	have no more of something
show up	appear, be seen, arrive at a place
sit down	get into a seated position
stay out	remain out of the house, especially at night
stay up	remain awake, not go to bed
take off	leave (usually by plane)
turn up	appear
wake up	stop sleeping
work out	exercise vigorously

16 Phonetic Symbols

Vowels

i	**see** /si/	u	**too** /tu/	oʊ	**go** /goʊ/
ɪ	**sit** /sɪt/	ʌ	**cup** /kʌp/	ər	**bird** /bərd/
ɛ	**ten** /tɛn/	ə	**about** /əˈbaʊt/	ɪr	**near** /nɪr/
æ	**cat** /kæt/	eɪ	**say** /seɪ/	ɛr	**hair** /hɛr/
ɑ	**hot** /hɑt/	aɪ	**five** /faɪv/	ɑr	**car** /kɑr/
ɔ	**saw** /sɔ/	ɔɪ	**boy** /bɔɪ/	ɔr	**north** /nɔrθ/
ʊ	**put** /pʊt/	aʊ	**now** /naʊ/	ʊr	**tour** /tʊr/

Consonants

p	**pen** /pɛn/	f	**fall** /fɔl/	m	**man** /mæn/
b	**bad** /bæd/	v	**voice** /vɔɪs/	n	**no** /noʊ/
t	**tea** /ti/	θ	**thin** /θɪn/	ŋ	**sing** /sɪŋ/
ţ	**butter** /ˈbʌţər/	ð	**then** /ðɛn/	l	**leg** /lɛg/
d	**did** /dɪd/	s	**so** /soʊ/	r	**red** /rɛd/
k	**cat** /kæt/	z	**zoo** /zu/	y	**yes** /yɛs/
g	**got** /gɑt/	ʃ	**she** /ʃi/	w	**wet** /wɛt/
tʃ	**chin** /tʃɪn/	ʒ	**vision** /ˈvɪʒn/	x	**Chanukah** /ˈxɑnəkə/
dʒ	**June** /dʒun/	h	**how** /haʊ/		

Glossary of Grammar Terms

ability modal *See* **modal of ability.**

active sentence In active sentences, the agent (the noun that is performing the action) is in subject position and the receiver (the noun that receives or is a result of the action) is in object position. In the following sentence, the subject **Alex** performed the action, and the object **letter** received the action.

Alex mailed the letter.

adjective A word that describes or modifies the meaning of a noun.

the **orange** car   a **strange** noise

adjective clause *See* **relative clause.**

adjective phrase A phrase that functions as an adjective.

These shoes are **too tight.**

adverb A word that describes or modifies the meaning of a verb, another adverb, an adjective, or a sentence. Adverbs answer such questions as *How? When? Where?* or *How often?* They often end in **-ly.**

She ran **quickly.**   She ran **very** quickly.

a **really** hot day   **Maybe** she'll leave.

adverb of frequency An adverb that tells how often a situation occurs. Adverbs of frequency range in meaning from *all of the time* to *none of the time.*

She **always** eats breakfast.   He **never** eats meat.

adverbial phrase A phrase that functions as an adverb.

Amy spoke **very softly.**

affirmative statement A positive sentence that does not have a negative verb.

Linda went to the movies.

agent The noun that is performing the action in a sentence. *See* **active sentence, passive sentence.**

The letter was mailed by **Alex.**

agentless passive A passive sentence that doesn't mention an agent.

The letter was mailed.

agreement The subject and verb of a clause must agree in number. If the subject is singular, the verb form is also singular. If the subject is plural, the verb form is also plural.

He comes home early.   **They come** home early.

article The words **a, an,** and **the** in English. Articles are used to introduce and identify nouns.

a potato   **an** onion   **the** supermarket

auxiliary verb A verb that is used before main verbs (or other auxiliary verbs) in a sentence. Auxiliary verbs are usually used in questions and negative sentences. **Do, have,** and **be** can act as auxiliary verbs. Modals (**may, can, will,** and so on) are also auxiliary verbs.

Do you have the time?   I **have** never been to Italy.

The suitcase **was** taken.   I **may** be late.

base form The form of a verb without any verb endings; the infinitive form without *to.* Also called *simple form.*

sleep   be   stop

clause A group of words that has a subject and a verb. *See also* **dependent clause** and **main clause.**

If I leave, . . .   The rain stopped.

. . . when he speaks.   . . . that I saw.

common noun A noun that refers to any of a class of people, animals, places, things, or ideas. Common nouns are not capitalized.

man   cat   city   pencil   grammar

communication verb *See* **reporting verb.**

comparative A form of an adjective, adverb, or noun that is used to express differences between two items or situations.

This book is **heavier than** that one.

He runs **more quickly than** his brother.

A CD costs **more money than** a cassette.

complex sentence A sentence that has a main clause and one or more dependent clauses.

> When the bell rang, we were finishing dinner.

conditional sentence A sentence that expresses a real or unreal situation in the *if* clause, and the (real or unreal) expected result in the main clause.

> If I have time, I will travel to Africa.
> If I had time, I would travel to Africa.

contraction The combination of two words into one by omitting certain letters and replacing them with an apostrophe.

> I will = **I'll**   we are = **we're**   are not = **aren't**

count noun A common noun that can be counted. It usually has both a singular and a plural form.

> orange — oranges   woman — women

defining relative clause *See* **restrictive relative clause.**

definite article The word **the** in English. It is used to identify nouns based on assumptions about what information the speaker and listener share about the noun. The definite article is also used for making general statements about a whole class or group of nouns.

> Please give me **the** key.
> **The** scorpion is dangerous.

dependent clause A clause that cannot stand alone as a sentence because it depends on the main clause to complete the meaning of the sentence. Also called *subordinate clause.*

> I'm going home **after he calls.**

determiner A word such as **a, an, the, this, that, these, those, my, some, a few,** and **three,** that is used before a noun to limit its meaning in some way.

> **those** videos

direct speech *See* **quoted speech.**

embedded question *See wh-* **clause.**

future A time that is to come. The future is expressed in English with **will, be going to,** the simple present, or the present continuous. These different forms of the future often have different meanings and uses. *See also* **future continuous.**

> I **will** help you later.
> David **is going to** call later.
> The train **leaves** at 6:05 this evening.
> **I'm driving** to Toronto tomorrow.

future continuous A verb form that expresses an activity in progress at a specific time in the future. It is formed with **will** + **be** + main verb + **-ing.**

> **I'll be leaving** for Hawaii at noon tomorrow.

general quantity expression A quantity expression that indicates whether a quantity or an amount is large or small. It does not give an exact amount.

> **a lot of** cookies   **a little** flour

general statement A generalization about a whole class or group of nouns.

> Whales are mammals.
> A daffodil is a flower that grows from a bulb.

generic noun A noun that refers to a whole class or group of nouns.

> I like **rice.**
> **A bird** can fly.
> **The laser** is an important tool.

gerund An -ing form of a verb that is used in place of a noun or pronoun to name an activity or a situation.

> **Skiing** is fun.   He doesn't like **being sick.**

identifying relative clause *See* **restrictive relative clause.**

***if* clause** A dependent clause that begins with **if** and expresses a real or unreal situation.

> If I **have the time,** I'll paint the kitchen.
> If I **had the time,** I'd paint the kitchen.

***if/whether* clause** A noun clause that begins with either **if** or **whether.**

> I don't know **if they're here.**
> I don't know **whether or not they're here.**

imperative A type of sentence, usually without a subject, that tells someone to do something. The verb is in the base form.

> **Open** your books to page 36.
> **Be** ready at eight.

impersonal *you* The use of the pronoun **you** to refer to people in general rather than a particular person or group of people.

> Nowadays, **you** can buy anything on the Internet.

indefinite article The words **a** and **an** in English. Indefinite articles introduce a noun as a member of a class of nouns, or make generalizations about a whole class or group of nouns.

> Please hand me **a** pencil.
> **An** ocean is **a** large body of water.

independent clause *See* **main clause.**

indirect question *See* **wh- clause.**

indirect speech *See* **reported speech.**

infinitive A verb form that includes **to** + the base form of a verb. An infinitive is used in place of a noun or pronoun to name an activity or situation expressed by a verb.

> Do you like **to swim**?

information question A question that begins with a **wh-** word.

> Where does she live?   Who lives here?

intransitive verb A verb that cannot be followed by an object.

> We finally **arrived**.

irregular verb A verb that forms the simple past in a different way than regular verbs.

> put — put — put   buy — bought — bought

main clause A clause that can be used by itself as a sentence. Also called *independent clause.*

> I'm going home.

main verb A verb that can be used alone in a sentence. A main verb can also occur with an auxiliary verb.

> I **ate** lunch at 11:30.   Kate can't **eat** lunch today.

mental activity verb A verb such as **decide, know,** and **understand,** that expresses an opinion, thought, or feeling.

> I don't **know** why she left.

modal The auxiliary verbs **can, could, may, might, must, should, will,** and **would.** They modify the meaning of a main verb by expressing ability, authority, formality, politeness, or various degrees of certainty. Also called *modal auxiliary.*

> You **should** take something for your headache.
> Applicants **must** have a high school diploma.

modal of ability **Can** and **could** are called modals of ability when they express knowledge, skill, opportunity, and capability.

> He **can** speak Arabic and English.
> **Can** you play the piano?
> Yesterday we **couldn't** leave during the storm.
> Seat belts **can** save lives.

modal of possibility **Could, might, may, should, must,** and **will** are called modals of possibility when they express various degrees of certainty ranging from slight possibility to strong certainty.

> It **could** / **might** / **may** / **will** rain later.

modal auxiliary *See* **modal.**

modify To add to or change the meaning of a word.

> expensive cars (The adjective **expensive** modifies **cars.**)

noncount noun A common noun that cannot be counted. A noncount noun has no plural form and cannot occur with **a, an,** or a number.

> information   mathematics   weather

nondefining relative clause *See* **nonrestrictive relative clause.**

nonidentifying relative clause *See* **nonrestrictive relative clause.**

nonrestrictive relative clause A relative clause that adds extra information about the noun that it modifies. This information is not necessary to identify the noun, and it can be omitted. Also called *nondefining* or *nonidentifying relative clause.*

> Rick**, who is seven,** plays hockey.

nonseparable Refers to two- or three-word verbs that don't allow a noun or pronoun object to separate the two or three words in the verb phrase. Certain two-word verbs and almost all three-word verbs are nonseparable.

Amy **got off** the bus.

We **cut down on** fat in our diet.

noun A word that typically refers to a person, animal, place, thing, or idea.

Tom   rabbit   store   computer   mathematics

noun clause A dependent clause that can occur in the same place as a noun, pronoun, or noun phrase in a sentence. Noun clauses begin with **wh-** words, **if, whether,** or **that.**

I don't know **where he is.**   I wonder **if he's coming.**

I don't know **whether it's true.**   I think **that it's a lie.**

noun phrase A phrase formed by a noun and its modifiers. A noun phrase can substitute for a noun in a sentence.

She drank **milk.**

She drank **chocolate milk.**

She drank **the milk.**

object A noun, pronoun, or noun phrase that follows a transitive verb or a preposition.

Steve threw **the ball.**   She likes **him.**

Go with **her.**

object relative pronoun A relative pronoun that is the object of a relative clause. It comes before the subject noun or pronoun of the relative clause.

the letter **that / which** I wrote

the man **who / whom** I saw

passive sentence Passive sentences emphasize the receiver of an action by changing the usual order of the subject and object in a sentence. The subject (**The letter**) does not perform the action; it receives the action or is the result of an action. The passive is formed with a form of **be** + the past participle of a transitive verb.

The letter was mailed yesterday.

past continuous A verb form that expresses an action or situation in progress at a specific time in the past. The past continuous is formed with **was** or **were** + verb + **-ing.** Also called *past progressive.*

A: What **were** you **doing** last night at eight o'clock?

B: I **was studying**.

past modal A modal that is used to express past certainty, past obligations, and past abilities or opportunities. It is formed with a modal + **have** + past participle of the main verb. Also called *perfect modal.*

He **must have arrived** late.

I **should have called,** but I forgot.

We **could have come,** but no one told us.

past participle A past verb form that may differ from the simple past form of some irregular verbs. It is used to form the present perfect, present perfect continuous, past perfect, past perfect continuous, and the passive.

I have never **seen** that movie.

He's **been** working too much lately.

By noon, we had already **taken** the exam.

She had **been** working since 8:30.

The letter was **sent** on Monday.

past perfect A verb form that expresses a relationship between two past times. The past perfect indicates the earlier event or situation. It is formed with **had** + the past participle of the main verb.

I **had** already **left** when she called.

past perfect continuous A verb form that is like the past perfect, but it emphasizes the duration of the earlier event or situation. It is formed with **had** + **been** + main verb + **-ing.**

When I was offered the position, I **had been looking** for a new job for several months.

past perfect progressive *See* **past perfect continuous.**

past progressive *See* **past continuous.**

past phrasal modal Examples of past phrasal modals are **ought to have, have to have,** and **have got to have.**

past unreal conditional sentence A **conditional** sentence that expresses an unreal condition about the past and its imaginary result. It has an **if** clause in the past perfect and a main clause with **would have** + the past participle of the main verb.

> If I had been smarter, I would have complained to the manager.

past *wish* sentence A **wish** sentence that expresses a desire for something that didn't actually happen in the past. It is formed with a **wish** clause + a past perfect clause.

> I wish I had moved to Colorado.

perfect modal *See* **past modal.**

phrasal modal A verb that is not a true modal, but has the same meaning as a modal verb. Examples of phrasal modals are **ought to, have to,** and **have got to.**

phrasal verb A two- or three-word verb such as **turn down** or **run out of.** The meaning of a phrasal verb is usually different from the meanings of its individual words.

> She **turned down** the job offer.
> Don't **run out of** gas on the freeway.

phrase A group of words that can form a grammatical unit. A phrase can take the form of a noun phrase, verb phrase, adjective phrase, adverbial phrase, or prepositional phrase. This means it can act as a noun, verb, adjective, adverb, or preposition.

> The **tall man** left. Lee **hit the ball.**
> The child was **very quiet.** She spoke **too fast.**
> They ran **down the stairs.**

possibility modal *See* **modal of possibility.**

preposition A word such as **at, in, on,** or **to,** that links nouns, pronouns, and gerunds to other words.

prepositional phrase A phrase that consists of a preposition followed by a noun or noun phrase.

> on Sunday under the table

present continuous A verb form that indicates that an action is in progress, temporary, or changing. It is formed with **be** + verb + **-ing.** Also called *present progressive.*

> I**'m watering** the garden.
> Ruth **is working** for her uncle.
> He**'s getting** better.

present perfect A verb form that expresses a connection between the past and the present. It indicates indefinite past time, recent past time, or continuing past time. The present perfect is formed with **have** + the past participle of the main verb.

> I**'ve seen** that movie.
> The manager **has** just **resigned.**
> We**'ve been** here for three hours.

present perfect continuous A verb form that focuses on the duration of actions that began in the past and continue into the present or have just ended. It is formed with **have** + **been** + verb + **-ing.**

> They**'ve been waiting** for an hour.
> I**'ve been watering** the garden.

present perfect progressive *See* **present perfect continuous.**

present progressive *See* **present continuous.**

pronoun A word that can replace a noun or noun phrase. **I, you, he, she, it, mine,** and **yours** are some examples of pronouns.

proper noun A noun that is the name of a particular person, animal, place, thing, or idea. Proper nouns begin with capital letters and are usually not preceded by *the.*

> Peter Rover India Apollo 13 Buddhism

purpose infinitive An infinitive that expresses the reason or purpose for doing something.

> **In order to operate this machine,** press the green button.

quantity expression A word or words that occur before a noun to express a quantity or amount of that noun.

> **a lot of** rain **few** books **four** trucks

quoted speech The form of a sentence that uses the exact words of a speaker or writer. Written quoted speech uses quotation marks. Also called *direct speech.*

> **"Where did you go?"** he asked.

real conditional sentence A sentence that expresses a real or possible situation in the **if** clause and the expected result in the main clause. It has an **if** clause in the simple present, and the **will** future in the main clause.

> If I get a raise, I won't look for a new job.

receiver The noun that receives or is the result of an action in a sentence. See **active sentence, passive sentence.**

> **The letter** was mailed by Alex.

regular verb A verb that forms the simple past by adding **-ed, -d,** or changing **y** to **i** and then adding **-ed** to the simple form.

> hunt — hunted   love — loved   cry — cried

rejoinder A short response used in conversation.

> A: I like sushi.
> B: **Me too.**
> C: **So do I.**

relative clause A clause that modifies a preceding noun. Relative clauses generally begin with **who, whom, that, which,** and **whose.**

> The man **who called** is my cousin.
> We saw the elephant **that was just born.**

relative pronoun A pronoun that begins a relative clause and refers to a noun in the main clause. The words **who, whom, that, which,** and **whose** are relative pronouns.

reported speech A form of a sentence that expresses the meaning of quoted speech or writing from the point of view of the reporter. **Wh-** clauses, **if/whether** clauses, and **that** clauses are used to express reported speech after a reporting verb.

> He explained why he was late.
> He said that he was tired.
> We asked if they could come early.

reporting verb A verb such as **say, tell, ask, explain,** and **complain** that is used to express what has been said or written in both quoted speech and reported speech.

> Tony **complained,** "I'm tired."
> Tony **complained** that he was tired.

restrictive relative clause A relative clause that gives information that helps identify or define the noun that it modifies. In the following sentence, the speaker has more than one aunt. The relative clause **who speaks Russian** identifies which aunt the speaker is talking about. Also called *defining* or *identifying relative clause.*

> My aunt **who speaks Russian** is an interpreter.

separable Refers to certain two-word verbs that allow a noun or pronoun object to separate the two words in the verb phrase.

> She **gave** her job **up.**

short answer An answer to a *Yes/No* question that has *yes* or *no* plus the subject and an auxiliary verb.

> A: Do you speak Chinese?
> B: **Yes, I do. / No, I don't.**

simple past A verb form that expresses actions and situations that were completed at a definite time in the past.

> Carol **ate** lunch.   She **was** hungry.

simple present A verb form that expresses general statements, especially about habitual or repeated activities and permanent situations.

> Every morning I **catch** the 8:00 bus.
> The earth **is** round.

social modals Modal auxiliaries that are used to express politeness, formality, and authority.

> **Would** you please open the window?
> **May** I help you?
> Visitors **must** obey the rules.

stative verb A type of verb that is not usually used in the continuous form because it expresses a condition or state that is not changing. **Know, love, resemble, see,** and **smell** are some examples.

subject A noun, pronoun, or noun phrase that precedes the verb phrase in a sentence. The subject is closely related to the verb as the doer or experiencer of the action or state, or closely related to the noun that is being described in a sentence with *be*.

> **Erica** kicked the ball.
> **He** feels dizzy.
> **The park** is huge.

subject relative pronoun A relative pronoun that is the subject of a relative clause. It comes before the verb in the relative clause.

> the man **who** called

subordinate clause *See* **dependent clause.**

superlative A form of an adjective, adverb, or noun that is used to rank an item or situation first or last in a group of three or more.

> This perfume has **the strongest** scent.
> He speaks **the fastest** of all.
> That machine makes **the most noise** of the three.

***that* clause** A noun clause beginning with **that**.

> I think **that the bus is late.**

three-word verb A phrasal verb such as **break up with, cut down on,** and **look out for.** The meaning of a three-word verb is usually different from the individual meanings of the three words.

time clause A dependent clause that begins with a time word such as **while, when, before,** or **after.** It expresses the relationship in time between two different events in the same sentence.

> **Before Sandy left,** she fixed the copy machine.

transitive verb A verb that is followed by an object.

> I **read** the book.

two-word verb A phrasal verb such as **blow up, cross out,** and **hand in.** The meaning of a two-word verb is usually different from the individual meanings of the two words.

unreal conditional sentence A sentence that expresses an unreal situation that is not true at the present time, and its imaginary result. It has an **if** clause in the simple past and a main clause with **would** + main verb.

> If I had the time, I'd walk to work.

used to A special past tense verb. It expresses habitual past situations that no longer exist.

> We **used to** go skiing a lot. Now we go snowboarding.

verb A word that refers to an action or a state.

> Gina **closed** the window.
> Tim **loves** classical music.

verb phrase A phrase that has a main verb and any objects, adverbs, or dependent clauses that complete the meaning of the verb in the sentence.

> Who **called you**?
> He **walked slowly.**
> I **know what his name is.**

voiced Refers to speech sounds that are made by vibrating the vocal cords. Examples of voiced sounds are /b/, /d/, and /g/.

> **b**at **d**ot **g**et

voiceless Refers to speech sounds that are made without vibrating the vocal cords. Examples of voiceless sounds are /p/, /t/, and /f/.

> u**p** i**t** i**f**

***wh-* clause** A noun clause that begins with a **wh-** word: **who, whom, what, where, when, why, how,** and **which.** Also called *indirect question* or *embedded question.*

> I would like to know **where he is.**
> Could you tell me **how long it takes**?

***wh-* word** Who, whom, what, where, when, why, how, and which are **wh-** words. They are used to ask questions and to connect clauses.

***wish* sentence** A sentence that has a **wish** clause in the simple present, and a simple past clause. A **wish** sentence expresses a desire to change a real situation into an unreal or impossible one.

> I wish I had more time.

***Yes/No* question** A question that can be answered with the words **yes** or **no.**

> Can you drive a car?   Does he live here?

Index

be (continued)
  with adjectives
    for behavior, 18
    and preposition + gerund, 243,
      244, A-7
    and classifying or describing
      nouns, 263
  in continuous tenses
    future continuous, 52, 53
    future with present continuous,
      53
    present continuous, 6, 7
  contractions with, A-11
  after *it* as subject, 233
  with modals
    modals of possibility, 148–149
    past modals, 170
  omission of
    in newspaper headlines, 222
    in relative clauses, 289, 295
    in passive sentences, 194–195,
      214–215, 224
    in unreal conditionals, 331
be able to, in unreal conditionals, 341
because, and past perfect and past
  perfect continuous, 136
been
  in past perfect continuous,
    124–126
  in present perfect continuous, 104,
    105
before
  with future, 67
  in past time clauses, 131
  with simple past, 41
begin, with gerunds and infinitives,
  238
be going to
  forms of, 53
  contractions with, A-11
  in future passive, 214, 215
  meaning and use of, 61–62, 65–67
    in discourse, 71
    in noun clauses, 385
    for plans and intentions, 61, 66
    for predictions and expectations,
      62, 65–66
    for scheduled events, 62
Behavior, and *be* + adjective, 18
being, in passive sentences, 195
Beliefs, and stative meaning, 17

but
  and past unreal conditionals, 360
  and wishes about past, 355
by
  later time expressed with, 131
  in passive sentences, 194–195,
    214–215
by the time
  with future time clauses, 67
  in past time clauses, 131

C

can't, see also *can't have*
  and certainty, 155, 160
  as modal of possibility, 148–149
  and surprise or disbelief, 155
can't have, as modal of past
  possibility, 176, 177
Cause and effect
  and real conditionals, 336
  and simple past, 41
Certainty, *see also* Uncertainty
  and modals of future possibility,
    160–161
  and modals of present possibility,
    153–155
  and real conditionals, 335–336
Changing situations, 13
Classification, with generic nouns,
  272
Clauses, *see* Dependent clauses;
    if clauses; *if/whether* clauses;
    Main clauses; Noun clauses;
    Relative clauses; Result clauses;
    that clauses; Time clauses;
    wh- clauses
Combining sentences
  with *and,* and present continuous, 8
  with relative clauses
    with object relative pronouns,
      305
    with subject relative pronouns,
      284, 293
Comma
  with *if* clauses, 330, 331, 354
  with nonrestrictive relative clauses,
    283, 305
  with quoted speech, A-10
  with time clauses, 32
Complaints
  and present continuous, 13
  and wishes, 344

Completed actions
  and past perfect, 136
  and present perfect continuous, 114
  and simple present, 93
Conclusions
  and modals
    modals of past possibility, 177
    modals of present possibility,
      153–154
  and past perfect and past perfect
    continuous, 136
  and present perfect continuous, 110
Conditionals, 325–368, *see also* Past
  unreal conditionals; Past wishes;
  Real conditionals; Unreal
  conditionals; Wishes
Conditions, *see also* States
  and simple present, 17
constantly, 13
continue, with gerunds and
  infinitives, 238
Continuing actions, and past perfect
  continuous, 135, 136
Continuing time up to now
  and present perfect, 89, 113–114
  and present perfect continuous,
    109, 113–114
continuously, and simple present vs.
  present continuous, 13
Continuous tenses, *see also* Past
  continuous; Past perfect
  continuous; Present continuous;
  Present perfect continuous
  infinitives with, 238
Contractions, A-11
  with *be,* A-11
  with *be going to,* A-11
  with *did,* A-11
  with *do,* A-11
  in future forms, 52, 53
  with *had,* A-11
  with *have,* A-11
  with modals, A-11
    modals of possibility, 148–149
    past modals, 170–171
    phrasal modals, A-11
  in passive sentences, 194–195,
    214–215
  in past continuous, 30–31
  in past perfect, 124–126
  in past perfect continuous,
    124–126